Rethinking Anti-racisms

The last two decades have seen not only the rapid growth of economic global-isation and transnationalism, but also a rise in ethnic conflict and forced migration. With this global social change there has been a transformation in the ideas and practices of racism and, in tandem, the old national focus of anti-racist theory and practice has become increasingly outmoded.

This fascinating new collection seeks to rethink anti-racism in the light of these social changes and in terms of new theoretical debates and the potential they hold for fighting racisms. The theoretical chapters critically evaluate some of the most important developments in the field. These include theoretical interventions in debates on citizenship, multiculturalism, hybridity, diaspora, globalisation and social movements. As well as chapters on such theoretical interventions, *Rethinking Anti-racisms* has chapters covering important substantive developments within:

- anti-deportation campaigns
- anti-fascism
- education
- the Southall Black Sisters
- the contradictory use of ethnicity as a way of tackling racism.

This book will be essential reading for students, academics and policy makers working in the areas of racism and anti-racism.

Floya Anthias is Professor of Sociology at the University of Greenwich, London. **Cathie Lloyd** is Senior Research Officer at Queen Elizabeth House International Development Centre, University of Oxford.

Rethinking Anti-racisms

From theory to practice

**Edited by
Floya Anthias and Cathie Lloyd**

London and New York

First published 2002
by Routledge
11 New Fetter Lane, London EC4P 4EE

Simultaneously published in the USA and Canada
by Routledge.
29 West 35th Street, New York, NY 10001

Routledge is an imprint of the Taylor & Francis Group

Typeset in Galliard by Exe Valley Dataset Ltd, Exeter
Printed and bound in Great Britain by
Biddles Ltd, Guildford and King's Lynn

British Library Cataloguing in Publication Data
A catalogue record for this book is available
from the British Library

Library of Congress Cataloging in Publication Data
Rethinking anti-racism: from theory to practice/edited by Floya Anthias and Cathie Lloyd.
    p. cm.
    Includes bibliographical references and index.
    1. Racism. 2. Multiculturism. 3. Racism–Great Britain. 4. Great Britain–Race relations.
    I. Anthias, Floya, 1945– II. Lloyd, Cathie.

HT1523.R36 2001
305.8'00941–dc21   2001041605

ISBN 0–415–18337–5 (hbk)
ISBN 0–415–18338–3 (pbk)

Contents

Contributors

Floya Anthias is Professor of Sociology at the University of Greenwich, London.

Gargi Bhattacharyya is a lecturer in the Department of Cultural Studies at the University of Birmingham.

John Gabriel is Professor of Sociology and Head of the Department of Sociology and Applied Social Studies, London Guildhall University.

Nadeem Hai is a researcher on social welfare.

Jim House is a lecturer in French at the University of Leeds.

Susie Jacobs is a senior lecturer in sociology at Manchester Metropolitan University.

Cathie Lloyd is Senior Research Officer at Queen Elizabeth House International Development Centre, University of Oxford.

Pragna Patel is a trainee lawyer and a member of Southall Black Sisters.

Nora Räthzel teaches at the Department of Sociology, Umea University, Sweden.

Howard Winant is Professor of Sociology, Temple University, Philadelphia, USA.

Nira Yuval-Davis is Professor of Gender and Ethnic Studies, School of Social Sciences, University of Greenwich.

Preface

This book is a product of discussions we have had over a long period and particularly over the last decade. An important landmark in these discussions was the racist murder of Stephen Lawrence, a black school student, on 22 April 1993, in Eltham in south-east London. Following this horrendous crime, there were major mobilisations for a full inquiry into racist police methods and against the presence of the fascist British Movement's headquarters in south-east London. In September of that year we organised a European conference at the University of Greenwich (10–11 September 1993) in order to begin to understand the new dynamics of racism. Since then our own professional trajectories have informed the interests we address in the present volume. These reflect the growing interest in the global dynamics of racism and anti-racism, and new ways of thinking which move beyond race-conscious policies, on the one hand, and identity politics on the other. We hope that the book will help to further develop theories and practices that challenge binary and essentialised categories, and encourage politics and policies that can more effectively attack the dehumanisation of racisms and other forms of social degradation, inferiorisation, violence and inequality.

Acknowledgements

We would like to acknowledge COST Committee of the European Commission, the Centre for Research in Ethnic Relations at the University of Warwick and the School of Social Sciences at the University of Greenwich for support for the original conference which gave rise to some of the ideas and discussions in this book. We would particularly like to thank all those who participated in the conference and who contributed to the coming together of this book. Nira Yuval-Davis was involved with us in the organisation of the conference, and in the early discussions for this book, and we would like to thank her for her contribution. We would also like to thank all our colleagues in the anti-racist and feminist movements (especially in the UK and France) for the practical lessons they have taught us over the years. Finally, we would like to dedicate this book to the Stephen Lawrence Campaign and all those struggling against racism and violence throughout the world.

1 Introduction

Fighting racisms, defining the territory

Floya Anthias and Cathie Lloyd

This book aims to consider new ways of thinking about anti-racism and how they impact on anti-racist political practice. Our aim is to push the debate forward and to intervene in theoretical and political arguments that are of central importance today. We draw on new approaches and theoretical debates relating to, amongst others, citizenship, multiculturalism, hybridity, diaspora and social movements. In so doing, the book explores the extent to which these approaches can offer frameworks that provide some alternative conceptual bases for addressing the problems of racism and anti-racism in Western societies. The book also analyses how these approaches might help us to understand more fully contemporary forms of ethnic conflict and hatred, and how they can provide tools for addressing and combating racism and xenophobia at a broader, international level.

Widespread ethnic conflict has been one of the most significant developments since the end of the 1980s, and it has had an impact both on ideas and practices of racism and on the flows of people fleeing violence and persecution in many parts of the world. Our book aims to bring together issues of theory and practice. It contains a number of chapters on political culture and discourse and how they relate to racist and anti-racist politics. In addition, a number of chapters focus on specific arenas for anti-racist politics such as local political campaigns, women's campaigns and higher education.

Some of the contributions focus on conceptual and theoretical ways which help us to rethink the anti-racist project away from the binaries constructed by the earlier discourse which set up anti-racism as the radical voice of the black disadvantaged and multiculturalism as the soft hand of liberal conscience. Others focus on more substantive or practical struggles. There are a variety of voices and views in this book and we do not necessarily agree with all of them. However, they all constitute important contributions to ongoing debates on racism and anti-racism. The theoretical debates are on recent developments, with the emphasis on issues of hybridity and diasporic processes (Anthias), citizenship (Yuval-Davis), social movement theory (Lloyd), the contradictory nature of using ethnicity as a way of tackling racism (Räthzel), and globalisation (Winant). The more practical or concrete aspects deal with anti-fascist campaigns (House), the important work of the Southall Black Sisters (Patel), anti-deportation campaigns (Bhattacharyya and Gabriel) and education (Jacobs with Hai).

It is our view that, along with other binaries, those set up by debates on 'multi-culturalism versus anti-racism' must be refused. The critique of multiculturalism for reifying and essentialising culture and the related critique of anti-racism for reifying and essentialising 'race' categories have set the parameters. In this chapter we will consider the impact of the rejection of these binaries, and ask: what type of politics and theory can help to transcend the vacuum that currently exists?

Transnationalism and globalisation

Any contemporary analyses of racism and anti-racism should be placed within the social context of increasing transnationalism. People are in movement all over the world. New forms of communication mean that their relations with their countries of origin are qualitatively different from those of earlier generations, and com-munications are not only faster, but even instantaneous with the use of the internet by some social groups. Transnationalism is, however, often accompanied by increased expressions of inequality, uncertainty, ethnic conflict and hostility (Bulmer and Solomos 1998).

Globalised networks now characterise modern societies at all social levels, including the cultural and the economic. Although this does not minimise the importance of ethnic and cultural ties, it does mean that these ties operate increasingly at a transnational rather than merely national level. Population move-ments of different kinds have gone hand in hand with a growing circulation of money, capital and information tied to a range of entrepreneurial activities. Groups involved are also at the leading edge of the emergence of hybrid cultural forms. However, we must be careful not to treat hybridity, as Floya Anthias argues in this book (Chapter 2), outside the parameters of unequal power relations that exist between and within cultures. Diasporic groups have been thought of as particularly adaptable to a globalised economic system (Cohen 1988). They draw their strength from advanced technologies of transport and information flows, and by being able to pool resources and exchange information and contacts. These enable them to operate successfully in emerging markets with the proviso that it is important to consider such groupings as neither essentially constituted in this way, nor as undifferentiated, as Anthias warns us.

The increasing importance of global networks has changed the context for political and economic policy and requires that we consider both formal and informal transnational networks. There is growing work (Cohen 1988) on the economic power of some diasporas (such as the overseas Chinese with a combined economic output close to $600 billion: see *Financial Times*, June 1996). Diaspora groups also have political influence as many countries that traditionally export migrants, such as the Philippines, Latin American countries and countries in South-East Asia, are heavily dependent on remittances. Moreover, those defined as classical diasporas, like the Greeks and the Jews, are powerful political lobbyists, particularly in America and the European Union (EU). Floya Anthias's chapter critically interrogates some of the arguments about the implications of diasporic developments for ethnicity and racism and the potential these hold for the fight against racism. Cathie Lloyd discusses the impact of these changes on the mobilising capacity of social movements and anti-racist organising (Chapter 4).

Whatever the value of the arguments about the potential of diasporic developments, there is no doubt that policy decisions need to take account of the growth of transnational communities and networks as well as the increasing multi-layering of identity with the growing hybrid nature of culture, for young people in general, and second- and third-generation migrants in particular. Policy decisions on foreign investment, labour market regulation, immigration and citizenship all need to take into account the implications for transnational groupings and strategies. Regarding global economic networks, the patterns of investment and exchange, portable skills and unrecorded international trade must be seen in relation to the collective strategies of transnational groups within the international as well as national arenas.

Citizenship, civil society and social movements

Awareness of the broader international frameworks of international migration and the impact of new forms of ethnic conflict and globalisation have had a major influence on our understanding of civil society and of social movements as transnational in scope. These form an important part of the political and social context in which anti-racist struggle takes place. In recent years, for instance, many anti-racist mobilisations have broadened their concerns to include asylum-seekers and forced migrants. These developments have also encouraged writers to think about the broader application of anti-racist ideas. At the same time there have been theoretical and practical challenges to the claims of anti-racism to represent universal values. The Unesco initiatives against racism in the 1950s stemmed from a determination of the General Conference 'to study and collect scientific materials concerning questions of race; to give wide diffusion to the scientific information collected; to prepare an educational campaign based on this information' (Unesco 1951: 4). At this time Unesco sponsored debate which encouraged a pluralist anti-racism moving from a post-war focus on anti-Semitism to a broader focus on issues arising from decolonisation and immigration, closely linked to educational programmes (Unesco 1972, 1980, 1982a, 1982b).

International initiatives such as the United Nations (UN) Technical Symposium on International Migration and Development in 1998 have reviewed the potential for international co-operation in a new context. There have been significant advances such as the growth of understanding of the multiple dynamics involved: the role of social networks and 'social and cultural capital' in the migratory process and the need to reflect the complexity of migrant communities – such as the abuse of migrant women. This initiative emphasised the need for better public information and education about migration and settlement as a means of combating racial discrimination (Castles 1999). Concerns about ethnic conflict and human rights violations have given rise to new initiatives linked to anti-racism at the levels of international governance.

At the time of writing, these issues are being debated in the UN World Conference on Racism, Racial Discrimination and Xenophobia. This aims to set an international agenda with important implications for anti-racist struggle. Key issues are the establishment of legal protection against racism and discrimination, the policies and practices at sub-national and national levels against racism and discrimination, education against racism and discrimination at different levels, and the role of information, communication and the media (United Nations 1997). As in earlier UN world conferences, there is recognition of the importance of non-governmental organisations' (NGOs) participation, in order to keep the debate as inclusive as possible. The remit of the conference involves a broadening of our understanding of racism – understood as a tool to gain and maintain power, linking the origins of racism in colonialism and slavery to its contemporary forms within globalisation. Current important issues are the growth of inequality through globalisation, questions about the restriction of different forms of immigration, the growth of ethnic conflict and the rights of indigenous peoples (International Council on Human Rights Policy 2000; International Human Rights Law Group 2000).

There are also parallel developments at the European level (Council of Europe 2000). In Chapter 4, Cathie Lloyd explores the impact of European structures on grass-roots civil society mobilisations against racism. Other studies have considered the extent to which migrants in other European countries relate to these initiatives. The contextual factors that shape collective organisation are paramount. Writing in the French context, Olivier Filleule has analysed the 'receptivity or vulnerability of a given political system to the action of a contesting group and the degree to which these actors enjoy formal access to institutions and resources' (Fillieule 1993) while maintaining that their actions are still influenced by their original frameworks and know-how (Tarrow 1995). There is growing evidence of the cross-fertilisation of campaigns, such as those of the '*sanspapiers*' across Europe (Lloyd 1997; Simeant 1998).

Compared with the mechanisms for the control of migration, the European space for anti-racist mobilisations remains fragile and under-exploited. This is despite the formation of organisations such as the EU Migrants Forum in 1991 to facilitate dialogue and exchange information. There was a relatively low response from migrant associations to funding opportunities during the European Year against Racism. One study concluded that the ability of groups to take these opportunities is defined by the interplay of opportunities at different national levels and arenas. These depend greatly on the national context and the use of informed gate-keepers to facilitate fundraising (Danese 1998). Recently arrived migrant, asylum-seeking and refugee groups suffer from social and economic insecurity and instability in their lives, and are forced to concentrate on their primary needs. Despite initiatives around 'Social Europe' and the European Mediterranean Policy following the Barcelona Declaration, which have aimed to enhance the role of NGOs in forms of decentralised co-operation, it has proved difficult to transcend national approaches, while ethnic minority groups have competed for leadership (Kastoryano 1994).

Jim House's contribution to this book (Chapter 7) helps us explain the constraints of these national approaches within a historical perspective. Using the case of anti-racism in France, he shows how the various strands of anti-racism have appealed to but also challenged the ideologies of the republican nation-state. Thus anti-racists engaged with key political, social and cultural expressions of modernity. House shows how anti-racism has been re-worked at different times: during the Dreyfus affair at the turn of the nineteenth century, within an anti-fascist discourse in the 1930s, or later in the context of struggle for decolonisation. Rather than being easily categorised, anti-racism appears as a contradictory, sometimes ambivalent discourse which does not always fulfil its own promise. This theme is taken up in Nora Räthzel's chapter (Chapter 5), which argues that ethnic identities can hold both a promise and a danger in terms of the achievement of anti-racism and social justice. The double-edged weapon of ethnicity is at the centre of much anti-racist discourse. Räthzel puts us on our guard against suggesting any blueprints for anti-racist struggle; she insists that this must be struggled for in terms of the complexity of particular contexts.

Several of the chapters offer an assessment of the way in which transformations are working their way through at national level in the UK. The 1980s and 1990s saw the rise and fall of local authority 'race' units, and some of the processes, difficulties and ambiguities are highlighted in different ways in this book in the chapters by Patel, Bhattacharrya and Gabriel, and Jacobs with Hai (Chapters 8, 9 and 10). Will the new London authority give rise to new practices in the same way as the Greater London Council (GLC) did in the 1980s? To what extent is the emergence of black-led national structures in the UK a response to the development of European structures or does it represent a new stage in anti-racism? Pragna Patel's account of the work of the Southall Black Sisters offers some ways forward here. This perspective acknowledges the dilemmas, contradictions and tensions that arise from the experiences of black women. Southall Black Sisters have always challenged the orthodoxies of both the anti-racist movement and state social welfare policies. This is a perspective which offers a way out of the fragmentation of diversity through an approach to wider alliances.

Such rapid change also creates opportunities for an enhanced and more democratically informed citizenship. Nira Yuval-Davis (Chapter 3) relates to some of the major theories and debates on citizenship within political science in order to tease out the specific issues that are important for the construction of a citizenship-oriented anti-racist approach. Issues are raised in relation to the boundaries of collectivities, equality and difference, and the relationship between citizenship and human rights. For instance, citizenship is posed in a new way within Europe because the European framework offers an alternative to the usual assumption of an essentialised link between social rights and national membership. Some of the most important mobilisations in recent years have been for the recognition of rights which should accompany residence, but which are often denied migrants because of their status as foreigners. Migrant and refugee groups have considerable resources in their unique social networks, which often form part of transnational social and political networks. We would fully acknowledge that ethnic mobilisations have their own dynamic and cannot be subsumed into anti-racism (Anthias and Yuval Davis 1992; Gilroy 1992; Rex and Drury 1994). However, these networks and organisations provide important resources, which can be used in mobilisations which we might include under the anti-racist banner, such as movements that demand equal rights and recognition (Joppke 1996). One of the most striking movements in recent years, discussed in Cathie Lloyd's chapter, is the undocumented or *sanspapiers* migrants' movement in Europe and their use of internet communication and other forms of publication (Cisse 1996; Cisse 1999; Diop 1997; Fassin *et al.* 1997; Lloyd 1997).

There are many other important interfaces between anti-racism and other struggles, such as migrant women's international networks of resistance against religious fundamentalism (Connolly 1991; Helie-Lucas 1993; Lloyd 1999a). Pragna Patel's chapter, as noted earlier, focuses on the implications of women's struggles, drawing on the experience of the Southall Black Sisters, for multiculturalism and anti-racism. Other examples of transnational mobilisations are those of indigenous peoples for land or environmental protection against development-induced displacement, which involves assertions of their rights to self-determination against multinationals which may ride roughshod over their interests and may be taken up in anti-racist struggle.

Debates on anti-racism and multiculturalism

These global dimensions of anti-racism may pose problems for earlier conceptualisations of anti-racism that often assumed the guise of a Eurocentric, Enlightenment-derived universalism (Lloyd 1994). We are increasingly aware of the transnational history of anti-racism with its origins in the international movement against slavery and the struggles for decolonisation, anti-apartheid and civil and human rights. Once these antecedents are admitted it is no longer possible to portray anti-racism as uniquely Western. Throughout the 1980s and 1990s we have seen tensions between anti-racism and multiculturalist valorisations of cultural difference. Discussions about the conceptual status of the category 'race' have heightened these tensions and given rise to much controversy (Anthias 1992a; Gilroy 1998). In his most recent writing Paul Gilroy has suggested that we may need to think outside the straitjacket of race and instead champion a new humanism which is global and cosmopolitan (Gilroy 2000).

The British anti-racist movement of the 1980s stressed structural racism rather than the targeting of individual prejudice, and was contrasted to different types of multiculturalism which promoted cultural tolerance and the celebration of cultural difference as modes of struggling against racism. To this end anti-racists stressed 'race' difference and awareness and a critique was launched against the colour blindness of liberalism as well as the culturalism of the emphasis on ethnicity found within multiculturalism.

The chapter by Howard Winant discusses the continuing importance of 'race' markers in both local and global spheres, and the uneasy co-existence of formal commitments to racial equality and the heritage of centuries of white supremacy. This is a challenging and important argument and there is no doubt that racialisation processes become amplified and transformed at the global level. Their impact in a wide range of different societies is discussed. Unlike Winant, however, we do not take the view that because of the continuing importance of 'race' markers, the most *effective* way of challenging racisms is to continue to develop and improve race-conscious policies. These might be strategic tools in particular contexts but caution is needed. This is because one of the difficulties of all 'race-conscious' policies is the deep theoretical and political ambivalence to 'race' markers (Goldberg 1993). For example, a position may be created whereby 'race' (or 'cultural' difference) is treated in an essentialising and static way. Some of these problems were echoed in the critique of anti-racism which rapidly emerged from both the right and the left in the UK. The right hailed 'universalism' to argue against positive action or political correctness on the basis that these were incompatible with liberal democracy. The panic of the right can be arguably likened to a contemporary take on 'reds (or blacks) under our beds'. The left, on the other hand, argued that the anti-racist movement failed to provide a forum for effective political mobilisation. Radical black writers critiqued the incipient culturalism and essentialism particularly endemic to race awareness policies and practices (see Gilroy 1992). There was also, very importantly, the critique by Hall (1992) of the 'essential Black subject'. A problem identified with both multiculturalism and anti-racism was that they treated racism as a set of fairly systematic but false ideas related to the disadvantaged economic position of the working class (Rattansi 1992). Whilst anti-racism, unlike multiculturalism, stressed the importance of institutional racism rather than prejudice, it also assumed that racism could be fought by a rationalist and interventionist approach.

The focus of anti-racism was two-pronged: on the one hand corrective action was to be taken in relation to special categories of the disadvantaged who were seen to require differential treatment on the basis of their special needs; on the other hand, racist ideas in school and the media were to be tackled not so much through teaching the culture of groups (this being a major shortcoming of multiculturalist education), but by making white people aware of their own racism. Moreover, the limited project of an anti-racism that was insensitive to sexism was rejected by feminists and others. There was concern about the failure to think through crosscutting exclusions to do with gender and class, and the failure to think in more positive terms about the type of society that would be fought for. The way anti-racist politics constructed 'race' in terms of a unitary black subject (rejected particularly by those who argued against the submergence of the Asian category under the notion of 'black'; see Modood 1992) was also an issue. The privileging of colour racism over other forms of racism was also an important critique made by a number of writers in relation to anti-Irish and anti-Cypriot racism (Anthias 1992b; Hickman and Walter 1997).

Multiculturalism on the other hand saw ethnic difference as a cause for celebration and thereby failed to acknowledge the gender-specific and indeed at times sexist elements of ethnic culture, or the ways in which both ethnic and race boundaries were exclusionary. Claiming difference and celebrating it has been one way of fighting racism, particularly in various forms of multiculturalism. Such a position may have the effect of ethnicising and producing modes of struggle that focus on culture and identity, repeating for themselves the static and ahistorical nature of racialised definitions (Anthias 1994). This is found within a range of discussions on the limits of identity politics (MacLaren and Torres 1999).

The project of maintaining culture potentially created a notion of a static and totalising culture. One could argue that groups wishing to maintain their culture should do this in ways which reflect the diverse political and other interests within any self-proclaimed group. Whilst public validation of different ways of life is important, the role of the state should not be to promote some notion of the culture of the group: who are to be the voices for defining this, in any case? As Southall Black Sisters work shows, discussed in Pragna Patel's chapter, it is often the traditional male voices that are given the role of acting to represent the cultural needs of groups. Whilst it is important to recognise that ethnicity is important for groups, this does not require us to treat it as either a necessary or sufficient means for pursuing various social and political ends. Moreover, uncovering the hidden ethnicity of the dominant groups is as important as validating the ethnicity of minority groups. In addition, multiculturalist policies could be seen as a way of managing ethnic diversity and although race discrimination was central to this project, state practices around this have sat uneasily with the kinds of policies related to migration and the failure to tackle institutional racisms.

Pluralities and limits: defining racisms

It is commonly acknowledged that to overcome the problems identified in the critiques of corporate anti-racism it is important to identify the range of social processes which could be defined as racism and which need to be tackled. There is a large range of repertoires from which racism can draw, which includes those of ethnicity. Indeed racism is opportunistic, it is relational to other social processes, and it is therefore a fluid and shifting phenomenon which evades clear and absolute definition in a once-and-for-all-type of way. A recent definition of racism is that '*racism*' . . . *advantage[s] or disadvantage[s] people because of their colour, culture or ethnic origin*' (Macpherson 1999: 6.4). The positing of *ethnic* origin raises the issue of the targets of racism being diverse and not restricted to groups defined in racial terms. However, such a definition provides little scope for discussion of the economic, political or ideological conditions within which racism operates as a sphere of social relations (rather than a set of advantages/disadvantage). Moreover, the constructed, rather than essential or fixed nature of the boundaries of 'colour', culture and ethnicity needs to be incorporated into any such focus.

Much discussion has in fact focused on the different markers that are deployed in racist discourse, for example whether the focus is colour or culture (say Islamic religion and identities). Issues around a broader conceptualisation of exclusion and inclusion, as well as differential social and economic access to resources become blurred, however, by questions about which is the population that most experiences racism rather than what are the processes by which this happens (Anthias 1998b). This is because in order to understand and fight racism (as opposed to sorting out empirically who are its targets at any particular point of time), it is important to focus on processes, structures and outcomes, through looking both at changing configurations of ideas about fear, threat, otherness, undesirability, *and* at how groups who are targeted may be responding to these challenges.

Although racisms as forms of discourse come in different guises, they are underpinned by a notion of a natural relation between an essence attributed to a human population, whether biological or cultural, and social outcomes that do, will, or should flow from this (Anthias 1998b). It is not possible to seek an exhaustive list of racisms and their empirical identification as though we can discover their essential truths. Culture is also a product of specific institutional sites at the international, national and local level. This includes processes and policies impacting differentially on minority ethnic groups, serving to disadvantage or exclude them. An example may be (social) council housing. For example, in Britain, state housing allocation is usually made on the basis of a range of criteria that will include the length of time individuals have been on a list. If some ethnic groups lack information on the criteria for council house allocation, or if they are less likely to stay in an area for the amount of time required, this may produce racist effects (this could discriminate against refugees or migrants particularly).

Another example might be the failure to provide enabling opportunities where issues of language proficiencies and cultural insider knowledges may be aspects of inclusion. The lack of such opportunities to acquire skills may become the basis for practices that produce racist effects – i.e. lead to harassment, discrimination, lack of legal rights, or exclusion from opportunities or allocations.

The differential treatment of women, particularly as it intersects with race, must be attended to. This involves not turning a blind eye to sexist violence and inferiority in the name of upholding the cultural traditions of groups, for example as in the treatment of Asian women and girls by the public services (cases quoted in the activities of Southall Black Sisters in this book). As Floya Anthias argues in her chapter, there is a need to fight against all those constructions of difference and identity that exclude and devalorise, and against all those social practices that construct identities and differences in naturalised, collectivised and binary ways and in terms of hierarchical otherness, unequal resource allocation and modes of inferiorisation (see also Anthias 1998a). These practices relate therefore to the projects of equalisation and democratisation at all social levels

Institutional racism

In the sociological literature the existence of institutional or structural racism has informed much debate, although some influential writers, such as Robert Miles (1989), have rejected it, with the accusation that it entails a conceptual inflation of 'racism'. The most recent attempt to think through, at least in the British context, the category of 'institutional racism' is found in the Macpherson Report of 1999. This report resulted from the furore and scandal relating to the police investigation into the murder of the young black teenager, Stephen Lawrence in southeast London. It exemplifies some current thinking in the UK which is echoed in race-conscious policies elsewhere, particularly the United States.

The Macpherson Report took on board some difficult conceptual, policy and political issues around racism in British society. Racism is regarded as pervasive not only within the police force but in other institutions such as the criminal justice system and education. In order to tackle such racism, there is an emphasis in the report on the need to monitor the police force's treatment of racially motivated crimes, and on the provision of race awareness training to foster the awareness of cultural diversity. Such training should be undertaken by police officers, and the personnel within the criminal justice system.

Amongst other recommendations, the Macpherson Report believes that people should be trained to become aware of 'cultural diversity'. Race consciousness is promoted, for example in the recommendation to keep records of the ethnicity/race of those subjected to 'stop and search', and other forms of ethnic record keeping and monitoring. Other forms of race consciousness are promoted through policies related to education. In the Macpherson Report it is suggested that training in ethnic diversity be incorporated within the National Curriculum as a provision, through the education system, for all. Ways of tackling racism within higher education in particular is the focus of the chapter by Susie Jacobs and Nadeem Hai (Chapter 10). They discuss pedagogical and theoretical problems and strategies in teaching 'race', ethnicity and anti-racism in social science higher education in Britain. The chapter considers, among other issues, definitions of terms such as 'race', ethnicity, racism, nation, black, white and the deconstruction of the term 'race'; whether different types of racism are included as issues in course syllabi/teaching strategies; and how the racialised/ethnic (and gendered, class/ed) position of the lecturer/teacher affects the content of the course and the students' experience of it.

One of the most discussed notions in the Macpherson Report is *institutional racism* which probably for the first time publicly and officially acknowledges the deeply entrenched and invasive nature of racist practices and outcomes. As such this notion recognises the importance of focusing on racist *outcomes* as well as *intentions,* and the importance of the culture of racism embedded in social arrangements.

The Macpherson Report defines institutional racism in the following way:

> 'Institutional Racism' consists of the collective failure of an organisation to provide an appropriate and professional service to people because of their colour, culture or ethnic origin. It can be seen or detected in processes, attitudes and behaviour which amount to discrimination through unwitting prejudice, ignorance, thoughtlessness, and racist stereotyping which disadvantage minority ethnic people.
>
> (6.34)

Quoting Carmichael and Hamilton (1968) that racism 'permeates society on both the individual and institutional level, covertly or overtly', the report fails, however, to place it in the context of collective social power and domination within which Carmichael and Hamilton locate it. In the report, the unwitting racism of institutions is a product of individual attitudes, exacerbated by a disinclination to critically self-examine actions. For Carmichael and Hamilton, on the other hand, among others (Sivanandan 1974), it stems from the structural features of a capitalist society and involves the class domination of whites over blacks and therefore the locus of effectivity is quite different.

Whatever the problems and difficulties with the notion of institutional racism, there is no doubt that the pervasiveness of institutional power makes accountability one of the most vital issues for anti-racist practice. Although there are few, if any, situations in which people are wholly powerless and they are not mere victims, having of course agency, this does not mean that they will be able to counter the power of institutions. Gargi Bhattacharyya and John Gabriel (Chapter 9) argue that in Britain, widely held media and political anxieties around immigration have coexisted alongside a largely unwritten history of the struggle against immigration and asylum laws. In their chapter, on an anti-deportation campaign in the West Midlands in the UK, the role of the campaign against the institutional racism of the immigration system is examined through histories of successful and as yet unresolved cases. These are put in the context of both recent changes in domestic law and policy and, despite Euro-sceptic rhetoric to the contrary, the harmonisation of European-wide policies on immigration and asylum. The chapter ends by looking at recent developments in campaigning tactics and the future of apparently local campaigns in a European context. This chapter focuses on community-based campaigns and aims not to romanticise the 'community' and its capacities for resistance. Instead it emphasises what is effective in certain situations in order to salvage a sense that despite all the problems with public institutions concerned with immigration, community politics can make a difference. This chapter clearly shows the role of agency by individuals and groups in struggling against racism.

Anti-deportation campaigns are an important part of the fabric of the resistance to institutional racism. Such campaigns, undertaken by NGOs, but also by temporary groups formed around families and other networks, provide focal points for alliances which can bring together different kinds of actors – trade unions, local community groups, family and other social networks in campaigns – which sometimes endure and sometimes lie dormant for years only to spring into new action in response to events. They provide an important interface between informal groups within local communities and the more organised anti-racist groups.

These campaigns respond to the way in which power is embedded in society in even more diffuse ways than that found in institutions such as immigration law. Power is institutionalised and exists in the very fabric of common sense taken-for-granted understandings of a society. Knowledge and access are a form of power. Underclass 'white' youths, as individuals, may have access to neither jobs nor positions of power. Indeed they may be excluded from access to these, through their position in class relations and through class and gender discourses about competencies in a society in the throes of economic recession and cultural crisis. Racist and violent behaviour may indeed be symbolic of the very little power they still have, manifested in their concern with territory, which may be a mode of contesting the threat to their own ethnicity (Bauman 1991; Cohen 1988). Working-class white youth may redefine themselves as an ethnic English collective claiming a greater share of the scarce resources of the working-class urban areas they inhabit. The collapse of employment structures and other infrastructures for young men may be part of the reason for some of the symbolic and other violence (the defiling of the Stephen Lawrence memorial, for example, mirrors the desecration of Jewish graves and attacks on mosques in many parts of the world).

These developments are not unique to Britain, but have been frequently identified as reactions to the homogenising effects of globalisations. Local particularities and identities, ethnic violence and extreme nationalist ideologies such as neo-fascism may provide refuge for marginalised populations. Chapters in this volume by Nora Räthzel and Cathie Lloyd (Chapters 5 and 4) document some of these developments and the reactions to them by national and European policy-makers. Over the past decade, within a global context of increased ethnic conflict, we have seen alarmingly high levels of racist violence, physical attacks on asylum-seekers and electoral support for the extreme right (in Austria, Belgium and France for instance). These developments are often concentrated where large numbers of young men come together, notably in violence between football supporters.

Masculinity is an important issue here, since the perpetrators of most racial attacks are young men attacking other young men. Racial violence functions within a racialised space where the importance of the masculinist culture of the school playground can be transported to claims over territory outside the school, a point noted by the Macdonald inquiry (MacDonald *et al.* 1989) into the murder of an Asian pupil at Burnage High School in Manchester. Racialised relations are complex (Back 1996) and there may be a link between racialised violence and male bonding (Rattansi 1999). Similar dynamics can be seen across Europe: in France, for instance, there is a serious debate about unacceptable levels of violence in schools, colleges and public transport which often follow ethnic divisions.

Moreover, there is an ambivalence about racism, found for example in the emulation of black popular culture, particularly music. Racist name-calling may be used as a taunt between friends and may function psychically as a means of bonding as well as be part of a negotiation of identities and testing grounds for those friendships. Available interpretative repertoires inevitably are drawn upon in inter-'racial' and inter-ethnic relations and friendships, and thereby their meaning may be fluid and transformed. Within this, issues of class and gender are central components of power relations. But the existence of multiple identities does not mean that individuals do not have different investments in different identities at different times. As Floya Anthias has argued elsewhere, they are: 'not like cloaks that we can don and then discard but like different layers that can be worn, some on top and some below at different times' (Anthias 1998c: 507). Moreover, the existence of hybridity or liminality (Bhabha 1994), as Floya Anthias notes, cannot presuppose that these identities will be able to transcend racism and ethnic absolutism, for they do not have any necessary political effects, despite the claims that have been made about their transformatory or transgressive potential (for a critique see Anthias 1998a).

The limits of multiculturalism, group rights and inclusive citizenship

With the failures of anti-racism and liberal multiculturalism, new ways of thinking about the project of fighting racism are needed. A liberal multiculturalist frame-work means that the dominant group within the state is able to set the terms of the agenda for participation by minority ethnic groups and involves a bounded dialogue where the premises themselves may not be open to negotiation. This is one reason why there has been increasing debate around the issue of multi-culturality (Parekh 1993) and critical and reflexive multiculturalism (May 1999; Parekh 2000; Rattansi 1999). Multiculturality or critical/reflexive multicultural-ism, unlike liberal multiculturalism, is concerned with the removal of barriers to the legitimacy of different ways of being and is compatible with transnational and transethnic identities as well as those that have been discussed using the notion of hybridity.

A starting point in debates on critical multiculturalism is that it must move away from the idea of one dominant culture that lays the frame of reference for the existence of tolerance towards other cultures. As such it must maintain a view of citizenship where the boundaries of citizenship are not coterminous with belonging to a community in the singular, discussed in the chapter by Nira Yuval-Davis. It has been argued that Marshall's idea of citizenship, as entailing full membership of the community, assumes a homogeneous community (Marshall 1950). How is the latter to be defined? Who constitutes the membership and who defines the boundaries? Who are its representatives? Who are able to speak within it (Anthias 1998b; Anthias and Yuval-Davis 1983; Lister 1997)? Some claims made in Western Europe have included the notion of collective rights of minority ethnic groups. In the case of Muslim minorities around the Rushdie affair in Britain, claims have been made for separate legal systems and Muslim law as central parameters of the social and political rights of particular (in this case Muslim) individuals.

Indeed, the issue of collective rights as citizenship rights has been debated regarding Western Europe in terms of multiculturalism (Kymlicka 1995; Parekh 1993; Parekh 2000). Early or incipient forms of this are found in positive action programmes such as those relating to special provisions. These have been critiqued both for reproducing categories of disadvantage (Anthias and Yuval-Davis 1992) and for being incompatible with the notion of equal human rights. Others have argued strongly that group rights are central for disadvantaged groups (Goldberg 1993; Winant 1994; Young 1989). Howard Winant (Chapter 6) remains convinced that policies need to be aware of group differences relating to 'race'. There are multiculturalist policies that work with some notion of group rights in Canada, USA, India, South Africa and Britain.

Ideas about a group having the right to pursue its culture, to be able to reproduce itself, raise a range of questions: what is that 'culture'; who defines its primary elements; do all the cultural practices embody other principles that a participatory democracy advocates (such as anti-sexism)? Therefore issues are raised about group representation, the management of internal conflict and external clashes about cultural and political values, the compatibility of different universes of meaning, and so on. There is also the question of whether the rights of a group identified through culture or 'race' have prominence over the rights of a group identified under the banners of class, political ideology or gender.

Will Kymlicka (1995) differentiates between 'two kinds of group rights': minority rights which safeguard the interests of minority groups and those which *aim to impose restriction on their own members*. Whilst supporting the former, he regards the latter as more difficult. Indeed, the principles embodied in the state may differ from and be oppositional to the rules upheld by a minority. On the other hand, rejecting the cultural rules of minorities through espousing the notion of universality could mean that the values of minorities are excluded from the public domain (Pateman 1988a). But both claims mentioned by Kymlicka raise the issue of who represents the group's authentic experience or culture, and which voices are to be listened to, for he fails to note the differentiations of gender and class within groups.

Feminism and multiculturalism

Over the last twenty years feminists, in particular black and third world feminists have pioneered the task of looking at issues of difference of ethnicity and racialisation and some of the intersections between feminism and multiculturalism. There has been a recent debate prompted by the white American feminist Susan Moller Okin's (1999) claim that 'multiculturalism' may be 'bad for women'.

Okin takes the position that traditional cultures often subordinate women and that universalist human rights should be prioritised. There have been three broad responses to her argument. First it has been pointed out that all cultures oppress women, albeit in different ways. Whilst some cultural practices referred to by Okin do subordinate women, many oppressive cultural practices are also found in cultures which pay lip-service to universalist human rights. This is the case for Western democracies which are premised on universalist ideals of liberty and equality but in practice are generically sexist and racist. Anti-racists remind us that cultures are racist and the foundation of Western rationality is racist; and the latter is also sexist, as Sandra Harding (1991) and Carole Pateman (1988a) have argued in different ways.

The second response therefore sees it as necessary to pay much more attention to what is meant by culture in the argument by Okin. By delimiting culture to certain groups which are those 'othered' already by the discourse and practices of the 'West' she is reproducing stereotyped and potentially racist representations of groups that do not conform to the liberal Western ideal. Issues around genital mutilation and forced marriages deprive women of rights and should not be tolerated. But focusing on these to make the argument against multiculturalism is not adequate. The issue of culture is much more complex and there are a range of practices in all cultures that would not stand the test if they are judged in terms of giving women autonomy or developing human capabilities. There can be no absolute consensus on these issues and they are emergent rather than given; women themselves need to engage in much more dialogue around them.

A third related criticism is the danger of cultural imperialism, found in arguments that Western universalist notions of human rights are able to yield principles of justice that should apply everywhere. The very fact that this recent debate has completely excluded reference to the plethora of writing by black and third world women is suggestive of another form of cultural imperialism by American feminism. It is a view from above. It also disguises the role of Western imperialism in countries where minorities perpetrate forms of violence against women. Moreover, condemning practices is not the same as condemning so-called cultural groups and failing therefore to think about the potential of new forms of multiculturalism. On the other hand the critique of universalism may emerge as culturally relativist (and not just relationist) and therefore justify (on grounds of cultural difference) violations and violence against the person found in forms of honour killings or domestic violence found all over the world in different forms. In addition cultures are dynamic and therefore open to change.

Pragna Patel's account of the work of Southall Black Sisters (Chapter 8) shows that black women's struggles for self-determination are at the centre of these debates, challenging the orthodoxies (especially multicultural) of both the anti-racist and the white feminist movement. This requires connections to be made between movements against racism, sexism and other forms of social exclusion at many different levels.

These difficult issues make any exhaustive approach to citizenship difficult. One answer to some of these questions is given by a concern with dialogic politics (Collins 1992; Giddens 1994; Yuval-Davis 1997c). However, effective dialogue requires social conditions which maximise equal intersubjective and represent-ational power: this can only happen effectively when incumbents of positions are able to meet on equal terms. Indeed effective dialogue requires an already formulated mutual respect, a common communication language and a common starting point in terms of power. Attempts to bridge universes of meaning cannot be fully successful if they are not accompanied by a serious concern with redressing economic and social inequalities. In any attempt to find commonalities in difference through forms of dialogic politics, there is also a range of unresolved difficulties such as the base line by which different cultural or group rights should be defined and the points at which the cultural practices of groups should be policed *vis-à-vis* sexism, for example. In this regard, polygamy and cliterodectomy are some of the most difficult issues.

Tackling racisms

It is widely acknowledged that new forms of cultural racism have turned univers-alist and differentialist arguments to their own advantage by making claims for a human nature which supposedly dictates that populations 'naturally' prefer to interact with their own (national-cultural) kith and kin. Superimposed upon these difficulties are problems of possible neutralisation by incorporation by the state, fragmentations within racialised communities, and divisions over strategy and leadership.

Some writers have been tempted to make very sweeping claims for anti-racism. Alastair Bonnet, for instance, includes 'every-day anti-racism', psychological anti-racism (including racism awareness training), multiculturalism, representative anti-racism (affirmative action) and radical approaches to anti-racism, which focus on challenging the structures of power and privilege (Bonnett 2000). We would be more guarded than this. We would argue for a definition of anti-racism which necessarily varies with specific contexts and changing circumstances of different racisms (Lloyd 1998b: 245). The key problem about approaches such as multi-culturalism is whether they really negate or simply coexist with racism. Are we to limit anti-racism to the *recognition* of difference or to the *transformation* of social relations?

One fruitful way of approaching this is to understand the discourses and practices of anti-racist associations and thus the diversity of approaches that are labelled anti-racist. Stephan Feuchtwang refers to anti-racism as starting from 'the politics of civil liberty and civil rights' (Feuchtwang 1990: 23). We would suggest that anti-racism constitutes a set of polycentric, overlapping discourses and practices which combine a response to racism(s) with the construction of a positive project about the kind of society in which people can live together in harmony and mutual respect. The commitment of anti-racism to social justice was apparent in the anti-fascist and anti-colonial struggles and in the campaigns for the rights of immigrant workers and their descendants. It has informed the broadening of discourses of discrimination (which were inevitably cast in oppositional terms) and the transformation of concepts of representation. The themes of solidarity and hegemony directly embody anti-racism's progressive social project.

Such broader strategic issues of building a more inclusive and just society need to be able to provide guidelines for specific and targeted policies. Ways of tackling racism at this level have included policing racist language or the expression of race hatred. This highlights the tension between the rights of individuals to free speech and the rights of others to be free from verbal abuse. In Britain, as in many countries, racist language is illegal if it relates to action, i.e. if it is an incitement to action or a verbal threat (defined in the Public Order Act section 4 and 5 as language that may 'threaten, provoke or generate fear of violence'). This raises the issue of how racist motivation is to be identified. If there is no racial abuse does this mean that an action is not racially motivated? If a black person is involved should the assumption always be that it is racially motivated? This raises both the issue of the nature of evidence for judging racist motivation, and the question of the means of attaining it.

At the broader level, the category of inclusion can be no more than approximate since not every individual and group can or indeed wants to be included in all social spheres. Differential but equal inclusion seems the best that can be formulated, from this point of view, with the proviso that equality of access should be accompanied by enabling mechanisms. An earlier formulation of Isaiah Berlin (1956), around the dyad *freedom from* and *freedom to*, still seems particularly useful in thinking through issues of citizenship in tandem with the issue of universalist human rights that can be marshalled in *appropriate circumstances and contexts* (Anthias 2000). This might include rights to be free *from* economic, political and cultural forms of discrimination and their institutionalised variants. Freedom *from* exclusion on the basis of racialisation may be thought of as part of this freedom. Social rights to be free *from* poverty, labour market exclusion, and exploitative forms of economic activity (extending further Marshall's right to work) may also be seen as part of these freedoms, involving therefore freedom *from* particular forms of *inclusion* in marginal areas of the economy.

Freedom *to* exercise rights of active political participation as well as its facilitation, where one constructs oneself as a member of the polity, may be usefully thought of as one of the rights *to* citizenship. Rights *to* practices of group culture, to a way of life, may also form part of these rights of citizenship, where these do not conflict with human rights to autonomy and self-realisation on the basis of those freedoms *from* indicated above on the basis of gender, age, disability or racialisation. In other words freedoms *from* need to be formulated before freedoms *to*, and should function in a more categorical and absolute way than freedoms *to* which may be more contingent and differentiated.

Another useful dyad is that between the idea of citizenship as a status and citizenship as a practice. This again raises the issue of the ways by which an individual's participation may be enabled and facilitated and the issue of active versus passive forms of citizenship. There is a problem though of defining *practice* or active political participation because this could exclude the informal politics of oppressed groups, for example in their negotiation with welfare state institutions. Moreover, political participation must not be defined too narrowly otherwise groups such as women may be effectively excluded.

What is clear is that a more inclusive notion of citizenship within a multi-cultural participatory democracy would not be based on the idea of nations as essentially monocultural, as Nira Yuval Davis points out in her chapter. Moreover, anti-racisms need to work on a number of fronts in terms of socio-material conditions, the discursive apparatus and mechanisms of subjective identification. These relate to a focus on specific *issues* rather than *identities* and require in our view the re-examination of the role of class inequalities and the psycho-social mechanisms attached to the increasing economic, political and identity crisis amongst young people, particularly young men (Anthias 1998c). The issue of identity choices made by the young needs to be seen also in relation to the contexts within which these come into play and as strategies rather than essential identities which are fixed.

Concluding remarks

It is now acknowledged that we do not always need to find a racist intentionality or a racist imagination to be able to refer to racist practices and racist outcomes in society. These racisms do not only depend on us studying ethnic relations and being aware of 'cultural diversity', but studying the modes in society by which inequalities and inferiorisations are produced and sustained and the interaction between gender, class, ethnicity, race and the state (to name the major parameters for inequality and division).

Whilst there is a need to reinforce penalties for the perpetrators of violence, there is also the need to examine the ways in which available discursive elements become harnessed within local youth cultures (Back 1996; Cohen 1988; Hewitt 1996) and the social movements they relate to, either explicitly or implicitly. In other words, a constellation of social meanings and political forces are inscribed in racist violence and these cannot be addressed purely through rational models of intervention (Rattansi 1992) nor purely through legal prohibition. The identific-ation of a crisis in anti-racism does not mean the abandonment of mobilisation over specific issues like racist violence but the need to link this within a broader-based appeal to democratic forces.

The more extensive introduction of race or ethnic conscious policies (following in the footsteps of the US) is at times offered in the UK as an answer to colour blind policies which have failed. It is important to be aware of some of the pitfalls of race awareness and cultural diversity arguments, found in anti-racisms and various forms of multiculturalisms that are already around. Some time ago, Miles alerted us that the issue is not one of race relations but one of racism (Miles 1989). We would also argue that the issue of racism includes issues about structures of *power*, the function of attributions and identifications using ethnic claims in general and the easy slide from the 'identity' of a group to exclusion and subordination. Therefore race awareness should be interpreted as an awareness of how power is socially distributed and not just as a reification of already existing racial categories.

This is particularly important in relation to recognising the links between such distribution of power along 'racialised' dimensions and those of class and gender. Racisms are forms of subordination and exclusion and work in tandem with class-related and gender-related forms of subordination and exclusion although they differ from them (Anthias 1998c; Anthias and Yuval-Davis 1992). They entail subject positions, intersubjectivities, discourses, practices and outcomes. Racism and cultural difference have a different salience and outcome in relation to wider social forces. The differential *effects of racialisation vis-à-vis* economic disadvantage and racial violence and prejudice as well as identity are by now well known. For example, different groups manifest different trends in employment and self-employment, with the differences within minorities as great, if not greater, than those between minorities and non-minorities (Modood 1997). Some groups have a higher socio-economic profile than 'whites', and some are systematically under-represented in the higher social categories. Despite this diversity, some categories of minority ethnic groups suffer particular disadvantages economically.

The recognition of the class and gender dimensions of racism does not imply that the fight against racist harassment or promoting cultural diversity is any less urgent: quite the opposite. Some of the implications of working on one level, such as racist harassment, need to be considered in terms of working on other levels, such as economic inequality and sexism, however.

In terms of contemporary Europe, large numbers of young people, particularly from the black and white working classes, have been disenfranchised through permanent unemployment in inner city spaces. This requires a much greater emphasis on economic and political processes than the debate on multicultural diversity (either liberal or critical) has been able to deliver. The struggles for social inclusion are an important component of anti-racist work. In France these have focused on mobilisations for access to housing which brought together activists for the Right to Housing (Droit au Logement) and migrant groups protesting against high levels of exploitation in substandard housing (referred to in Cathie Lloyd's chapter), and initiatives to reduce unemployment by limiting the working week to thirty-five hours. While housing has been a potent focus for mobilisation, attempts to reduce levels of unemployment hold the danger of a *two-speed* society which fails to address the problem of people in insecure employment, particularly in the service sector.

Cross-national research has attempted to disentangle the threads in analysing commonalities and differences between different anti-racist movements and to show how the legacy of the Enlightenment is as much at stake in this context as in the debates about modernity and postmodernity (Lloyd 1994). We need to confront the possibility that a new European anti-racist politics of citizenship cannot be created without a transformation and reconstruction of the ideas of liberty, equality and fraternity inherited from the Enlightenment.

We would suggest that any future research agenda should address the current dearth of empirical studies on this subject. Research needs to consider anti-racism in its local, national and international or transnational dimensions. There are many questions unanswered. When we talk about anti-racism are we referring to a specifically Western phenomenon or is it more widespread? Do individuals and organisations who mobilise against ethnic and racial hatreds use similar or very different assumptions? What are the resources that different cultures contribute to the emergence of societies which are more tolerant of difference? Other recent work raises the question of whether we can identify a common factor which unites all forms of anti-racism.

The contributions to the book

Critiques of notions of ethnicity and identity that are fixed, stable, monolithic and exclusionary have led scholars and activists to embrace new ideas of hybridity and diaspora. In her contribution, Floya Anthias considers these ideas and the extent to which they potentially create a space for forms of anti-racism that can harness multiple notions of being and challenge the fixity of boundaries that characterise racist practice, culture and identities. The aim is to analyse their usefulness for providing alternative ways of thinking about anti-racist politics, and their dialogical potential. The chapter calls for caution in the espousal of these concepts and offers the notion of 'translocational' positionality as a more adequate means for thinking about belongings.

Citizenship debates have over the last few years provided an important forum for the discussion of social inequalities and exclusions. In her contribution to this book, Nira Yuval-Davis examines the centrality of citizenship debates to struggles against racism. From these debates the chapter teases out specific issues for a construction of a citizenship-oriented anti-racist approach, in particular issues relating to boundaries of collectivities, individual and collective rights and responsibilities, and the relationship between the notion of citizenship and human rights. Issues are discussed which relate to the boundaries of collectivities (sub-cross- and supra- as well as national), equality and difference and the relationship between the notions of citizenship and human rights.

Cathie Lloyd interrogates recent debates on anti-racist social movements in Britain, France and more broadly in Europe. She argues that one of the main obstacles to the study of anti-racism as a body of ideas and practices in its own right, is the way in which anti-racism has been trapped in the dichotomy racism/anti-racism. The study of civil society, transnational networks and social movements provides the means to overcome this problem. What is required is a wider understanding of the interface between informal social movements, more formally organised associations and mainstream political formations. Such an approach helps to understand the different political levels at which anti-racism operates.

Using political debates about the dangers of racism and populism in contemporary Germany as her starting point, Nora Räthzel discusses the flexibility of ideas of the nation and of ethnic formation. A new consensus developed in the 1990s with the reunification of Germany, but different social groups still defined themselves in terms of (different) Other groups. Räthzel argues that the homogeneity and heterogeneity of the nation-state are two sides of the same coin. While the existence of different ethnic groups within a nation-state is not a problem, the construction of ethnic groups as *not belonging* is. She argues that both dominant and subordinated ethnic groups attempt to represent themselves within a national project, structured by social and gender hierarchies, a myth of origin and an emotional attachment to the group which itself may be internally fractured. Given the pressures of globalisation, Räthzel argues that it is impossible for us to secure social justice by campaigning at the national level alone and that it is essential to break through by campaigning at the transnational level.

Howard Winant addresses the changing dynamics of race and racism at the global level. Using comparative historical sociology, he considers the aftermath of decolonisation, minority social movements and systems of racial stratification and their impact on political conflicts across the world. The chapter gives a historical and theoretical account of the emergence of what Winant terms the 'modern world racial system' and then moves on to a group of contemporary case studies (the US, South Africa, Brazil and Europe). In the final section he considers the enduring relationship between race and modernity, and the uneasy coexistence of formal commitments to racial equality and the heritage of centuries of white supremacy.

Jim House examines the ways in which anti-racist discourse and action have been moulded and channelled by various aspects of French political culture, notably Republicanism. He shows how strands of anti-racism have in the French context appealed to and challenged the ideologies of the republican nation-state as a key political, social and cultural expression of modernity. House discusses 'republican anti-racism' which emerged at the time of the Dreyfus affair. Anti-racism has been reworked within an anti-fascist discourse in the 1930s and later in the context of struggles for decolonisation. Arguing that these examples of previous anti-racist action in France from the 1930s and 1960s can inform the present, he proposes a methodology to account for the changing forms of racism and anti-racism in modern and contemporary France, examining concepts such as 'race' and 'difference' and the various meanings assigned to these terms in social discourse since the 1930s. The influence of this Republican discourse can help explain the confused reaction to the many forms of opposition to racism that have emerged from the counter-cultural national liberation movements and negritude, leading to the marginalisation of opposition to colonial and then post colonial racism.

Pragna Patel's chapter is concerned with some of the struggles involved in the important campaigning work in Britain of Southall Black Sisters, which celebrated its twenty-first anniversary in 2001. A central issue is how the group can take advantage of the space that has opened up through the Stephen Lawrence inquiry to redefine and formulate anti-racist strategies to help to create a new politics of resistance in the face of inequality and social justice. The account is of the dilemmas, contradictions and tensions that arise from their experience as black women, which challenges the orthodoxies of the anti-racist movement and of state social welfare policies which are predicated on notions of diversity and multi-culturalism. Patel sees the struggle as a fragmenting one, which suffers because of a political vacuum. This highlights the need actively to seek wider alliances.

Gargi Bhattacharyya and John Gabriel argue that, in Britain, widely held media and political anxieties around immigration have coexisted alongside a largely unwritten history of the struggle against immigration and asylum laws. In the main, anti-deportation campaigns have been concentrated at a local level. This chapter looks in detail at the particular practice of one organisation, the West Midlands Anti-Deportation Campaign. The role of the campaign is examined through histories of successful and as yet unresolved cases. These are contextual-ised in recent changes in domestic policy and law and the harmonisation of European-wide policies on immigration and asylum. This chapter focuses on community-based campaigns and aims not to romanticise the 'community' and its capacities for resistance. Instead it emphasises what is effective in certain situations in order to salvage a sense that despite all the problems with public institutions concerned with immigration, community politics can make a difference.

Susie Jacobs, with Nadeem Hai, discuss pedagogical and theoretical problems and strategies in teaching 'race', ethnicity and anti-racism in social science higher education in Britain. Concepts of 'race', ethnicity, racism and nation are discussed, as well as whether different types of racism are included as issues in course syllabi/teaching strategies. They also consider how the racialised/ethnic (and gendered, class/ed) position of the lecturer/teacher affects the course and students' experience. Jacobs and Hai cover some of the broader anti-racist issues raised in the deployment of terms like 'white' and 'black', colour racism and anti-Semitism. They also raise central problems relating to broader issues around standpoint theory; *who* has legitimacy to research and teach issues of racism; and the relationship between the pedagogic process and racism and racialisation in the classroom.

2 Diasporic hybridity and transcending racisms

Problems and potential

Floya Anthias

The contextual and situational role of culture and identity in the struggles against racism has been one of the main issues within policy and academic debates. It is also an important element in the rejection of the old polarity between anti-racism and multiculturalism. Anti-racist politics have tended to pay little attention to the role of culture by focusing on the institutional, economic and political levels and have tended to be socially determinist and neglected the role of agency (and therefore the possibilities of change) in relation to both the victims and the perpetrators of racism (another polarity assumed in the discourse of anti-racism). By working too much with fixed racial categories, particularly the binaries of 'black' and 'white', such politics have tended to reify racialised categories. By being too tied to the 'anti', anti-racisms have generally neglected thinking through the goal of building a more just and fair society for all. Multiculturalism, on the other hand, has been critiqued as embedded in fixed and static notions of culture and recently contrasted with a more reflexive or critical multiculturalism (see May 1999; Rattansi 1999; Parekh 2000). This recognises both the fluid nature of cultural identities as well as their location within racialised social structures and specific social sites.

With these developments, a focus becomes possible on the multi-layered means whereby new forms of social and cultural practice and structures can emerge, paying attention to forms of democratisation and citizenship as well as new sites for anti-racist practice and struggle. Debates on hybridity and diaspora can be located very much in terms of the critique of social and economic determinisms (for example the Marxist or Marxisant emphasis on the role of 'capital', both economically and as represented in the state), and a critique of the traditional liberal multiculturalism that 'museumises' culture (Bakhtin 1986).

A focus on the cultural domain is symptomatic of the present position in both policy and academic debates. Hybridity and diaspora postulate shifting and potentially transnational and transethnic cultural formations and identities. These new identities can be located within a globalised and transnational social fabric rather than one bounded by the nation-state form. If one of the most virulent forms of racism is to be found in the very nature of modern exclusivist ethnicity with its culture of fixed boundaries, then we might envisage that progress can be made with forms of cultural identity that are more fluid and synthetic, such as those that have been characterised as hybrid and diasporic.

In this chapter,[1] I will therefore look at developments within approaches to diaspora and hybridity and consider their dialogical potential. For it is in the concept of dialogue, the focus on interaction and communication, and the shifts in position that become possible through this process, that a potential may be found in revealing the fluidity of boundaries and their social rather than natural construction. Such a process can encourage notions of a self which is multiple, not just in terms of an accretion of different identities, but one that can encompass otherness. In such a model, the self and the other are no longer experienced as eternal binaries but are aspects of each other.

Racisms need to be countered in terms of a number of interrelated processes and important within these is the dismantling of fixed identity boundaries. It is in this light that ideas of diaspora and hybridity may be able to create a space for forms of anti-racism that can harness notions of multiple belonging (sometimes referred to as hyphenated identities) to the task of challenging the fixity of boundaries which characterise racist practice and racist cultures and identities. One issue, however, is the need to be cautious in espousing concepts such as hybridity and diaspora as unproblematic and endemically anti-racist. It is therefore important to explore some of the ways in which such developments within a global and transnational world can be harnessed to the struggle against racism.

I want to begin by noting some of the debates around the concepts of hybridity and diaspora. Second, I want to reflect critically on the extent to which shifts in identity (and therefore a discourse about culture and identity) are adequate ways of thinking about racism and anti-racism. I suggest that they need to be tied much more carefully to wider structural processes and resource claims also involving forms of politics around class and nation and democratisation more generally.

A critical evaluation of hybridity and diaspora, moreover, may be an important frame for evaluating the degree to which change has occurred in the paradigms used to understand forms of migration and settlement in the modern era. Hybridity and diaspora (Anthias 1998b), have become fashionable terms and commonly hailed. To a large extent such terms are used in order to counter the essentialism found in many traditional approaches to ethnicity and racism, and as critiques of static notions of ethnicity and culture. I will argue that diasporic hybridity, although denoting important developments and challenges to static and essentialist notions of ethnicity, migration, culture and identity, presents important conceptual and substantive difficulties when it is tied to anti-racism. The key problems relate to the location of culture as the core element for defining identity and community as well as in the fight against racism. Such culturalisms problematise the struggle against racisms. Not only does the notion of culture need much more specification than is found in debates on diasporic hybridity, but culture and identity need to be disassociated.

It is vital to distinguish between the problematic of culture and that of identity and the formation of solidary projects. Whilst identity formation and re-iteration involve narratives of belongingness which may use cultural attributions, this does not mean that identity processes are synonymous with shared cultural practices: identities do not depend solely on cultural practices or beliefs. The forms of ethnicity hailed by the notion of hybridity therefore require delineating: to what extent does hybridity signal the end of ethnicity, in the sense of struggle around the ethnic boundary? Hybridisation as 'the ways in which forms become separated from existing practices and recombine with new forms of new practices' (Rowe and Scheling 1991: 231) may be seen as a depiction of all culture and therefore neither new nor essentially related to diasporic experience or diasporic space (Brah 1996). What, if any, is the new and transgressive potential to be found within hybridisation processes? A central theme of my chapter will be the continuing links between the notion of hybridity and traditional conceptions of ethnicity, particularly in their culturalist variants, and the continuing links between hybridity's sister notion, diaspora, and the traditional concern of ethnic categories with origin and homeland.

Hybridity, cultural globalisation and interculturality

It is worth saying that in discussing hybridity I am not concerned with approaches and discussions of 'mixed race' identities (A. Wilson 1987; Tizard and Phoenix 1993; Root 1996) that are often depicted through the term 'hybrid'. These are concerned with the issue of mixed parentage. They tend to work with the binary distinction between black and white 'races', and may suggest that those of 'mixed race' are 'in between', thereby pathologising their subjects. I am concerned rather with approaches that find hybrid social forms to be results of interculturality and diasporic relations, or what Hall (1990) calls cultural diasporisation, and which claim that these signify new forms of identity which are potentially destabilising of racism and are able to transcend ethnic particularisms. The new use of the term hybridity implicity rejects the idea of pre-existing pure categories. On the other hand, if all cultures are by definition hybrid because they are not 'pure', the term loses its specific analytic usefulness. If we look at it in relation to a postmodern framework for approaching issues of culture, identity and race, it comes to make more sense.

Hybridity is a central term in post-structuralist cultural theory and in some variants of globalisation theory. It is tied to the idea of cultural syncretism, rather than the cultural difference solidified by multiculturalism. In some versions hybridity is depicted as transgressive (e.g. Bhabha 1990, 1994; Rassool 1997). Clearly, the examination of new forms of identification and the construction of more synthetic cultures are an important focus of study in contemporary Europe. For example, Britain along with many other European countries has a large range of more or less permanent transnational populations and their descendants. Much of the literature on issues of migration and ethnicity has tended to see the latter as being 'between two cultures' or they have been researched in terms of their assimilation or integration within mainstream society and the extent to which they retain the culture of their parents. There now exists a growth of interest in the ways in which young people's identities emerge in specific locales (Back 1996; Hewitt 1996). Those who write within the new tradition reject the old paradigms for understanding the social relations and the lived experiences of this new generation, and may deploy the term 'hybridity'.

Cultural globalisation

The debate on cultural globalisation and the focus on hybridity are clearly related and indeed dependent to some extent on each other. Globalisation processes have been characterised as political, economic and cultural and regarded as a challenge to the nation-state, although also seen as generating ethnic and cultural parochialisms and localisms, or *glocalisation* in Roland Robertson's own 'hybrid' term (Robertson 1995). It has been argued that the boundary of the nation-state is traversed in the multiple ways identified by the movement of capital; the growing penetration over the globe of transnational financial capital; the growth and penetration of new technologies; the export and movement of communication modes including media forms and images; the growth of transnational political and juridical groups (e.g. the EU and its potential); growing international resistance and action groups (e.g. the Beijing Conference of Women); and penetration of ideologies producing a 'world system' (Wallerstein 1990) or global village (McLuhan 1964). One key element of globalisation theory is the identification of cultural globalisation as a core contemporary facet. Diaspora groups or communities are seen to embody the transnational principle, moving ethnic and solidary organisation from the confines of the nation-state to the global arena. The nation-building project of nationalism (never fully successful anywhere) of marrying the boundaries of ethnicity, the boundaries of the state and the boundaries of the nation-state becomes challenged. In addition, diaspora groups, it has been claimed (Gilroy 1993a; Clifford 1994; Brah 1996), are characterised by the growth of synthetic or mixed cultural elements, taking selectively in succeeding generations from a range of cultural resources. It has been claimed that the global cultural is constituted in and through hybridisation (Pieterse 1995).

It is useful to reiterate some of the claims of globalisation theory since this is the peg on which debates on hybrid interculturality are often hung. Globalisation theory is a diverse and unsystematic array of positionings with a highly diverse set of interrelated foci. Whether it is a new process or an old one, whether it exists or not (Hirst and Thompson 1996), whether its character is imperialistic or democratising, and the extent of hybridisation (Pieterse 1995) are all currently debated issues. What is generally regarded, however, as a unique feature of the modern or postmodern globalisation process is its acceleration and amplification and the role given to self-reflexivity and cultural mobility. It is here that notions of hybridity and diaspora, developed most fully within post-structuralist cultural theory, have their central role. McLuhan's view that 'this is the world of the global village' (1964: 93), stressing the existence of a global consciousness, is echoed in Robertson's claim that: 'Globalisation as a concept refers both to the compression of the world and the intensification of consciousness of the world as a whole' (1992: 8). One of the substantive historical problems with the idea of transnationalism (translated often as hybrid heterogeneity) is that religion, ideology, capitalism and 'communities' (such as Gypsies, Jews, Greeks and blacks) have existed in the transnational sphere prior to the identification of new forms of globalisation. Therefore the idea of the globalisation of self-reflexivity and culture seems to be the most qualitative, as opposed to quantitative, change signalled by the globalisation debate.

Waters, in his useful book *Globalisation*, defines it as 'A social process in which the constraints of geography on social and cultural arrangements recede and in which people become increasingly aware that they are receding' (1995: 3). Whilst ethnic and other fundamentalisms have been seen as a reaction/contradiction to globalisation, the issue of diasporic hybridity is seen as a substantive consequence of increasing cultural interpenetration allied to self-reflexive or 'open to the other' cultures. These are epitomised by cosmopolitanism, as found in Bhabha's counter-narrative (1994) and Friedman's (1997) cosmopolitan. In these respects, Giddens's (1991) emphasis on the global cosmopolitanism of the modern world, and the self-reflexivity of its individual and institutional actors, reverberates with some of the themes of post-colonial cultural studies.

For some, like Giddens (1991), globalisation is a 'consequence of modernity', which in turn is identified with Westernisation. Others have seen globalisation as uneven, divergent and contradictory (Robertson 1995; Appadurai 1990). Robertson uses the term glocalisation to denote the connections between the local and the global. This implies not only global production in different local spaces. It signals the ways in which global consciousness affects local conditions, giving rise to claims for a unique difference, human rights, national autonomy and so on. As he puts it, there is a 'global institutionalisation of the expectation and construction of local particularisms' so 'that the cultural idea of the nation state is a social fact' (Robertson 1995, p. 34). In this context, local nationalisms (as in Catalonia, the Basque Country, old Yugoslavia, Sri Lanka) are not counter-global developments, but are part of the spread of the universalising tendencies of those very global developments.

Whilst the demise of the nation-state form is heralded within globalisation theory, in approaches to hybridity there is a depiction of moving or travelling cultures, where boundaries between ethnic forms are transgressed by intermixing, and borders are dismantled. Globalisation as hybridisation then comes onto the agenda head on: with the dismantling of national borders, there is the dismantling of ethnicities, and a new openness to translation and dialogue. However, hybridity in the sense of interculturality is not a new phenomenon; it is intrinsic to the process of migration and dislocation, as Simmel (1950) and Schutz (1996), amongst others, have shown. Nor does it necessarily lead to transgressivity or empowerment: even where individuals adopt some of the cultural traits of the new society, they may remain marginalised and seen as 'strangers'.

The stranger and interculturality

Interculturality and the crossing of cultural borders has been an ongoing concern in sociology. The role of border crossings in dismantling the 'barbed wire' of monolithically constituted ethnic absolutisms is found centrally in the work of a number of classical social theorists, but particularly in the work of Simmel and Schutz on the 'Stranger'. This earlier discourse was more concerned with specifying some of the epistemological aspects of culture contact rather than their potential in dismantling fixed notions of identity and culture. In addition, the models used by Simmel (1950) and Schutz (1996) focus on the stranger as immigrant or sojourner, and are concerned with the individual condition created by the crossing of cultural and social borders, rather than on wider social outcomes, unlike the more recent work on hybridity and diaspora.

Whilst not attending to the cultural heteroglossia which have historically produced all societies, both Simmel and Schutz attend to the process of distantiation, objectification and the acquisition of translation skills by strangers or travellers from one society to the other, as a form of skilled management of the condition of marginality. Simmel defines the stranger as 'the wanderer who comes today and stays tomorrow . . . [whose] position in the group is determined essentially by the fact that he has not belonged to it from the beginning' (1950: 402). The prototype here is the outsider/trader, epitomised for Simmel by the European Jew. He is mobile and comes into contact with, but is not organically connected with, any one person. Simmel also refers to the stranger's objectivity in as much as he is not radically committed (like Mannheim's (1929) free floating intellectual), but this: 'does not simply involve passivity and detachment; it is a particular structure composed of distance and nearness, indifference and involvement' (1950: 404). 'Objectivity means that he is bound by no commitments which could prejudice his perceptions, understanding and valuation of the given' (1950: 405) which makes him 'contain many dangerous possibilities'.

The stranger is often accused of inviting transgression, for as an observer of culture, he possesses a dual and contradictory character, being 'close to us, in so far as we feel between him and ourselves common features of a national, social or generally *human* nature' (406). But Simmel uses the example of Greeks and Barbarians to argue that the stranger may be disallowed this last feature (i.e. the commonality of 'the human') if he is seen as a member of a group of strangers, rather than as an individual. Simmel thereby distinguishes the occasional stranger from group migration and identification. Simmel underplays the potential culture conflict and the diverse ways in which strangers are received and relate. However, asymmetry is a key area (this becomes complex when the stranger is the *dominant* stranger – as the coloniser or the foreign capitalist).

Schutz, on the other hand, sees the 'Stranger' as having the intention to 'interpret cultural patterns of a social group which he approaches to orient himself' (1996: 339). He is defined as 'an adult of our times and civilization who tries to be permanently accepted or at least tolerated by the group' (1996: 339). The prototype is the immigrant who has to adapt to a new world, and learn its world-view, i.e. that of the hegemonic culture. Crossing cultural boundaries involves a cultural disabling; to become enabled, the stranger must learn to see the world through the indigene's eyes. The stranger needs to learn new recipes, not yet tested by experience, and must be involved in a continuous process of translation. The conflict of universes of meaning is resolved by cultural adaptation and assimilation. In this sense the contemplation of the original homeland, and its sets of meanings in Schutz, the taken-for-granted typifications or sets of recipes for making sense of the world, become displaced and their relativisation becomes possible. The past of one place can then be interrogated by crossing the border, to use Gloria Anzaldua's (1987) term, showing it to be constructed as opposed to being essentialised, and open to change. In Schutz, there is an epistemological privilege given to this process of displacement and replacement. Unlike the epistemological privilege of the 'free-floating intellectual' in Mannheim's work (1929), which derives from being able to see all points of view because s/he lacks a fixed class location, it is precisely the experience of dislocation and relocation that enables privileged knowledge production. Schutz recognises that there are differential opportunities to use cultural understandings, and that they can be used for differentiated individual and collective ends. In the process, Schutz notes two aspects: the development of objectivity, and the stranger's neutral positioning in terms of loyalty to the group, which he calls 'doubtful loyalty'. The objectivity derives from the stranger's 'bitter' experience of 'the limits of thinking as usual' (1996: 347). This doubtful loyalty 'is especially true when the stranger proves unwilling or unable to substitute the new cultural pattern entirely for that of the home group. . . . Then the stranger remains . . . a cultural hybrid on the verge of two different patterns of group life, not knowing to which he belongs' (347).

In this way, Schutz focuses on the incommensurability of two cultures, which are seen as closed universes. Incommensurability is not treated as a moral imperative (as in the writing of the new right in contemporary Western societies) but rather in terms of a sociology of knowledge which treats knowledge as social product and contextually relevant only. The experience of the stranger involves a crisis of orientation. This may be related to Park's notion of marginal man (in Stonequist 1937), who is on the border of two cultures. This conflict is resolved by cultural innovation possibly embodied most by Weber's notion of a pariah population, and middle men minorities (see Stone 1985; Bonacich 1973).

Stranger, in the sense of *xenos* in Greek, means both stranger and outsider/guest. In the latter sense, hospitality is due to the stranger, and there is honour in this without an expectation of reciprocity, but there is the expectation that the stranger will leave. There is a diverse number of ways in which strangers are received, however, which relate partly to their mode of arrival, their relative temporality and the degree to which they are seen to be part of an Othered group. Asymmetry is a key area, particularly where the stranger is the dominant stranger (as a coloniser), or alternatively where the stranger is here to stay. The ideas of Schutz and Simmel are interesting in suggesting reactions and responses to individuals who cross borders. However, the relations between strangers, either from the same origin or group or from others, are neglected. The importance of negotiation and the existence of different cultural rules for family/kin, and for outsiders (recognised in the Greek sense of *xenos*), is also relevant. In the modern period, it is difficult to use the insights of Schutz and Simmel when explaining group movement and settlement. Indeed, globalisation involves a growth in the numbers of movement, which both intensifies strangeness and normalises it. The condition of 'overall strangeness' becomes the condition *par excellence* of global society. However, as stressed by both Schutz and Simmel, the incommensurable facets of culture are important constrainers of the optimism found in 'hybrid' models of culture, and lead us to return to the idea of culture as patterned within structures of dominance. The importance of 'asymmetry' and hegemonic cultural discourses needs to be considered by the new approaches to the issue of interculturality, found in the idea of cultural hybridity, which will now be looked at more closely.

The new hybridity theorists

Stuart Hall (1990), Paul Gilroy (1997) and Homi Bhabha (1994) each present rather different versions of 'hybridity', although they share a concern with developing an anti-essentialist framework for understanding culture and identity. Stuart Hall rejects the essential black subject and wishes to consider racialised identity as constructed out of an experience of colonialism and oppression and as a way of forging resistance. Paul Gilroy is keen to stress the connectedness of the 'Black Atlantic' in diaspora as a product of racist violence and as an identity of resistance. Homi Bhabha, on the other hand, is concerned with the diasporic intellectual who is able to transcend the boundaries of a given national culture and occupy the space of the 'in between', a space of displacement which refuses all cultural belongings, and yet is able to exist in all of them.

In Hall's work, hybridity is particularly linked to the idea of 'new ethnicities' (Hall 1992), which attempts to provide a non-static and non-essentialised approach to ethnic culture. Whilst the 'new ethnicities', it is argued, involve a search for roots and grounding, they are not stymied by a search for identity on the basis of origin. Ethnicity, in this sense, relates both to the homeland, and to the society of settlement, and is reconfigured within a diasporic space. It has been argued that this can produce a more effective cultural intervention in racialised discourse (Hall 1990). From this position, it is a small step to argue that such a rearrangement of identities and cultures opens up a space for interpenetration and translation; this is depicted through the concept of hybridity. Such identities are never complete and are being continuously made and remade. The term hybridity also designates the formation of new identities that may have a more transethnic and transnational character. For example, new British Muslim identity is not confined to an ethnic group, but is an amalgam, neither purely religious nor specifically ethnic, that may be linked to forging identity as a culture of resistance. Being black, or part of the African diaspora, stresses experience, rather than origins, and constructs a transnational identity (Gilroy 1993a). Young white adolescents are synthesising the culture of their white English backgrounds, with the cultures of minorities, to forge new cultural forms in music, and inter-racial friendship networks and movements (Hewitt 1986; Back 1996). Young Asians are producing new forms of Anglo-Indian music (Sharma *et al.* 1996). Young Cypriots are keener to abandon the ethnocentricity of their parents, and are forging links with young Turkish Cypriots, and with other marginalised and ethnicised youth (Anthias, forthcoming).

Gilroy's book *The Black Atlantic* (1993a) probably presents the most sustained theoretical defence of the concept of diasporic hybridity. Gilroy's concern is to reconstruct the history of the West through the work of black intellectuals like Du Bois and Richard Wright whom he sees as inhabiting 'contested "contact zones" between cultures and histories'. Intermediate concepts like hybridity and diaspora 'break the dogmatic focus on discrete national dynamics' which has characterised modern Euro-American cultural thought and reinstate the role of 'intercultural positionality' (1993a: 6). Like Hall, he rejects the notion of an essential black subject and the unifying dynamic of black culture. Instead he relies on the concepts of hybridity and diaspora as a heuristic means to focus on the difference and sameness of the connective culture across different national black groups. The connective tissue is seen to lie in a discourse of racial emancipation on the one hand and the conflictual representation of sexuality on the other, constructing communities that are 'both similar and different'. He relies for much of the argument on the hybrid but distinctive forms of music and performance as expressive of a double consciousness (using Du Bois's famous phrase) which constitutes a relatively privileged knowledge space. He contrasts it to prevailing ethnic absolutism and sees it as the theorisation of 'creolisation, metissage, mestisaje and hybridity' (1993a: 2). Despite, however, referring to the centrality of gender and the representation of sexuality in constituting 'the changing same', Gilroy fails to give women any agency within the black diaspora and is more interested in the male gaze (see also Helmreich 1992).

Bhabha (1994) sees the transgression of national or ethnic borders as the key to the condition of hybridity; a double perspective becomes possible. This portrays the migrant artist/poet/intellectual as the voice that speaks from two places at once whilst inhabiting neither. This is the space of liminality, of 'no place' or of the buffer zone of 'no man's land'. For Bhabha (1994: 38) the space of the 'inter' is 'the cutting edge of translation and negotiation, the *in between* space'. This always produces a counter-narrative or 'Third Space' to 'elude the politics of polarity and emerge as others of ourselves'. Bhabha therefore sees hybrids as cultural brokers. It is clear that this does not occur out of a simple process of accretion nor is it ever complete; it is full of discontinuities and ruptures.

Notions of hybridity retain a concern with cultural contents and style (such as art, music and language), rather than the ethnic boundary. Hybridity is treated as a challenge to dominant homogenous cultural forms. However, the West, as opposed to the rest, to use Hall's terms (Hall *et al.* 1992), is an amalgam from a position of dominance of the opportunistic pillage of other cultural forms that may be put to new ends. This constitutes a form of hybridity also. From this it becomes clear that asymmetric social relations produce particular configurations of cultural elements, not merely the form of the hybrid but particular constellations of the hybrid. Exploring the different forms of the hybrid, produced within different positionalities in relation to unequal resources and power, would turn our attention to different class and gender groupings as well as those of race, migration and ethnicity. It is the missing elements here that then require us to look further into the ways in which the term culture is deployed within the hybridity framework.

Culture

The notion of hybridity begs a much clearer definition of culture than is being offered by any of the new hybridity theorists. Culture is a heavily used and contested concept and it is impossible to give a comprehensive account here of the multiple meanings it has been given and the multiplicity of perspectives that give the term its particular resonance. What we can signal here is that there are at least three main ways in which the term 'culture' has been used in sociology:

1   Culture as a set of cultural attributes or artefacts, of a locality or a particular group, denoting its symbols and practices. Here there may be a distinction between high culture (music, literature, art, poetry), expressing the production of universalisable meanings in local form, and low culture (that of the masses): *culture as content or product.*
2   Culture as a world-view, involving an orientation to the world (Mannheim 1929), perhaps depicted as ways of being and doing or what Banuri (1990: 77) calls 'software'. A culture is the pool of components from which forms of culture or cultural products/resources are drawn but is not coterminous with these products: *culture here is a process or mechanism.*
3   Culture as patterned ways of knowing and doing. These are institutionalised within hegemonic processes and structures. Transgression of the central core elements leads to forms of social regulation, prohibition, exclusion, or banishment. This may be linked to Durkheim's notion of social facts: *culture as form or structure.*

In addition there are notions of culture as emergent (see Bourdieu on 'habitus' (1990), which links it with agency), culture as a set of typifications or recipes (in Schutz 1970), and culture as 'performative' (Butler 1990). This schematic delineation constitutes a few of the ways in which the notion of culture may be used in sociology. Given the range of different meanings that have been attached to the notion of 'culture', the object of reference in debates on global culture needs differentiating and specifying.

As I have already suggested, the notion of culture within debates on cultural hybridity is confined (in a rather incoherent and unclear fashion however) to the first definition above, in terms of cultural products or attributes. I would also suggest that hybridity functions on an assumption of an essential unity of the two or more cultural forms from which it is composed, for if all culture was recognised as intercultural, then the term would become redundant. Moreover, it does not attend to the *meanings and uses* of the cultural elements, and to the combinatory of elements, since the assumption is that the syncretic nature of hybrid cultures, in and of itself, constitutes an anti-essentialist achievement. This fails to consider the role of context and agency. It is useful here to interject by referring to two distinctive meanings of hybridity noted by Pnina Werbner (1999, using the work of Bakhtin 1986), that of hybrid culture as an organic synthesis, a bringing together, a merging, and that of hybrid culture as producing a space for the endless refusal of any unity, any bringing together. In the work of the hybridity theorists referred to here what is being signposted is the latter. But because the focus is on culture as the means for its achievement, there is little scope for addressing the mechanisms whereby the disruptive break is constituted. The transcendance or refusal of any cultural belonging, as a political outcome (as opposed to an existential position), requires a situated account of embodied positionalities which is not purely reliant on the cultural domain. From this point of view, cultural artefacts *or* practices do not have singular or fixed meanings. Hybridity in the transgressive sense cannot be examined in terms of the inter-mingling of cultural components, without considering the question of how they are used and in what contexts. For example, the hybrid nature of much pop music is discussed, divorced from the question of agency. Such hybridities cannot be judged as either transgressive or progressive, without paying attention to their deployment (e.g. see Hebdidge 1979, who argues for the co-optation role of new youth styles relating to music). There is no necessary political belonging therefore to this type of interculturality.

Furthermore, there occurs a conflation between recognising the syncretic character of cultural discourse and practice, and its positive evaluation. Hybrid cultural forms are not necessarily more desirable or progressive than others. As noted earlier, a number of writers have noted the 'progressive transgressive' and countering tendencies of border crossings. Others, however, have pointed out that hybridity is not necessarily progressive (Solomos and Back 1996). For example, racism too may be ambivalent or hybrid (Rattansi 1992) and fascism may be a reactionary version of hybridity. Ahmed (1997) argues that being positioned as hybrid produces the effect of being inadequate to any available cultural identity. Rassool (1997) adopts Giddens's use of reflexivity; hybridity is the 'key variable within this process of redefinition' and challenges the idea of the homogeneity of dominant cultures. However, she rightly says that this process cannot be thought outside the context of racist exclusions. Hybrids are not always the 'new world of bricoloeurs' that Cornel West (1992: 36) refers to and may be tied to violence and alienation, as receivers or producers.

It is also possible to distinguish between the problematic of culture, and that of identity and the formation of solidary projects. The synthesis of cultural elements relating to music, popular culture, friendship networks and movements (Hewitt 1986; Back 1996) amongst adolescents does not necessarily produce significant changes of identity, or undermine racialised relations. The pick and mix of cultural elements does not necessarily signify, therefore, a shift in identity or indeed the demise of identity politics of the racist or anti-racist kind. The whole area of the link between culture in terms of patterns and products, and the issue of identity and boundaries of belonging, requires much more systematic analysis.

Bhabha's idea of the 'in between space' constructs a 'third space' inhabited by the cosmopolitan who lacks a central cultural narrative. However, cosmopolitanism may not be the primary condition produced through transnational movements. Through migration and diasporisation, the opposite to hybridity can occur: a ghettoisation and enclavisation process, a living in a 'time warp', a mythologising of tradition (Shukla 1997). Hall, following Robins (1991), acknowledges that this may be the alternative adaptation to that of translation (where new more trans-gressive forms emerge). In addition, a concern with homeland and its national project, or what Anderson (1995) calls long-distance nationalism, is found in the political projects of the Irish, the Jews, and the Greeks, amongst others. Such concerns are not confined to traditionalists but may also mark cosmopolitans: the space of cultural sophistication and urbanity does not preclude nationalistic fervour or identification, although it is more likely to. Moreover, the concept of hybridity assumes a free-floating person (as in Mannheim's free-floating intellectual). It is important to recognise the role of agency, on the one hand, but to explore also how it is exercised within a system of social constraints, linked to the positionality of actors (both individual and collective) within specific social contexts.

How does the discussion of hybridity relate to the notion of ethnicity? Ethnicity is a contested term, open to a range of definitions, but I have argued that it involves deploying the boundary of the ethnic category, as a central arena for struggle *vis-à-vis* resources of different types (Anthias 1992a, 1992b). This distinguishes the concept of ethnicity from the broader concept of culture. Ethnicity cannot be confined to questions of culture and identity, since it is evident that culture and identity need not take an ethnic form. The relational aspect of ethnicity is increasingly recognised in a literature that has now, not before time, largely abandoned the idea of ethnicity as primordial, fixed or just a question of culture and subjective identification. The idea of ethnicity as a boundary marker, found in the work of Barth (1969) and others (e.g. Wallman 1979), treats 'the cultural stuff' as its signifier but not its chief project (Anthias 1992a, 1992b). Ethnicity may be political (Cohen 1974; Hechter 1987; Rex 1986), drawing on cultural as well as other identity narratives and resources, such as economic niches and social networks, to pursue diverse political projects (Anthias 1990, 1992a). Cultural resources are only one of a set of resources used by ethnic groups.

However, ethnic groups are various and diverse. Ethnic groups may not necessarily be subordinate. They may be hegemonic, which is the case for those who are represented either exclusively, or as the majority in the state, and its institutions. For example the English are an ethnic group whose 'culture' is most fully represented in the British state. The relational identification of such ethnic majorities or dominant ethnic groups is in juxtaposition to the 'others' who are in a subordinate position. The term 'ethnic' group is always constructed relationally. It only makes sense in the context of the ethnicisation of another population and involves a process of differentiation. It could be argued that all individuals have an ethnicity. If this is the case, 'hybrids' also possess an ethnicity. If there are hybrid cultural forms then these hybrid social forms may or may not have a singular effect on the ethnic boundary: the case must rest with the investigation. Moreover, it may be that the hybrid condition is a transitory one and like all forms of ethnic identity, situational and contextual. Hybridity and cosmopolitanism, in this sense, may be just particular configurations of the shifting and dynamic nature of the cultural narrative contained in ethnic phenomena. However, some aspects of culture may be *incommensurable*; translation may not always be possible, a point noted by Schutz discussed earlier. Spivak (1993) makes a similar point when she points to the impossibility of translation between dominant and subaltern cultures: for the subaltern can't speak. Moreover, if hybridity is a product of a mix and a dialogue, under what conditions does it take place and what are those features of culture that can 'travel best' and for whom?

Not all aspects of culture have been equally malleable to globalisation (if that, as it often does, implies homogenisation, particularly around Western values and actions). Nor is the recognition of the influence of 'subaltern' cultures, in the domain of music for example, enough to hang the notion of a two-way dialogue. The mixed cultural patterns of second- and third-generation diasporic actors underplays the extent to which gender and religion, for example, serve different ends in different contexts (e.g. see Afshar 1994). The bringing together of different cultural elements syncretically transforms their meaning, but need not mean that dialogue between cultural givens is necessarily taking place. Moreover, it could be argued that the acid test of hybridity lies in the response of culturally dominant groups, not only in terms of incorporating (or coopting) cultural products of marginal or subordinate groups, but in being open to transforming and abandoning some of their own central cultural symbols and practices of hegemony. Until there is evidence of this, it seems somewhat over-enthusiastic to denote contemporary cultural forms as hybrid. This is particularly the case when the dimension of power over the deployment of different cultural symbols is rendered visible. Although there are hybridities to be found in the realm of music, art, fashion and food, amongst other cultural forms, there is very little evidence of dominant white culture seceding its role in defining the cultural domain. This is precisely the critique made of multiculturalism as a theory and a practice; not only does it reify cultural difference but it treats hegemonic culture as natural. I do not have the space to address these problems in detail but I want to summarise three central problems of the debate on cultural hybridity here:

1   It privileges the domain of the cultural as opposed to the material or the political (restricting its sense to that of cultural products) and therefore depoliticises culture. It loses sight of cultural domination; power, as embodied in culture, disappears. Hybridity may not be possible in the colonial encounter (see Spivak 1993).
2   It homogenises the group in not attending to differentiated hybridisation. The differential projects of diaspora groups or the divisions within them are not explored enough, particularly those of class and gender (see Anthias 1998b).
3   It focuses too much on transgressive elements and underplays alienation, exclusion, violence and fundamentalism as part of cultural encounters, particularly where there is social assymetry as in colonialism.

Given these difficulties, a range of questions needs to be substantively researched. Under what conditions is a synthesis of cultural elements possible? Which elements of culture become destabilised? To what extent do groups assert identity in the face of threat? Which social groups within are most reluctant to negotiate cultural rules and around which aspects of culture? Are some aspects of culture more difficult to mix? How important is the institution of family and kinship the position of women and religious and moral rules, particularly around sexuality? What are the difficulties of translation? Is there a truly radicalising potential? What are the different forms the condition takes?

Diaspora

Having explored some of the difficulties and contradictions found in the notion of hybridity, I now want to turn to its sister concept, that of diaspora. Hybridity and diaspora are terms that are often coexistent if not coterminous. Both denote an important reconfiguration of 'ethnic' boundaries and bonds and posit the growth of transnationalism. Diaspora is an old term, but has been rediscovered in order to be made to do theoretical work, in relation to the growth of new identities and experiences (e.g. Hall 1990; Gilroy 1993b; Bhabha 1990, 1994; Clifford 1994; Brah 1996; R. Cohen 1997). It may be seen as providing a less essentialised approach to 'ethnic' allegiances than those found within mainstream ethnic and race paradigms.

The term diaspora is a Greek word meaning the spreading of seeds. The contemporary revival of the term 'diaspora' can be largely attributed to the influential work of black writers like Stuart Hall (1990) and Paul Gilroy (1993b, 1997), writing within a cultural studies tradition and using a postmodern frame. 'Diaspora' has also been used as a descriptive typological tool for understanding migration and settlement in the global era (R. Cohen 1997), and to denote a social condition and a societal process (Clifford 1994) (for an extensive discussion see Anthias 1998a). The old usage of diaspora restricted it to population categories which have experienced 'forceful or violent expulsion' processes (classically used about the Jews), but in the modern usage it refers to a population category or a social condition entailing a particular form of 'consciousness' which is particularly compatible with postmodernity and globalisation, and, like hybridity, embodies the globalising principle of transnationalism (Waters 1995).

Stuart Hall has been concerned, over the years, to develop an analysis which is non-essentialist, and which validates the search for identity. This is linked to experiences of racialisation and posits the importance of narratives of identity for resisting racist exclusions. The concept of diaspora can allow a movement away from the notion of the essential black subject (Hall 1990), historicising it; 'histories have their real, material and symbolic effects' (1990: 226). These histories relate to the recognition 'of a necessary heterogeneity and diversity' and that identity 'lives with and through, not despite, difference; by hybridity' (1990: 235). In Hall's work, the black subject emerges through history as differently constructed and yet still identifiable on the margins, in the periphery, largely because of racialised experience and subjectivity.

Paul Gilroy's book *The Black Atlantic* (1993a), referred to in the discussion of hybridity, also constitutes the most used and developed approach to the new concept of diaspora as well. The defence of the notion of 'diaspora' hinges on its ability to transcend the emphasis on the borders of the nation-state. Gilroy suggests that diasporic positionality produces a form of consciousness that crosses the borders of given national, or ethnic, tunnel visions, constituting a double consciousness. In this sense for Gilroy, the diaspora is the collective space or site within which hybrid social forms flourish. Although highly original and insightful, it relies not so much on an analysis of the specificities of diasporic consciousness, but on the cultural products of this diasporic formation. This posits both continuities and discontinuities within the black cultural domain. The insights of Gilroy's approach have influenced many writers to use the term diaspora, which, it could be argued, has often been made to substitute theoretical work in substantive analysis. To what extent is it translatable into a general theoretical tool?

The notion of diaspora is placed centrally in many of the arguments about the connection between the local and the global, and the development of cultural globalisation, or glocalisation as Robertson (1995) calls it. One of the main ways in which the term has been used is as a celebration of the implications of diasporic models of consciousness and action. For example, Winant (1994: 273) notes 'the rise of diasporic models of blackness, the creation of pan-ethnic communities of Latinos and Asians . . . all seem to be hybridising and racialising previously national politics, cultures and identities'. Hall's idea of the role of the diaspora in 'translation' and R. Cohen's (1997) view that the diaspora can supersede the nation-state, as a form of social organisation, impute a radicalizing and destabilising character to the diaspora as a social force, and see it as a challenge to the nation state. Cohen (1993, 1997) sees a fit between diasporic processes and globalisation and notes 'the development of new creative energy in a challenging, pluralistic context outside the natal homeland' (1993: 5). He suggests (1993: 22) that the old diasporic practice of sojourning has become a feature of the new global economy. Cohen paints a fairly optimistic picture drawing also on Hall's depiction of the African Caribbean diaspora as undergoing a process of hybridisation 'through transformation and difference' (Hall 1990: 235). Clifford's (1994) view is that one way of conceptualising diaspora is to note what it defines itself against: the norms of the nation-state and the claims of indigenous tribal peoples. The nation-state is subverted by diasporic attachments which involve forms of hybridisation and cultural change, but without cultural assimilation. Contestation generally is over the rights to culture, to roots rather than for political representation. Such roots, Clifford claims, are not conceived as static. A degree of accommodation is achieved in as much as the permanent locale now becomes the place of settlement, rather than the homeland, and identity becomes more syncretic. Clifford refers to this as selective accommodation: the desire to stay and be different. The claims of belonging are a challenge to essentialist claims of the authentic ties to the land made by 'natives'.

I will examine various issues here in order to pinpoint some difficulties with the notion of diaspora particularly with reference to its underlying assumptions.

Transnationality and transethnicity

It has been suggested that diasporas think globally but live locally. There is an assumption, however, of a unitary community of actors whose commonality derives from an original 'seed' or fatherland. The original father(land) is a point of reference for the diaspora notion which precedes the affirmation of bonds with the siblings in other countries. I argued earlier that hybridity deploys a particular notion of 'culture' (as content or product). Diaspora also deploys a notion of ethnic bonds as primarily revolving around the centrality of 'origin', seeing these being played out in a transnational arena. Therefore, there is a subtext which involves privileging the point of 'origin' in constructing identity and solidarity. If this is the case, then it sits uneasily with the view that diasporas can transcend the orientation to homelands. Indeed in some analyses, the continuing attachment to the idea of ethnic and therefore particularist bonds is underestimated. Diasporas may derive legitimation and strength from global connections. The legitimacy of the claims may be sought in a more global international context. There may be an overarching concern with the homeland and its national project, which Anderson calls long-distance nationalism. This may be found in the political projects of the Irish, the Jews and the Greeks (Anderson 1995). However, they may be essentially reconstituting a form of local, and particularist, ethnic absolutism. Many writers emphasise the importance of transnational bonds and see these as positive and useful in undermining ethnic and national divisions. However, such bonds may weaken transethnic bonds with other groups which share a more local or national context of contestation and struggle. I have argued elsewhere (Anthias 1998b) that the concept of diaspora fails to pay adequate attention to transethnic, as opposed to transnational, processes. The concept of diaspora also neglects the aspects of ethnicity that are exclusionary, for the commonality constructed by racism is different, and indeed may be transethnic rather than transnational. Transethnic, as opposed to transnational, commonalities and processes are pushed to the background in discussions of 'diaspora' and this sits uneasily with the idea of hybridisation as transethnicity. So whilst hybridity and diaspora are often conjoined within approaches, the connection and tension between them is ignored.

Homogeneous communities and diversity within

I have also argued (Anthias 1998a) that the focus on diasporic attachments forecloses a concern with differences of gender, class and generation within diasporic groups. The category of diaspora fails to provide a class and gender analysis of the processes of migration, settlement and accommodation. Class is a missing term in the discourse of the diaspora. For example, the image of the diasporic individual in Bhabha (1990, 1994) is of the cosmopolitan individual, most likely to be an intellectual. With regard to gender, the role of men and women in the process of accommodation and syncretism may be different; this issue is not explored.

The concept of diaspora may be able to deliver a concern with cultural change, changing identities (or new identities), globalisation, travel, movement and dispersal. However, it may limit a concern with inter-ethnic allegiances within the nation-state and the systematic appraisal of forms of racism. Moreover, it does not interrogate ethnic rootedness and belonging as forms of exclusion.

Hybridity, modernity and globalisation

Hybridity, hybridisation and diaspora have been central to the debate about cultural globalisation, and have functioned to celebrate it. Such a cultural globalisation has been seen as a challenge to ethnic essentialisms and absolutisms and therefore as a potential weapon in the fight against racism. Interpenetration is a feature of social relations but the combinatory of different elements produces new but highly heterogeneous effects. This does not only mean that a homogeneous culture does not exist, as Pieterse (1995) rightly claims. Neither does it mean that hybridisation, in the sense of interpenetration, can be read into processes of cultural spread, without paying attention to the array of social places, political projects and social divisions that will encounter them and imbue them with local and particular meanings. Also, if, as Pieterse says, the one distinguishing feature of the present phase of globalisation is that no single mode has overall priority, is this not to deny the forms of cultural and ideological hegemony (Laclau and Mouffe 1985) structured in and through capitalist penetration, that is, the dominance of the West?

If, within nation-states, localisms are emerging as the embodiment of universal or global particularisms, how might hybridity and diaspora be seen to involve border crossings and the 'in between function'. I have argued that both concepts, whilst being anti-essentialist, have not been able to move convincingly away from old notions of culture and ethnicity which still lie at their heart. The need to investigate more substantively these processes, whilst not idealising and mytho-logising them, is urgent. Whilst movement across cultures may empower, and enable a more global world-view, distanced from ethnic insularities and fundamentalisms, this needs to be explored in the light of specific and contextual relations of particular diasporic spaces, and cannot be theorised in the abstract.

Taking all these problems into account might urge us to identify a more fragmented and discontinuous picture of 'cultural globalisation' (Featherstone 1990) than that presented within some versions of globalisation theory. It also presents a much more discontinuous notion of the self and identity in high modernity than the one espoused by Giddens (1991). A large number of the diaspora are not exposed to the self-reflexivity that Giddens identifies with modernity, or alternatively, the hybridisation which is seen to characterise the globalisation process by other writers. This applies particularly to certain categories of the excluded, subordinated and disadvantaged: to women, especially working-class and racialised women; those who live within ethnic niches or economies; older migrants; and those transnationals who are not cosmopolitans, some of whom may be ethnic chauvinists. We may have global imagery, but these global images are read through local eyes. Not all those eyes are self-reflexive or would recognise Giddens's risk society!

A singular absence within this literature is the discussion of the shaping of patriarchy by the hybridisations of globalised capital. Feminism has not dealt with globalisation, largely because of the retreat from ideas of a common sisterhood. However, there is a trend to 'hybridities' in the recent debate around transversal or dialogical feminist politics (see Hill Collins 1990), as espoused by Italian feminists and others (e.g. Yuval-Davis 1997c). However, global images of women (as represented by a recent issue of *Cosmopolitan* magazine, on its twentieth anniversary, reprinting covers of world-wide *Cosmopolitan* issues including India, Russia, Japan and Greece) show how homogenous the images of women are, despite subtle differences in nuance. Woman as sex-goddess is clearly a globalised image which can only however be accessed by a select few. This reminds us that we need to distinguish between the existence of the global image and its differential transmission, availability and relevance in a world dominated by illiteracy, poverty and disease.

At the level of the construction of new forms of collective identity, the term hybridity merely denotes another, possibly more 'open' and 'in between' cultural configuration, but this third space is also located rather than 'free-floating': it must be seen in the context of fluidity, diversity and situational context, as well as the political nature of identities in general. A view of hybridised diasporas, which neglects the political and power dimensions of social relations, falls into the same culturalist essentialist traps as earlier notions of ethnicity.

As a counter to notions of hybridity and diaspora, as well as Giddens's notion of the global 'we' identity and the 'pure relationship', I would like to suggest the continuing importance of the social relations of 'othering' on the one hand, and resource struggles on the other. These may take particular forms in the period of 'high modernity'. Some of these may yield reflexivity in recognising multiple selves and others (hybrid/diasporic), but even here there are potentially contradictory processes in terms of struggles around resource allocation; such struggles may take place along the lines of the relations of gender, 'race' and class. Understanding new forms of identity and consciousness, within a global context, requires even more that we attempt to think through the implications of the articulation of gender, ethnicity, 'race' and class. I have argued elsewhere that this understanding lies at the heart of social theory (Anthias 1996, 1998a) and requires not merely the recognition of a proliferation of identities (found in the postmodern frame), nor a conception of the 'self' as befitting high modernity (found in Giddens), nor a notion of hybridised identities and diasporic consciousness, but an analysis that can indicate their connections in producing specific social outcomes.

I have maintained that the problematic of hybridity and hybridisation is inadequate in addressing the issue of the multifarious nature of identifications, since it constructs identity in a singular, albeit synthetic form. It does not acknowledge that the acid test of hybridity might be the extent to which the dominant culture is open to elements that may challenge its hegemony. Nor does it begin to evaluate the progressive potential of different types of synthesis or interculturality. The political projects, to which so-called hybrid social forms are harnessed, have not been adequately explored nor are the potentially violent and dislocating aspects of the hybrid or diasporic condition effectively addressed. But more importantly, the concerns of hybridity and diaspora are essentially those of culture and consciousness, rather than social inequality and exclusion. The focus on the latter has been displaced by the postmodern emphasis on difference and identity, on hybridity and diaspora. The materialist, as opposed to culturalist, bases of racist subordinations, inequalities and exclusions have been marginalised through the new hegemony of this postmodern discourse within the social sciences. A refocus on these requires specific and local analyses of differentiated social outcomes, looked at through the complex interweaving of the social relations related to hierarchical positionality, and not just through a focus on culture and identity. I will therefore now turn to postulating an alternative conception which acknowledges the role of interculturality on the one hand but attempts to move beyond this in the discussion of anti-racism.

Anti-racism and the issue of identity and difference

One of the most useful insights of the debates sketched above relates to the issue of boundaries of identity as central elements in racist practice. Hence the idea of ethnic categories as implicit in racialised social relations, whilst contested in the 1980s and much of the 1990s, has now become acknowledged. Indeed, Hall's own notion of 'new ethnicities', the work of writers like Modood (1994a) on the category 'black' and the problem of giving a common 'naming' to racialised groups, the recognition of culture as a central element in racism through the notion of cultural racism but also of a racist culture (Goldberg 1993) – all these constitute important advances. The critique of multiculturalism as fixing culture, the failure to acknowledge fully the constructed and shifting nature of ethnic categorisations (e.g. the use of the term Asian is an attribution rather than an identification which uses common signifiers), is also linked to the failure to recognise different positionalities around class, gender and politics. Hybridity theory has refined older debates about the conditions by which cultural monism can be transcended, and the subversive role of culture contact where it is not premised on the colonial encounter and as enriching the traveller (although not necessarily the native). The discussion of diasporic space in the work of writers like James Clifford (1994) and Avtar Brah (1996) optimistically transforms the facts of such a space (i.e. that indeed people are all transformed by transnational population movements) into a progressive outcome in relation to people being opened up to the imaginative possibilities of such a mixing and interaction.

Dialogue is an essential element in this process. But dialogue can not be guaranteed by the coming together of different cultural groups or when there are different interests around resources such as those of representation and recognition as well as the more obvious economic and cultural resources. Nor can it be simply guaranteed by a formula such as being rooted in one set of cultural idioms whilst respecting and acknowledging the other, i.e. as an ethical encounter, where asymmetric relations exist. The conditions for 'voice', of being allowed to speak from a different 'place', are important. However, what is central is being able to make effective the claims of the voice. It is neither simply a matter of asking under what conditions allegiances or alliances can be forged: the very notion of allegiance already presupposes the investments in the 'difference' that allegiances are to be made 'between'. The notion of hybridities (unlike that of diaspora, which retains a notion of a distinctive place of origin by which one is to be defined, despite a multiple belonging and engagement somewhere else) already assumes that the difference has been overcome or at least that the difference is no longer one between people but within them, and therefore validated when discovered between them also. Such differences can no longer therefore have an equal ontological status. The reason this is not enough is because it ignores the other constructions of difference and identity within which positionalities are made, those of gender and class.

A focus on location and translocation (see Anthias 2001) rather than culture or identity is able to redress some of these problems. This recognises the importance of context, the situated nature of claims and attributions and their production in complex and shifting locales. It also recognises variability with some processes leading to more complex, contradictory and at times dialogical positionalities than others. The term 'translocational' references the complex nature of positionality faced by those who are at the interplay of a range of locations and dislocations in relation to gender, ethnicity, national belonging, class and racialisation (see Anthias 1998a). It is therefore able to move more effectively away from the residual elements of essentialisation and culturalism retained within the concept of 'hybridities'.

What has usually been thought about as a question of identity (collective identity) can be understood as relating to *boundaries* on the one hand and *hierarchies* on the other. Not only do 'identities' such as ethnicity/'race' (as well as gender and class) entail categories of difference and identity (*boundaries*), they also construct social positions (*hierarchies*), and involve the allocation of power and other resources. What characterises such categories as boundaries is *relationality, naturalisation and collectivisation* (for an extended discussion see Anthias 1998a). Relationality involves the construction of categories that involve dichotomy and function as mutually exclusive; to identify is to differentiate from and vice versa. Cultural constructs around these categories tend to use binaries, common in Western thought (self/other, male/female, black/white). Naturalisation involves the formation of categories which are taken as indisputable and given. The construction of collective attributions and the production of unitary categories are a particularly salient aspect of ethnic and gender divisions and construct those inside (and often outside) in unitary terms. Constructions of sexual or 'racial' difference in terms of a biological or somatic difference come to signify or postulate necessary social effects, to produce gendered or racialised depictions and dispositions.

What this suggests is that anti-racism, as the fight against those constructions of difference and identity that exclude and devalorise, requires a concerted effort against all those social practices that construct identities and differences in naturalised, collectivised and binary ways and in terms of hierarchical otherness, unequal resource allocation and modes of inferiorisation (see Anthias 1998a). This includes engagement at a political level around the following:

- Naturalisation: a denaturalisation of difference and identity by showing the ways they are located historically and as social constructs. This involves not only culture contact but a concern with addressing all those institutional ways in which such naturalisation is constructed, from the assumptions made in the legal and political systems to unequal resource distribution across various social categories.
- Collective attributions: a recognition of differences within individuals in terms of the interaction between ways in which they are constructed and construct themselves situationally and contextually: therefore an emphasis also on gender, class and other forms of categorisations. A refusal to construct people or selves in terms of singular identities. Whilst identity is the narrative where one is constructed as a person with agency, this needs to be mitigated by a recognition of the importance of location and positionality in terms of

opportunities and constraints for the effective articulation (even at the necessary fictive level) of its performance or accomplishment.

- Hierarchical cultures: the development of legal and other state mechanisms
  which embody the principle of multiculturality where it does not conflict with
  the basic ethical principle of personal autonomy as a basic human right and
  where the collective claims of groups allow individuals to choose the legal and
  cultural framework within which they are embedded (e.g. education or legal
  pluralism) as long as this does not violate rules of human rights of individuals.
- Racial and ethnic categories: should not be seen unproblematically as having
  their own political voice. However, they must have rights to culture and ways
  of life as long as these do not conflict with overall principles of human rights.
- Rights and responsibilities: include ethical principles of responsibility to the
  human rights of others.
- Mechanisms of accountability within institutional frameworks: scrutiny of
  procedures in terms of outcomes as well as intentions and rules, so that
  racialised sexist and class unequal outcomes are made prominent even where
  no intentionalities are found, and redressed through corrective and sustain-
  able procedures such as positive action frameworks.

A concluding note on 'dialogue'

Such a framework brings me back to the notion of dialogue in terms of dialogic
positionalities. This involves asserting the role of talk and voice, the right to be
heard and the responsibility to listen. Such basic intersubjective competencies are
important to structure the framework of debate at all social levels, including being
a central element in the school curriculum: modes of persuasion, tolerance,
understanding, empathy, shifting of position and recognising the multiple nature
of the intersubjective encounter at the individual and group level are all important
facets of this. Intersubjectivity itself assumes the possibility of dialogue since it
involves being oriented to the other and the practical accomplishment of
communication and articulation. For Mead (1934) intersubjectivity or dialogue is
the basis of the construction of self and society. For Goffman (1974) dialogue
involves rituals of interaction and for Schutz (1970) dialogue is rooted in shared
taken-for-granted world-views. For Habermas (1985), on the other hand,
language in dialogue works towards consensus. His ethics of communicative
action requires rational minds oriented to understanding. In dialogue one is faced
with the 'other' and has to negotiate meaning. One could argue that this both
reveals otherness and submerges it, submerging the plural through misidenti-
fication and overdetermination. Bakhtin's (1981) dialogical sociality insists not on
Mead's generalised other but the social as heterogeneous with no unified core.
For dialogue to be possible, however, we must assume a common framework of
meaning. Effective dialogue requires the ability to establish equal positionalities
from which to speak and to be structured through rules of symmetry. This
assumes the goodwill of partners in dialogue, but goodwill already assumes an
imaginary dialogue, i.e. an orientation to the abstract or concrete other. In
dialogue you show who you are to yourself as well as to others; your meaning is

expressed to you after you have spoken and acted in the speech and in the action. If the other is an enemy or a threat, what kind of dialogue is possible? Dialogue becomes monologue in the colonial or hegemonic/hierarchised encounter (this may depend on rules and practices of hierarchy). In this case dialogue becomes a way of enabling power, i.e. as a legitimation tool.

This discussion shows that dialogue as an enactment is an important but not necessarily an adequate framework for thinking about anti-racism in the broader sense that I have suggested: as the fight against the border guards of difference and identity. Such performativity, of orientations to the other, of goodwill, of the ethical encounter (as in Levinas 1987), must be located within the rule of symmetry where access to resources of both a material and a symbolic nature involves effective participation and the autonomous self, i.e. this requires an emphasis on processes of equalisation at levels that include those of gender and class as well as ethnicity/race. However, such processes can only become possible under conditions where the dialogical imperative has been enabled and therefore we can reassert the notion of dialogue here in terms of a dialectical moment between establishing practices where dialogue is performative and working towards social arrangements which reinforce these processes. No blueprint is aimed at here. The debate must now be in terms of the forms of politics which will deliver such social arrangements: this brings back, as a central element of debate, the nature of the new politics which will deliver anti-racism from the tunnel vision of racism itself, both as a focus separate from other understandings of devalorisation and inequality, and as a social reality that dehumanises both culprits and victims.

Note

1 This chapter draws, in part, on my article 'New hybridities, old concepts: the limits of culture', *Ethnic and Racial Studies* 24 (4), 2001.

3 Some reflections on the questions of citizenship and anti-racism

Nira Yuval-Davis

As early as 1987 Paul Gilroy found 'anti-racist strategy' to be highly problematic. Bob Miles (1993) contemplated racism – and the fight against it – beyond the 'race relations paradigm' which has dominated the British anti-racist movement in some form or another since the 1960s. Michel Wieviorka (1997) has argued that following the rise of new racism, which does not necessarily use the terminology of 'race', it is not easy to detect, as it used to be, the difference between racists and anti-racists. In the 1990s 'racism is said to be everywhere, including among those whose intention it is to combat it; the references are confused while, at the same time, the evil is perceived as gaining ground' (1997: 141).

Obviously, such statements reflect a paradigmatical shift in the thinking about racism as well as anti-racism and need further reflection. This has been given further impetus by the Stephen Lawrence murder inquiry report (Macpherson 1999, see also the special issue of *Sociological Research On-Line*, Spring 1999) and the ways the public, the media and the state have been responding to it. The aim of this chapter is to examine what the new discourses around the notion of citizenship could offer to such a rethinking. Following the decline of class struggle and the rise of identity politics with their own particularistic agendas, citizenship discourse has gradually become the main inclusionary emancipatory discourse of the left. None the less, as Hall and Held noted (1989), questions of immigration and racism have kept debates on 'citizenship' going before it became a fashionable discourse in the late 1980s. If there is any common goal to anti-racist thought it is to enable all people in society to be full and active citizens (Jayasuriya 1991), to remove the fixed, immutable and naturalised boundaries of otherness involved in processes of racialisation (Anthias and Yuval-Davis 1992). The political and theoretical debates that are taking place concerning questions of equality and difference, to which Wieviorka (1997) alludes, relate to the question of what such an inclusive notion of citizenship might mean, as well as to the ways required to achieve it.

This chapter relates to some of the major theories and debates on citizenship that have taken place within various disciplines, such as political sciences (in particular the debates between liberals, republicans and communitarians); sociology and social policy (especially Marshall 1950; Edwards 1988; B. Turner 1990); pluralism (e.g. Kymlicka 1995; Jayasuriya 1991; Young 1989); feminism (e.g. Pateman 1988a, b; Lister 1998); and a conference at Greenwich on Women,

Citizenship and Difference which gave rise to a special issue *of Feminist Review*, 1997 (see also Yuval-Davis 1999).

This chapter will tease out of these debates the specific issues that are important for a construction of an anti-racist approach oriented to citizenship, in particular issues relating to boundaries of collectivities (sub-, cross- and supra- as well as national), equality and difference, and the relationship between the notions of citizenship and human rights. Its main argument is that an anti-racist notion of citizenship is that of a multi-layered citizenship (Yuval-Davis 1999). Such a notion of citizenship recognises, without essentialising and reifying, the different positionings of different citizens. It also acknowledges that today, more than ever before, states are not the only polities in which people are citizens, although they often are still the most powerful ones. An anti-racist notion of citizenship is a dialogical transversal citizenship (Yuval-Davis 1997a, 1997b; *Soundings* 1999; Yuval-Davis and Werbner 1999) that takes into consideration power relations between collectivities as well as between individuals, but does not confuse positionings with identities.

The nature of contemporary citizenship

The renewed interest in issues of citizenship accompanied the rise of 'the politics of recognition' (Taylor 1994a). In this politics, marginal elements in society who were previously excluded, formally or informally, from participation in the public political arena, have fought their way, largely by means of identity politics and social movements, into social and political recognition. Part of this process has been the establishment of multiculturalism as a transformative project of the welfare state (Schierup 1995), especially in Anglo-Saxon states.

This transformative project has taken place in the context of the far-reaching political and social restructuring which accompanied the disintegration of the Soviet Union, the rise of neo-liberal globalisation and the abandonment of class as the major tool of political resistance and organisation.

These geo-political changes have also affected the nature of citizenship itself (Turner 1999). However, the association of citizenship with 'nation-states' constructs an image in which the globe is divided into different territories, each of which belongs to a nation, which ideally has its own state. The reality, of course, has always been very far from such a fiction. There have always been waves of immigration of populations from one country to another, as a result of wars, natural disasters, persecution of particular religious or ethnic minorities and poverty. The association of specific nations with specific territories and specific states has always been a result of particular cultural-political processes and has often been contested.

Many people whose countries were under European rule before and after independence have migrated to Western countries. They, and other migrants from marginal European and Middle Eastern countries, were recruited to work in Western countries in the post-Second World War expanding economies, and became their new ethnic minorities from the 1960s onwards (Castles and Miller 1993). The members of these new ethnic communities established themselves in new diasporic communities and their membership in their states of residence needs to be understood from their specific historical, cultural and often legal positions in the country, as well as in their relationships to their countries of origin (Brah 1996). The demise of the 'iron curtain' and the many regional wars in Southern Europe, the Middle East and Africa have added to and accelerated these waves of international migration of both labourers and especially of asylum-seekers and refugees. The rise of new 'tiger economies' has directed immigrants to countries which traditionally were not used to recruiting external migrant labour. As Castles and Miller point out, contemporary international migration tends to be globalised, to and from a broad spectrum of countries, it is growing in number and is led by a variety of motivations, skills and countries of origin.

Formal citizenship is normally associated with the right to carry a passport of a specific state, which normally identifies the individual as 'belonging' to a specific nation-state. One of the signals of the super-state nation-building of 'Europe' has been the issue of a European passport for all EU members. While the formal intention has been to establish a 'borderless Europe', the transfer of responsibility of illegal immigration to the flight and shipping companies has resulted in many cases with even more scrupulous checking of passports than before. An international system of stratification has been created, at the top of which are found Western passports which can almost always guarantee their carriers the right of free international movements, and at the bottom of which are those who have no right to carry any passport at all. In parallel there has been a growth in the number of people who carry two, three or even more passports of different states. Interestingly, the practice of issuing passports, although so thoroughly 'naturalised', is only about a hundred years old and the use of passports as a way of controlling immigration is even younger.

Norman Tebbit, an ex-minister in Thatcher's government, argued that the support of British citizens of South Asian origin to the cricket teams of their countries of origin proves that they are not loyal British citizens, much to their indignation and resistance. In many parts of the world there exist immigrant communities that are culturally and politically committed to continue to 'belong' to their 'mother country' – or more specifically to the national collectivity from where they, their parents or their forebears have come. At the same time they see their own and their children's future as bound with the country where they live. When examining issues of citizenship of those migrants and their children, therefore, one needs to take into consideration not only their formal and informal status in the countries where they live, but also that in their countries of origin as well. Probably most important in determining their position would be the relationships between the two countries and their relative position of power in the international social order. A comparison between the relative power and freedom of, for example, a white American student and a Somali refugee living in London could illustrate this most forcefully.

Another whole set of citizenship issues is related to indigenous minorities in settler societies. The age of Western imperialism and colonialism has created 'settler societies', sponsored by European empires in South and North America,

South and North Africa, Australia and New Zealand (Stasiulis and Yuval-Davis 1995). In these states the indigenous populations were often persecuted, exploited, exterminated and in some cases until today have not received full citizenship rights. Moreover, indigenous peoples' movements have tended to challenge the whole basis of legitimacy of settler societies as they may see themselves as citizens in the communities of the stateless societies which existed in these countries before colonialism (e.g. Dickanson 1992; Reynolds 1996).

However, it is not just that in many societies indigenous populations have been very late, if at all, entrants to the formal citizenship body of the state. It is that if their claim on the country, in the form of land rights, was to be taken seriously and in full, this would totally conflict with the claim of the settler national collectivity for legitimacy. Attempts to solve the problem by transforming the indigenous population into another 'ethnic minority' have usually met with a strong and understandable resistance (de Lepervanche 1980). Formal treaties, which would institutionalise and anchor in law the relations between what Australian Aboriginals have been calling 'the imposing society' and the indigenous people, often create a complex situation in which there exist two national sovereign entities over the same territory: one that owns the state and one that attempts to establish a sovereign stateless society within it. There is a need to explore the implications of such conflicts for the citizenship of both the 'indigenous' and the settler communities, both in relation to their own communities and in relation to the state. Kymlicka's (1995) and Taylor's (1994b) proposals in this respect are far from satisfactory – as will be discussed later on in the chapter.

Somewhat similar, if less racialised, struggles are present in the many regionalist secessionist or irredentist movements which claim the right of national self-determination *vis-à-vis* their states which themselves have been constructed as nations. Such movements can be found both in Europe and outside it (e.g. in Northern Ireland, Former Yugoslavia, Quebec, Kurdistan, Northern Sahara, East Timor). The legitimacy and state of the struggle would determine the relationships between the citizenship of people in the two contesting collectivities. Their fate might be determined these days more and more by intervention of international NGOs and governmental agencies (probably the most extreme intervention of this kind to date has been in Kosovo).

The constraints on the state in many of the post-colonial states, by local and traditional communities on the one hand, and multinationals and international agencies on the other hand, would be even more noticeable than in the West. As a result of the above, I have been arguing (1991, 1997c, 1999) that citizenship needs to be understood as a multi-layered construct. One's citizenship in collectivities at different levels/layers – local, ethnic, national, state, cross- or trans-state and supra-state – is affected and often at least partly constructed by the relationships and positionings of each layer in specific historical contexts. This is of particular importance if we want to examine citizenship in a way which is not westocentric. Recent technological, economic and political developments have enhanced the need for such an analytical perspective.

The debate on citizenship and difference

The liberal theory of citizenship has been challenged from a variety of directions. One of the central debates in political sciences, especially in the USA, has been the debate between the liberals on the one hand and the republicans and communitarians on the other hand (see, for example, Avineri and Shalit 1992; Daly 1993; Oldfield 1990; Peled 1992; Roche 1987).

For the liberals, citizenship has been envisaged as a relationship between individuals and the state, constructed by a set of formal rights and obligations. For the republicans, citizenship is mediated by the 'moral community'. While Liberals assume the priority of 'right over good' (Sandel 1982), for the republicans citizenship means active involvement and participation in the 'determination, practice and promotion of the common good'. Thus, for liberals, citizenship is foremost a status of an individual in relation to the state, with no predetermined relationship with other citizens (and thus, in a way continuing the citizenship tradition of the Roman Empire). For republicans, citizenship is foremost an act of active participation in the political community and thus, in a way, continuing the citizenship tradition of the Greek *polis* and medieval cities (Shafir 1998). Communitarians go further than the republicans. For them it is not just a question of people living with each other as part of a community. Rather, they perceive people as products of the community in which they were socialised and constructed since the day they were born.

Several issues in this debate are important to the question of racism and resistance to it. One issue is whether or not the citizen is an abstract individual or a member of a particular community, with particular culture and tradition. It is not only liberals but also Marx (in his article on the Jewish question, 1975) who constructed citizens as abstract individuals and saw all particularisms as belonging to the arena of civil society rather than the political one. Such a universalist position can be seen as promising equal treatment and non-discrimination towards individuals, but as Balibar (1990) and others have pointed out, it does not take into account the fact that, given the different positioning of individuals, such a formal universalism would necessarily be exclusionary.

The question arises, then, to what extent the republican and communitarian models, which do recognise people as members of specific communities, offer a better alternative that would be sensitive to issues of racism. Unfortunately, as I have elaborated elsewhere (Yuval-Davis 1997a, 1997b), the communities to which the promoters of these models relate are usually the hegemonic historical national communities. Peled (1992), when discussing the republican community, distinguished between two distinct notions of community that can be discerned in the current revival of republicanism: a weak community, in which membership is essentially voluntary, and a strong, historical community that is *discovered,* not formed by its members. In a strong community its 'ongoing existence is an important value in and of itself' and becomes one of the most (if not *the* most) important imperatives of the 'moral community'.

Membership in such a community involves 'enduring attachment', a myth of common destiny and often a myth of common origin, and is clearly bonded by a myth of common destiny. In other words, this 'strong community' is the national 'imagined community' (Anderson 1983). There is no difference between republican constructions of the 'moral community' and the *gemeinschaft*-like constructions of the 'national community'.

The question arises, then, about what should happen to those members of the civil society who cannot or would not become full members of that 'strong community'. As mentioned above, virtually in all contemporary states there are migrants and refugees, 'old' and 'new' minorities, and in settler societies also indigenous people who are not part of the hegemonic national community (Stasiulis and Yuval-Davis 1995). In addition, there are many other members of civil society who, although they might share the myth of common origin of 'the community', do not share important hegemonic value systems with the majority of the population in sexual, religious and other matters.

Works like those of Ignatieff (1993), Kristeva (1993) and Habermas (1992) (see also Robert Fine's critique of their works on nationalism, 1994) smooth over the difference between the members of national communities who share in the hegemonic majority's 'myth of common origin' and those who do not. They perceive 'ethnic nationalism' as a negative characteristic of 'Others'. That things are experienced differently by the marginal Others in their 'nations without nationalism' (to use Kristeva's book name) is not taken, or not taken enough, into account.

Residents, and even formal citizens of the state, who are not part of these communities are excluded, at least partially, from full citizenship. In some cases the option of assimilation may be open for them, or at least for their children, and they become full citizens once the signifiers of difference between them and members of the citizenship community disappear. This is how J.-P. Sartre described liberal anti-Semitism, which is ready to accept Jews once there is nothing which specifies them as Jews any more (1948). At most, as Peled suggests (1992), those who are not members of the hegemonic 'moral' (or, rather, national) community may be offered liberal-like citizenship which gives them rights and responsibilities as individuals, rather than as members of the citizenship community.

Peled's suggestion (noted earlier) is similar to that of Taylor (1994a) and Walzer (1994), who have attempted to solve the problems within liberal discourse by differentiating between what they call 'liberalism 1' and 'liberalism 2'. Liberalism 1 is committed to individual rights and, calls for the absolute neutrality of the state. Liberalism 2, on the other hand, allows the state to promote the existence and flourishing of a particular culture, as long as the rights of all citizens would be defended (Walzer 1994: 99). Walzer argues that 'liberalism 2' actually fits more closely the European model of the 'nation-state' than that of liberalism 1 and does not seem to be perturbed by the necessarily exclusionary effects such a 'liberalism' might entail. Moreover, both Tamir (1998) and Burke (1999), in their different ways, point out that in reality there has not been such a difference between the two kinds of liberalism. In a way they both go back to Balibar's argument that any ideology, such as liberalism, that presents itself as universalist and neutral, is exclusionary without acknowledging this.

T. H. Marshall (1950, 1975, 1981), who has been the most influential social scientist theoretician of citizenship and the welfare state, and who defines citizenship as 'a full membership in the community', assumes, like other theoreticians of citizenship, the overlapping relationship between the boundaries of civil and political communities and, the nation. However, unlike liberals, republicans or communitarians, Marshall relates also to class differences among the members of the community. His approach to citizenship has two major advantages over the previous ones, which have been teased out and developed further by other citizenship scholars. One is that Marshall does not define citizenship explicitly in terms of the nation-state at all. This allows a theorisation of citizenship that views citizenship in the nation-state only as a historical phase in the history of citizenship which has existed in a variety of frameworks and polities – in cities (the Greek *polis* and medieval cities) and empires as well as in nation-states. With the evolving of the European Union, the UN and other inter- and supra-national polities, 'post-Fordist citizenship', to use Bryan Turner's expression (1999), is progressively relevant to other bodies than that of the 'nation-state'. As mentioned above, these different forms of citizenship should not be seen as mutually exclusive but rather, contemporary citizenship should be seen as a multi-layered construct. I shall come back to that point later in the chapter.

Marshall has also brought into the arena of citizenship the notion of difference among citizens, when he discussed citizenship social rights. The development of welfare rights was directly linked with differences in social needs. Marshall's notion of citizenship is constructed, to use Edwards's words (1988: 135), as 'treatment as equals rather than equal treatment'. Again, differences of ethnicity, nationality, race and culture are not mentioned in his work. However, his sensitivity to some differences among the members of the citizenship body opened the way for those who wanted to argue, especially within multicultural policy model, for the inclusion of these differences into the citizenship paradigm.

Social rights and social difference

As originally envisaged by Beveridge (1942), social welfare rights were aimed at improving the quality of life of the working classes (as well as the smooth working of capitalism). As Harris (1987) put it, welfare was conceived as the institutionalised recognition of social solidarity within the political community of the citizens.

As Evans (1993) points out, this social solidarity is being threatened by a variety of groupings, ethnic, racial, religious and sexual sub-collectivities which exist within the marginal matrix of society and 'which experience informal and formal discrimination consonant with their credited lower social worth' (1993: 6). A primary concern of many relevant struggles and debates (Gordon 1989; Hall and Held 1989) has been around the right to enter or to remain in a specific country. The 'freedom of movement within the European community', the Israeli Law of Return, and the patriality clause in British immigration legislation, are all instances of ideological, often racist, constructions of boundaries which allow unrestricted immigration to some and block it completely for others.

Even when questions of entry and settlement have been resolved, the concerns of ethnic minorities might be different from those of other members of the society. For example, their right to formal citizenship might depend upon the rules and regulations of their country of origin in addition to those of the country where they live, as well as the relationship between the two. Thus, people from some Caribbean islands who have been settled in Britain for years have been told that they could not have a British passport because their country does not recognise dual citizenship and because they had not declared (in time) their intent to renounce the citizenship of their country of origin after it received independence. Concern over relatives and fear of not being allowed to visit their country of origin prevents others (such as Iranians and Turks) from giving up their original formal citizenship. Women workers who have children in other countries are often not entitled to receive child benefits like other mothers. Countries like Israel and Britain confer citizenship on those whose parents are citizens rather than on those born in the country. Further, the right of entry to a country is often conditional on a commitment by the immigrant that neither s/he nor any other family member will claim any welfare benefits.

However, as Shafir (1998: 14) reminds us, one needs to differentiate between social rights that are universal, and welfare rights which are given only to those who need them. As Ruth Lister (1998: 50) comments, the question of social heritage raises the question of 'culture and tradition' and the extent to which people who belong to ethnic and national collectivities with different cultural 'heritage' to that of the hegemonic majority would be entitled to receive support from the state in relation to theirs. This question is under intense debate between the 'universalist' right who call for 'the separation of race and the state' (D'Souza 1995) and the multiculturalists who call for the state to support each cultural group according to their needs.

Therefore, the growing importance of multicultural policies in many of the Western states towards settled minorities, as well as the rise of identity politics, has raised the question of the extent to which differences other than class, age and health should be acknowledged among citizens. A lot of the discussion on this has been related to the social rights of citizenship, both individual and collective.

For instance, an important debate has taken place on how the state determine whether, what and how much resources it should distribute to each cultural minority. For some (like Harris 1987 and Lister 1990), the problem remains within the realm of individual, though different, citizens. This is in contrast to multiculturalist policies that construct the population, or rather, effectively, the poor and working classes within the population, in terms of ethnic and racial collectivities. These collectivities are attributed with specific needs, based on their different cultures as well as on their structural disadvantages in the marketplace (see Burney 1988; Cain and Yuval-Davis 1990).

Defining 'cultural needs'

Jayasuriya's answer (1991) to the question of how to define specific needs, following Edwards (1988), has been to differentiate between 'needs', which the state would provide, and 'wants', which should be provided in the civil and private spheres. This answer is, of course, unsatisfactory, as the difference between 'needs' and 'wants' is context-dependent and subjective at best. There is also no prima-facie way to determine which groups would be defined as groups that are entitled to receive resources from the state and which groups would be considered too small or insignificant to receive them. The British census, for instance, mentions less than ten categories of 'ethnic minorities'. The number of countries and language groups from which ethnic minorities' people emigrated to the UK is much larger, and health and welfare services, for example, offer translators only to a small percentage of them. Political, economic and social power relations – both in the wider societies and within the minorities' populations – determine the construction of minority collectivities and their boundaries within each polity.

The difficulty lies, then, in the processes involved in the construction of the minority collectivities and their boundaries in public and official discourse at any given moment. It also lies in the determination of what elements of these collec-tivities' perceived 'cultures' belong to the public or to the private domain. The conceptualisation of 'wants' and 'needs' as objective differences between essential and non essential cultural demands of specific sub-collectivities within the civil society, assumes a fixed a-historical essentialist model of what such cultures are. However, cultures are highly heterogeneous resources which are used selectively, and often in contradictory ways, in different ethnic projects which are promoted by members of specific collectivities, often in a way which disadvantages women (Sahgal and Yuval-Davis 1992).

A different mode of supplying 'cultural needs' developed largely within the realm of the market-oriented civil society in Thatcherite Britain. The Thatcherite notion of citizenship as consumerism (Evans 1993: 6) was not based, of course, on a completely free market model, in spite of its universalistic rhetoric. There are legal and moral constraints that have prevented a variety of marginal or minority groups from pursuing their religious and cultural beliefs or economic needs in equal measure. The state's management of these 'moral aliens' of various kinds who are to be found in the marginal matrix of citizenship, is exercised in social, political and economic arenas. This is the twilight zone between the liberal and republican constructions of citizenship, where religious, ethnic and sexual minorities are located outside the national 'moral community' but inside the civic nation. To those who can afford it, this is not a completely closed-off system. Evans describes how sexual minority groups have developed socio-economic 'community' infrastructures around their identities, organise to obtain further housing, insurance, medical, parenting, marital rights etc., and spend a significant proportion of their income on distinguishable lifestyles in segregated or specifically gay social and sexual territories (1993: 8). Multi-culturalism, aimed at ethnic minorities, can be described in similar terms. Stuart Hall (1998) described multiculturalism as 'an epistemological irritant'. Multi-culturalist policies are aimed at simultaneously including and excluding the minorities, locating them in marginal spaces and secondary markets, while reifying their boundaries. The growth of lucrative 'hybrid' leisure and enter-tainment industries can be seen as a successful manipulation of upwardly mobile entrepreneurial, mostly second-generation, minority members of such market openings.

Multiculturalist ideologies, including 'hybrid' forms, celebrating 'travelling cultures' and 'cultural diversity', however, have their limits (defined in this way in the clause on 'the limits of multiculturalism' in the Australian government document: Office of Multicultural Affairs 1989). Not all perceived 'needs' of ethnic minorities would be acceptable to the hegemonic majority. There are always cultural practices (from taking drugs to genital mutilation) that would not be accepted as legal practices in states where the hegemonic majority's moral code would reject these practices. Moreover, multicultural ideologies assume that beyond these 'extremes', the different cultures are compatible and that there is a prima-facie goodwill and interest in coexistence in a pluralist society – under the hegemony of the dominant collectivity, of course.

The 1989 'Rushdie affair' has been, in a way, a signal that things are not always that simple. It is not a question of conflicting cultures; as mentioned above, it has more to do with specific ethnic projects that use selectively specific cultural resources for particular political purposes. Rather, it is that while many celebrate the richness of multicultural societies, hybrid 'travelling cultures' and the ability to challenge authoritarian cultural and political traditions (Clifford 1992; Gilroy 1997), others look for ways to defend themselves from what they foresee as complete social disintegration and loss of cultural heritage and political autonomy (Stolcke 1995). Majorities fear being 'swamped' by racial and ethnic minorities and minorities fear assimilation and collective disappearance. In the context of the growing rate of mixed marriages among western Jews, the term 'demographic holocaust' has been known to be mentioned (Yuval-Davis 1987). At the same time racism, immigration legislation and what the Canadian government calls 'visibility' of minorities can often trap people in enforced identities from which assimilation, as a strategy of self-defence, is not possible. If citizenship is defined as full membership in the community, the lived experience of such people often would be dominated by encountering the varying ways and measures by which they are excluded from such membership (e.g. Wrench and Solomos 1993).

'Thin' and 'thick' multiculturalism

Yael Tamir (1998), following Walzer (1994), differentiates between what she calls thin and thick multiculturalisms. The first applies when different cultures share liberal values and the second also includes non-liberal cultures. Tamir argues that political/cultural neutralism of the state is an ideal that is inapplicable in reality, even if the cultural particularity is often invisible to members of the hegemonic majority who tend to naturalise it as 'human nature'. But there is no such a thing as just being 'human' – every social order is culturally constructed. Often, the choice, if any, which is open to members of minority groupings is whether to keep their cultural identity but remain on the margins of society where they develop ways to accommodate into the local situation, or whether, as part of upward social mobility, to become culturally assimilated into the hegemonic majority. The recent celebration of hybrid and diasporic cultures (Bhabha 1994; Gilroy 1997) is a sign of a certain success among minority intellectuals and artists in their efforts to resist such dichotomous choices, as well as constituting part of the effects of globalisation. However, there is a need to differentiate between such voluntaristic hybridity and that of the working-class and poor minority members, who have had to adapt to customs and institutions of the hegemonic societies as part of their strategies of survival (Werbner 1999). Moreover, in these days of 'culturalisation' (Ålund 1995; Schierup 1995; Yuval-Davis 1997b), it is important to remember that in addition to the cultural dimensions of the processes of racialisation, there are also political and economic dimensions, although at the same time one should not collapse questions of exclusion and discrimination into those of disadvantage (Anthias and Yuval-Davis 1992).

Iris Marion Young (1995) has tried to solve the contradiction between 'universalist' democracy and the reality of life of oppressed and disadvantaged groupings in society by transforming differences into political resources and bases of political representation in what she calls 'communicative democracy'. Kymlicka (1995), more sensitive than Young to power relations within and not just between communities and groupings, presented a two-layered structure of rights – of the cultural community from the state and of individuals from the cultural community. Unlike Walzer and Tamir, Kymlicka can include this as a consistent part of his liberal model because for him the right to cultural affiliation is, in practice, an extension of the right to personal liberty (Margalit and Halbertal 1998: 100).

In spite of this important reservation, Kymlicka, like most of the other participants in this debate, tends to naturalise and homogenise the minority collectivities and, even more, to reify and homogenise minority 'cultures'. Probably this is because the cultural artefact that most of the participants in this debate relate to, especially those who write about Quebec, has been that of language. Both the right to use one's mother tongue and the mother tongue itself seem to be unproblematic. And yet we know that the cultural 'stuff' of language is far from being fixed and uncontested and is subject to selective use, reflecting specific ethnic and national political projects. First, very often it is a highly political decision whether a certain dialect is considered an autonomous language or not. Second, nationalist movements, like in Ireland and Wales, very often reintroduce the 'mothertongue' as part of their educational projects to children whose mothers actually do not speak it. The most extreme case has been the use of Hebrew in the Zionist movement. It is a well-known tale that the son of Eliezer Ben-Yehuda, who wrote the first modern Hebrew dictionary, was kept away from other children for the first four to five years of his life. Only then could his parents be sure that he had Hebrew as his mother tongue, the only child in the world to have it at that time. Other Jewish children at that time tended to have Yiddish, Ladino, or local languages as their mother tongues.

If 'language as culture' cannot be reified, once we look closer at the ways it has been used as a resource in a variety of political ethnic and national projects, other cultural resources, from religion to fashion, cannot either. One of the problems of multiculturalist policy-makers with traditional and fundamentalist 'ethnic leaders' has been their acceptance of the version of culture presented by these leaders as the 'authentic culture'. This is also a problem that has not been solved by the writers of the Macpherson Report. They recommend that the police and other governmental agents should become 'sensitive to issues of cultural diversity' without referring to what they mean by this and who would have the authority to define the meaning (1999).

Encompassing equality by difference – anti-racism and transversal citizenship

As Gita Sahgal and I commented elsewhere (1992), some multiculturalist notions of difference create a space for fundamentalist leaderships to rise and gain legitimacy as 'representing' the community. This is a result of the tendency of multiculturalist policies often to homogenise minorities and to attribute to all their members the same relationship to their 'culture and tradition' (Anthias and Yuval-Davis, 1992).

This clearly has to be rejected. At the same time, as Balibar (1990), Iris Marion Young (1989) and Kymlicka (1995) have shown, among others, the classical liberal – and Marxist (1975) – notion of citizenship, which adopts an individualist 'universalist' approach in which differences among citizens are seen as irrelevant, becomes, as a result, exclusionary and discriminatory. People's membership in a state, their rights and responsibilities, are mediated by their membership in other collectivities and polities, sub-, cross- and supra-state. Therefore, their positionings in that respect, as well as in terms of their class, gender, sexuality, stage in the life cycle, ability etc., have to be acknowledged in any citizenship project that in principle, at least, would be inclusive and democratic. The Marshallian social welfare state catered for some class differences, but other modes of difference have been largely ignored (for more elaboration of this point see Yuval-Davis 1997a or 1997b).

In our introduction to the book *Women, Citizenship and Difference* (Yuval-Davis and Werbner 1999), Pnina Werbner 'imported' an anthropological theory by Dumont (1972) on 'encompassment'. This theory points out that often (in the case of Dumont he was discussing the Indian caste system) contradictory value systems do not exclude each other socially, but rather encompass each other. Essentialist notions of difference, promoted by ethnic and religious fundamentalist movements, are very different from the notions of difference promoted by those of us who believe in the importance of incorporating notions of difference into democracy. In the first case notions of difference replace notions of equality; in the second case they encompass it.

Notions of difference that encompass notions of equality are not hierarchical and assume a priori respect for other positionings – which includes acknowledgement of their differential social, economic and political power. This is the basis for dialogical transversal citizenship (Yuval-Davis 1994, 1997a, 1997b), the 'grammar for democratic conduct' (Mouffe 1992: 238). As the Italian feminists in Bologna taught us, such a grammar has to include 'rooting' and 'shifting' (Yuval-Davis 1994) – acknowledgement of one's own positioning(s) while empathising with the ways positionings of others construct their gaze at the world.

In transversal citizenship politics, therefore, differences encompass equality and perceived unity and homogeneity are replaced by dialogues that give recognition to the specific positionings of those who participate in them as well as the 'unfinished knowledge' (Hill-Collins 1990: 236) that each such positioning can offer. Crucial to such an epistemological and political approach is the differentiation between identification and participation as well as between identity and positioning. Group identities – ethnic, national, racial – tend to repress or marginalise differences among the members of the groupings, whether identified as 'us' or 'them'. However, the nature of participation of the citizenship of people in these groupings is thoroughly affected by their positionings – social, economic, political and legal.

Much of the impetus of the development of identity politics social movements, including the feminist movement, has been driven by such a recognition on a national scale, i.e. the recognition that nation-state citizenships are gendered, racialised, heterosexualised (as well as class differentiated, as has been recognised in the previous generation). However, such differences exist and affect the mode of participation of people also in other intersecting layers of collectivities in which people operate. And as mentioned above, people's citizenship in the nation-state is affected not only by their individual positionings but also by the positionings of the other collectivities in which they are members, whether these are other nation-states, local communities, cross- or supra-states. Religious codes can affect the lives of women just as much, and often more, than state legislation and soliciting the support of an international agency can sometimes be the recourse of women who are disempowered within their local communities. This is one of the reasons why continuing to relate to citizenship only in terms of the nation-state and not membership in other collectivities/polities makes incomprehensible the dynamics of contemporary nation-state citizenships themselves.

Transversal dialogue, therefore, is crucial for common political action. Transversal politics, nevertheless, does not assume that the dialogue is boundary-free, and that each conflict of interest is reconcilable, although, as Jindi Pettman points out, 'there are almost always possibilities for congenial or at least tolerable personal, social and political engagements' (1992: 157). The boundaries of a transversal dialogue are determined, however, by the message, rather than the messengers. In other words, in addition to differentiating between identity and participation, transversal politics differentiate between social identities and social values (Assitter 1996). Assiter also argues that emancipatory values should be given priority in transversal politics as they are the ones that would ensure 'an active commitment to listening to the voices of marginalized others . . . [which is] always underpinned by an evolving vision of emancipation' (1999: 50).

It is for these reasons that the discourse of citizenship, of multi-layered memberships in collectivities, with all the rights and responsibilities this involves, is of pivotal importance to the construction of any effective anti-racist strategy.

Some concluding ponderings

In her critique of the notion of diaspora, Floya Anthias challenged the reifying effect of this concept when dealing with issues of multiculturalism and anti-racism. Both as a descriptive typological tool and as a social condition, argues Anthias, the concept of 'diaspora' cannot attend fully to 'intersectionality', that is to issues of class, gender and transethnic alliances (1998a: 557). Gilroy (1993a) has used the notion as an alternative to the simplistic, unproblematic relationship between people, their community and their 'homeland'. However, an anti-racist construction of citizenship cannot deal with people only as part of smaller collectivities who are themselves part of the national collectivity. Avtar Brah (1996) has attempted to overcome this problem by using the term 'diaspora space' as a means of decentring any privileged positioning of the hegemonic majority. Nevertheless, there is also the need for any anti-racist citizenship framework to recognise people's affiliation with more than one collectivity and polity – where they live and in other territories where their polities govern.

If people belong to more than one collectivity that can be in and outside the state in which they live, and if the boundaries of these collectivities are constantly shifting, the question arises by whom or how can their citizenship rights and responsibilities be determined. The answer to this question lies in our understanding of the interrelationships between citizenship rights and human rights.

Citizenship and human rights are often discussed as two separate arenas. The first one as associated with the national level and the second one with the international one (Pateman 1996). However, I would argue that human rights discourse and legislation need to be viewed as a specific layer of supra-national citizenship – the global one, which progressively affects more and more the national level and, most importantly, individual citizens. This entails both mobilising politically around human rights discourse, and the growing use of human rights litigations in regional (e.g. the European Court of Human Rights) as well as international (e.g. the International War Crimes Tribunals) judiciaries by individuals, 'class acts' and international agencies (Ramsbotham and Woodhouse 1996). People's membership in supra-state polities is therefore, like in states, partly direct and individual, and to a great extent mediated by their membership in other collectivities and states.

The establishment of the League of Nations after the First World War, and even more so the United Nations after the Second World War, has launched an era of supra-state institutions and legislations. These institutions have acquired a growing amount of moral and legal authority over individual states and provided an important arena for new, especially post-colonial states to make their voices heard while not obliterating the political reality of the unequal power relations of international politics. The growing visibility and effectivity of the NGOs in recent United Nations conferences – on the environment in Rio, human rights in Vienna, population policies in Cairo and women in Beijing – have added an important element of the new social movements into international politics. Feminist activists who, for many years, have been part of autonomous movements started to find themselves listened to and sometimes recruited by the UN, the World Bank, official aid organisations, etc. This has presented opportunities as well as dangers of incorporation and co-optation for these activists. However, it is clear that even if sometimes it is only cosmetic, there has been a change of style, and occasionally of substance, in hegemonic discourses concerning a variety of important policy issues (e.g. the linkage of population policies with women's reproductive rights and health) (Yuval-Davis and Vargas 1999).

At the same time, however, as Yasmin Soysal (1994) has pointed out, there is a certain paradox in the growing importance of the supra-national authority of human rights declarations and treaties. While they are aimed at controlling and guiding state agencies, the executors of these international codes of rights and the members of international bodies are still the states and no international agency has the right to 'interfere in the internal affairs' of their states. Nevertheless, given that most recent wars have taken place within states between different ethnic/national groupings and not between states, and that the UN or other supra-state forces such as the North Atlantic Treaty Organisation (NATO) have gone to these countries as 'peace-keepers', even that accepted rule seems to be crumbling. The viability of states as representing the only significant political frameworks of populations is crumbling with it (Held 1995; Anderson 2001). This is despite the 'real politic' interests of states that usually determine where and how such interventions take place, and the very real violations of human rights that usually are involved in such 'peace-keeping' military interventions. As Francesca Klug (1999) has pointed out, human rights legislations have to be seen not just as essentially formal legal documents (or, I would add, a set of governmental and supra-governmental policies and actions), but also as a set of values, a type of secular ethics that is growing in importance, even if contested.

It is important to remember, however, that it is not only the UN and its associated organisations – NATO or even regional organizations like the EU, or much weaker ones like the Arab League, for instance – which constitute the only international forums which affect people's memberships in their communities and states. International religious organisations/projects like the Catholic Church or the Muslims Khalifa have important normative as well as political projects which affect people's affiliations and ways of life.

Similarly, sub- or cross-national collectivities, with their own internal norms and regulations, based on traditional and 'invented traditional' (Hobsbawm and Ranger 1983) power relations, would determine individual rights and responsibilities in gendered, aged and other ascribed ways (Yuval-Davis 1997a, 1999)

At the beginning of the chapter, I related to the paradigmatic shift that is taking place these days in academic and political circles in the thinking on racism and anti-racism, and wondered what, if anything, the current debates on issues of citizenship could contribute to such a shift. Several such contributions have been raised in the chapter, relating to issues such as individual and collective rights, social rights and social difference, transversal dialogue and the encompassment of equality and difference.

However, probably the most significant contribution lies in the recognition of the multi-layered nature of citizenship and the separation of issues of citizenship from the state. Such a recognition entails the acceptance that processes of racialisation operate not only on interpersonal or institutional levels but also on the level of collectivities and communities which often constitute powerful polities in themselves, autonomous if not often independent of the state. Such a recognition entails the acceptance that people and communities who are in the positionings of racialised minorities in one layer of their citizenship can be the ones who racialise ethnicised Others in another layer of their citizenship (as well as or alternatively excluding or subjugating others in other ways, such as on the basis of gender, age or class). Probably above all, however, such a recognition entails the acceptance that people's rights, including the right not to be racialised, are not negotiable.

4　Anti-racism, social movements and civil society

Cathie Lloyd

This chapter examines the ways in which anti-racism is developing in civil society and as a social movement at a time of momentous change. European economic, social and political integration has had a major impact on the issues facing anti-racists and the way in which they organise. While the main themes of the 1990s have been the increase in racism and xenophobia and the harmonisation of immigration controls, attention must now turn to the democratic deficiencies of the new systems of global governance.

Globalisation theory suggests that there has been a diminution in the scope of political activities as effective power shifts away from the sovereign nation state (Bauman 1998). This process is echoed in the decline in influence of and identification with traditional centres of political activity, particularly political parties and trade unions (Cloonan and Street 1998; Johnson and Pattie 1997). This chapter explores some of ways in which anti-racism has been developing within European nation-states and suggests new ways in which broader activities can take place through forms of networking within social movements.

We need to situate anti-racism within a historical and political context in order to be clear about what is at stake. A contextualised approach can help us to see the complexities behind the dualism racism/anti-racism suggested by the term anti-racism. The problem is that using the racism/anti-racism formulation involves taking anti-racism for granted and subordinating it to racism, which means that in theorising racism, anti-racism has been eclipsed. There is an implicit, yet unacknowledged recognition that anti-racism is always attempting to become something but is not always successful. The name 'anti-racism' suggests a realised project of how to overcome racism, whereas anti-racists are often groping towards an adequate response. In the next section I consider how analyses of racism have given rise to different forms of anti-racist response within the contemporary context of globalisation, which presents us with challenges but also new opportunities.

Racism and anti-racism in the contemporary context

With the discrediting of pseudo-scientific biological ideas of 'race' after 1945, a consensus was established around the idea that education, culture and social environment were the main determinants of differences between human groups (Kuper 1975; Unesco 1951). It was thought that racial prejudice could be educated out of existence. However the economistic left tended to focus on class struggle and migrant labour as the 'reserve army of labour' which served to postpone tackling the problem of racism (Castles and Kosack 1973). An important difference between the liberal and Marxist perspectives on 'race' and racism lies in the insight that ideologies of racism are not just matters of individual prejudice but can permeate structures. This gave rise to the concept of institutional racism which has opened up a wider field of possible social action against covert attitudes and structural forms of discrimination. Such an approach requires us to pay attention to the wider context in which anti-racist policies and initiatives operate.

Anti-racism therefore operates in a wide arena through public policy and legislation, within institutional structures, in civil society and social movements. My account here focuses on anti-racism which operates within civil society, through social movements, grass-roots organisations and the mobilisations of ethnic minority communities. I seek to explore who are anti-racists, how they organise and what they do (Lloyd 1998b). This gives rise to a further series of questions about the future of anti-racism. How will the traditional themes of anti-racism – opposition to racial discrimination, representation of and solidarity with people who experience racism, and the attempt to establish an anti-racist common sense (or hegemony, in the Gramscian sense) – fit into the political discourses of the twenty-first century, marked by post-colonialism and globalisation?

Globalisation and anti-racism both have a paradoxical relationship to universalism and particularism. In the processes of globalisation, increased consciousness of the international is accompanied by yearnings for the recognition of difference and identity (Held 1991: 149). The political aspects of globalisation involve an apparent loss of control of key aspects of sovereignty by the nation-state, leading to a focus on the control of its own population and its borders. Under these conditions it is thought that power leaves traditional political channels leading to opaque areas of decision-making, which involves political demobilisation and a loss of faith in the main political parties, a growth of social insecurity and a paradoxical swing between universalising and particularistic impulses. This presents social movements with new possibilities: if it is no longer useful to focus on individual states, instead movements may bypass their own target state and rely on international pressure and the transnational human rights movement to support them (Keck and Sikkink 1999).

These views are not uncontested: research points to a continuing high level of political participation in most countries of Western Europe; this is quite distinct from political identification or loyalty, which does appear to be increasingly unstable (Johnson and Pattie 1997; Wilkinson and Muglan 1995). Some commentators suggest that globalisation is used to paralyse reforming strategies, and that these developments are used by states to control the movement of poor people across their borders (Hirst and Thompson 1996).

Globalisation may indeed offer an opportunity to anti-racists since 'modern communications form the basis for an international civil society of people who share interests and associations across borders' (Hirst 1997: 180). This emerging international civil society, expressed through a growing number of transnational

NGOs, such as Amnesty International or the International League for Human Rights, collect and publish information about abusive behaviour in order to challenge offending parties (mainly national governments). These initiatives have been sustained by the validation of human rights conventions by the majority of governments. Thus 'the global spread of political democracy, with its roots in constitutionalism, makes those persons within the territorial space controlled by the sovereign state increasingly aware of their political, moral and legal option to appeal to broader communities in the event of encroachment on their basic human rights' (Falk 1995: 164). These developments may also be understood as transnational networks seeking to mobilise through international NGOs, such as Amnesty International or Anti-Apartheid, and which often operate like oppositional grass-roots movements.

A central feature of anti-racism is its diversity. Studies of anti-racism generally agree that it is a 'difficult issue' which is not easily accommodated within the policy-making process partly because its constituency is relatively powerless (Heineman 1972; Lloyd 1994, 1998a; Stedward 1997). As a political movement anti-racism may be best understood as occupying different points on a continuum between well-organised, bureaucratic organisations, pressure groups and protest or social movements which challenge dominant social practices and preconceptions. An assessment of its effectiveness as a constellation of pressure groups makes it clear that it does not fit neatly into any one category. For instance, in traditional pressure group theory, anti-racist groups fall somewhere between sectional or represent-ational and promotional or universalist organisations (Finer 1958). A view of the over-arching themes of anti-racist discourse helps to show how anti-racists can be a more clearly defined lobby. Most groups campaign on a variety of different issues: against unjust immigration controls, police harassment, racist violence, or inform-ation gathering. Some offer legal services; all tend to vary according to the social and political context in which they operate (Coutant 1997). For instance, in the UK, the existence of a (relatively) well-funded statutory body committed to enforcing the law against racial discrimination, the Commission for Racial Equality (CRE), has limited the priorities and scope of anti-racist organisations. In France, designated anti-racist associations, with tiny budgets, working with a largely voluntary legal advice service, are mainly responsible for the enforcement of the laws against racism.

The relationship between anti-racist organisations and policy-makers is not an easy one. While decision-makers may not always regard anti-racists as respectable or responsible, there may also be pressure from within the anti-racist movement to maintain a distance from the authorities. Both sides may be highly conscious of the disparity in terms of access to material resources and power. The nearer one approaches the social movement end of anti-racism, the more there is suspicion, antagonism and distance towards authority. These attitudes are bound up with analyses of the ways in which racism is rooted in institutional practices and cultures (Macpherson 1999). Anti-racist protest groups face the dilemma of wanting to make a practical impact on policy and keeping faith with their grass roots who are the receiving end of racism (often exacerbated by government policies). Vitriolic debates may take place over co-operation with official inquiries (as with the Scarman inquiry in 1981) or the politics of accepting government grant aid.

Not all anti-racist organisations are equally distant from centres of decision-making. In Britain, Race Equality Councils (RECs) are tied in to a structure funded by a mix of local authority and Home Office money through the CRE. In France some organisations have received large government grants: for instance SOS-Racisme and France-Plus had a very comfortable relationship with the Socialist government during the 1980s. The main focus of these grants was to organise major campaigns which were directed at young people, including lavishly produced 'rock' concerts and a national week of education against racism. These organisations carried out important campaigns during this period to encourage young people from immigrant backgrounds to register to vote. There are similar relationships between some anti-racist groups, political parties and churches in other European countries. Governments have increasingly recognised that civil society provides solidarity in a situation of social fragmentation, but this carries with it all the problems attendant on alliances or partnerships: in particular the risk of political manipulation and of co-option. Anti-racist groups' agendas may be distorted because funds may be available for one type of activity rather than another. Or they may become embroiled in political disputes which have little to do with their immediate concerns.

While groups may differ in their ability to benefit from subsidies and grants, another important factor of difference lies in the different resources at their disposal. While some groups may have few resources other than strongly motiv-ated members, others such as the Joint Council for the Welfare of Immigrants (JCWI) in Britain or the Groupe d'Information et de Soutien des Immigrés (GISTI) in France may have slender financial means, but benefit from supporters' professional activities based in law or social work. They are able to formulate demands in ways that policy-makers can understand and use, forming a sort of bridge between protest/social movement groups and policy-makers.

It is important to establish some of the broad characteristics of the different approaches to anti-racism in Europe before we can identify the ways in which wider transnational co-operation might be possible. The next sections of this chapter draw on research and participation in anti-racist activity in Britain and France, enabling this discussion to move from the debate about differences and similarities in approaches to anti-racism in both countries to an assessment of recent attempts to build a European-wide anti-racism.

Britain

In Britain, debates about anti-racism have focused on the problem of conflict between different types of political actor within anti-racist organisations, especially participation, representation and entitlements. Some studies have considered how to surmount the oppositional characteristics of anti-racism by broadening or expanding anti-racist issues, and establishing alliances. Historically anti-racism is associated with movements in support of decolonialisation, anti-fascism and struggles against discrimination and for immigrants' rights. What are the links between these different aspects and do they make some kind of coherent whole which constitutes anti-racism?

Anti-colonialism and anti-fascism were the most prevalent forms of anti-racism in the first part of the twentieth century. Anti-colonialism was so important that it was one of the central characteristics of the British left in the period 1918–64, according to Stephen Howe (1993). It marked an important transition between traditional radical attitudes towards international issues and the orientation of 'new left' politics of the 1960s. It also shaped the activity and forms of organisation of early black British political groups, many of which originated in the metropolitan activity of exiled or student anti-colonial leaders (Howe 1993: 25). Anti-fascism was another defining feature of the left, particularly between the 1930s and 1950s. It was however limited by the use of a restricted concept of racism as one among other features of the broader problem of fascism (Knowles 1992). This approach left a legacy which limited the scope for the recognition of ethnic mobilisation as part of anti-racism, and frequently reduced anti-racism to an aspect of anti-fascism. Anti-colonialism, anti-fascism and anti-apartheid involved activists in broader, international struggles which provided a world-view which could be adapted to accommodate the problems raised by globalisation (Seidman 2000).

In the 1950s and 1960s anti-racists began to turn to preoccupations closer to home, in particular the problem of racism against immigrants who had come to work in the UK (as in much of Western Europe) in response to the demand for labour for post-war reconstruction. These concerns tended to be dealt with by anti-racists on a country by country basis, although there was some international co-operation. In the UK the point of reference tended to be the USA.[1]

The Campaign Against Racial Discrimination (CARD) provided a base for activists in the 1960s who attempted to promote the cause of social equality and to organise the political representation of immigrants in Britain. In so doing it fell prey to conflicts over the power relations between the black and white liberals and the more radical community-based organisations (such as the West Indian Standing Conference, the National Federation of Pakistani Associations in Great Britain and the Indian Workers' Association). The CARD anti-racists were attracted to solutions which had developed in the very different conditions of the USA. CARD took its cue from the US civil rights movement to press for legislation against discrimination at the moment when this tactic was being superseded across the Atlantic by community action and Black Power. Consequently, the US experience can be seen to have distorted and undermined the British anti-racist movement, encouraging it to develop goals without fully relating them to specific British conditions (Heineman 1972: xi; Sooben 1990).

As a result of the failure of such broad-based anti-racist organisations during the 1960s, more specialist organisations such as the Runnymede Trust and the JCWI were formed. They worked on providing information, analysis and campaigning with other anti-racist groups and did not claim to represent but rather to serve the broader constituency. CARD had been racked by difficulties about issues of identity and representation among its members and leaders. This issue, articulated in different ways throughout the 1970s, found expression in the rivalries between competing organisations, which stressed different aspects of anti-racist work. During the mid-1970s when the extreme right National Front (NF) appeared to be making electoral headway, anti-racists found themselves negotiating two schools of thought, one (epitomised by the Anti-Nazi League) emphasising the importance of destroying the NF as an electoral force, and the other (perhaps best epitomised by the magazine collective CARF) emphasising the importance of a layered response to racism, which was in tune with experiences of the black community at the grass-roots while maintaining a critique of national policies (Lloyd 1998a; Sivanandan 1982).

From this point onwards, for anti-racists to be able to claim any sort of legitimacy they needed to show that they took their cues from the demands of ethnic minority groups and to work with them in some kind of alliance. In the UK the question of 'who are anti-racists' centres on this relationship. However, this is not a simple interface. John Rex has pointed out that ethnic mobilisation is wider and more ongoing than much anti-racism because 'at all times, and not only at moments of economic crisis, collective political actors emerge' (Rex and Drury 1994: 3; Rex 1996). Similarly the equation of anti-racism and the struggle for black liberation has been challenged by Paul Gilroy, who argues for a distinction between such struggle and responses to the everyday problems of black people (Gilroy 1987b: 115). Ethnic minority groups mobilise for different reasons, their lives are not solely determined by racism and the need to counter it. Such groups do not just mobilise to oppose racism and their choice to ally with other groups is one option among others. Ethnic mobilisation cannot be reduced to anti-racism or vice versa, but they are closely intertwined.

The race relations 'industry' in the 1980s, which was dominant in local authority politics, did tend to equate its anti-racist activities with the struggles of the black community in ways that led to bitter divisions and competition (Cain and Yuval-Davis 1990). Community representatives were co-opted onto committees to act as advocates in the process of consultation, with doubtful consequences. One of the central problems associated with these practices was an unproblematic construction of the central concept of the community. This policy tended to construct the black community as solely concerned with racism, which led to a too-rigid dichotomy between victims and oppressors as critiqued in the Burnage report on anti-racism in Manchester schools (MacDonald *et al.* 1989). The report emphasised the need for all sectors of the local community to take responsibility to oppose racism.

In the 1990s there has been increased awareness of the complexity and heterogeneity of ethnic mobilisation. Further, ideas of hybridity and plurality have undermined the idea of the unitary 'black' subject (Goldberg 1990: xiii; Hall and du Gay 1996: 113). The concept of 'black' as a universal category denoting the experience of oppression is challenged from a different position by Tariq Modood, who points to the way in which this discourse excludes certain groups, specifically Muslims (Modood 1996b).

Feminist analyses of anti-racism have drawn attention to the gender and class differences which run through the black and ethnic minority communities (Anthias and Yuval-Davis 1992; Brah 1996). Women's role in anti-racism has all too often been ignored. Feminist analyses confronted the differences between black and white women over the role of the family in their oppression, the difficulties posed for women attempting to discuss questions of domestic violence, and the policing of young women's sexuality by the family. Clara Connolly (1990) describes the failure of a young women's project attempting to be anti-racist which was working with the structures and concepts of multiculturalism, racism awareness training and fostering cultural identity. She suggests that a feminist anti-racism would involve a recognition of the nature of racism while also acknow-ledging the separate interests of women, and it would involve black and white women organising together (Connolly 1990: 63). Groups may operate with conflicting or competing priorities or within different communities, e.g. women against fundamentalism (Sahgal and Yuval-Davis 1992). Gender issues were however thrown into relief by the furore over the Rushdie affair and women's challenges to the right of community leaders to speak on their behalf (Patel 1999; Sahgal and Yuval-Davis 1992).

Given this fragmented field of action, the question of alliances between different groups with different motives for combating racism is raised. Caroline Knowles and Sharmila Mercer acknowledge that first-hand experience of racism confers a privileged position within anti-racist struggle while arguing that 'anti-racist politics needs to be built around issues and . . . the only qualification for membership needs to be a practical commitment to challenging racism' (Knowles and Mercer 1990: 137). They see 'temporary links between groups of subjects with interests and positions' (84) as constantly reconstructing anti-racist politics according to specific circumstances. In this they anticipate what Italian feminists and French activists term 'transversal politics' in which each participant in the dialogue brings with her the rooting in her own membership and identity but at the same time tries to shift in order to create an exchange with women who have different membership and identity (Yuval-Davis 1997b: 130).

Writing about earlier coalition politics, Stephan Feuchtwang suggests that this might mean

> an odd alliance between agencies of liberal justice, variously oriented to com-munity groups, workplace groupings, sections of unions, campaigns and often anti-reformist black groups and parties . . . it amounts to more of a criss-cross of pressures than an organised movement. But the pressures could be repercussive, beating against resistances.
>
> (Feuchtwang 1990: 153)

The British debate has been largely organised around the assumption that anti-racist activity is about opposition to colour-based racism (Brown 1984; Daniel 1968). There has been much less awareness about racism directed against different groups of people (such as the Jews or the Irish), even though their concerns have been covered in much anti-racist practice (Hickman and Walter 1997; Lloyd 1995). The scope of anti-racism has been largely determined by the central role of the CRE, which has responsibility for enforcing the law against racism and for conducting formal investigations into possible areas of racist practice. This has meant that anti-racist civil society focuses on areas which are essentially conflictual and problematic. At the same time anti-racism needs to build alliances and campaign around different *ad hoc* issues.

This self-limiting stance gives rise to two sets of problems: first that anti-racism risks remaining ineffective and tokenistic, unable to do more than make gestures in favour of lasting reforms, and second that it becomes embroiled in fragmentary politics without the benefits of alliance, which only serves to block its access to the political mainstream. Groups which are based mainly in the white left and which attempt to mobilise separately have been criticised in the past, as in 1993 when rival marches were organised by the white-led Anti-Nazi League and black-led Anti-Racist Alliance. Such rivalries have in the past posed serious problems for the establishment of national anti-racist coalitions in Britain, which have encountered problems due to London-centrism (which gives national status to groups without a broad-based implantation), divided or sectarian leadership, a tendency towards formalism and instrumentalism, and 'resolution politics' (Huq 1995).

While still viewing anti-racism as essentially defensive, Cambridge and Feuchtwang seek to understand how to go beyond ideas of resistance which involve 'emergent political forces which might combine to reduce and eliminate racist practices' (1990: ix). Feuchtwang argues that 'the politics of civil liberty and universal rights . . . are the starting position in contesting racism within the discourse and politics of government, civil society and population' (1990: 21). For him, anti-racism begins 'with the re-assertion of humanity, citizenship and social being. . . . The politics of demands for justice, against racialist exclusions and licence to scapegoat excluded populations, point in the direction of new concepts of sovereignty and of public policy' (1990: 21–4).

Developments in the late 1990s suggest that the anti-racist movement in Britain is beginning to reap some successes. Most notable was the campaign surrounding the murder of Stephen Lawrence, illustrating how anti-racist work, which has often operated at the margins, painstakingly collecting data about police racism and racist violence, and forming networks between anti-racist lawyers and campaigners, could bear fruit, given a window of opportunity with the Macpherson Report (Lloyd 1999b). Similarly after many thwarted attempts to form a nationally anti-racist co-ordination, the National Assembly Against Racism has shown considerable stability.

I will now turn to a discussion of approaches to anti-racism in another European country, France, in order to draw attention to some of the common issues and to highlight some important differences.

France

An overview of approaches to anti-racism in France can help us to understand continuities because there are several long-standing organisations which have existed since before the Second World War (or, if one includes the Ligue des Droits de l'Homme, the turn of the century).[2] French anti-racists claim to trace their antecedents back to the Enlightenment and the Revolution of 1789, pointing to precursor anti-racist views among some of the philosophers and the abolition of slavery and emancipation of the Jews during the Revolution (Lloyd

1996). The battles for social justice during the Dreyfus affair and opposition to anti-Semitism and fascism in the 1930s and 1940s were early forms of anti-racist activity, while as in Britain, anti-colonialism and struggles for the rights of immigrant workers have also played a large part in building the bases of resistance (Bouamama 1994; Noiriel 1992).

In the early 1980s anti-racists debated issues about who comprised the main body of activists. One of the key questions related to their affirmation of the positive aspects of the 'droit à la différence'. Commentators warned that this idea needed to be carefully qualified because it was open to misinterpretation and it was used to advocate segregation and oppose immigration by 'new right' groups (Guillaumin 1992; Taguieff 1979, 1980, 1991: 15).

Given the stability of the older anti-racist organisations, it has been possible to take the infrastructure largely for granted. Mobilisation, however, is recognised as presenting a more difficult set of issues. Social movement theorists offer a more detailed exploration of the social dynamics which give rise to anti-racist activity, which is particularly relevant to the French case. They emphasise the mobilising potential of ideas and values and the strategic aspects of political practices. Alain Touraine's theory of 'class struggle without classes' challenged the determinism of structural theories, and drew attention to the way in which political conflict could be neutralised if it became entrenched in institutions such as political parties (Touraine 1969). He was interested in the meanings produced and experienced by grass-roots participants and shifts in consciousness among them. His analysis of the new forms of domination in 'post-industrial' society regarded alienation as more important than economic exploitation. Thus he expected students and cultural workers to be at the forefront of the social movements of the 1970s, which he characterised as anti-institutional, spontaneous attempts to reconstruct the social order with a distinct and non-local identity (Hannigan 1985).

Influenced by the growth of racism in the form of the Front National (FN), urban riots and perhaps his own participation in the Commission of Experts on the Nationality Code (Long 1988; Silverman 1988: 10–16), Touraine turned his attention to questions of immigration and integration. Responding to riots against police harassment in the housing estates of Vaulx en Velin and Les Minguettes in 1990, he argued that 'ethnic categories are almost the only ones at present to produce collective action' (*Libération*, 15 October 1990). The social is increasingly viewed in cultural terms in fragmenting post-industrial societies, and people are defined by their ethnicity rather than their occupation or class.

Touraine's associates have taken this focus further: Michel Wieviorka focuses on popular racism, Jazouli on the mobilisation of suburban youth, and Dubet on the problems of life in the suburbs, particularly the 'galère'.[3]

Michel Wieviorka sees racism as a perversion of social action, a 'social anti-movement' which is incapable of structuring society. Anti-racism, however, offers an alternative social vision. He maintains that anti-racist action is only really effective if it involves those directly affected by racism rather than more detached groups acting in the name of democracy, human rights, humanist or religious values (Wieviorka 1993b: 418). This form of anti-racist mobilisation is based on the affirmation of identity grounded in racial categories produced by the very processes of racialisation which it is seeking to counter. Anti-racist action by groups who are not mobilising in terms of their own identity may play a useful political, legal or educational role but might also have to contend with racialised identities surfacing within the organisation (Wieviorka 1993: 419). Thus the familiar binary opposition between universalist anti-racism/relativist-differentialist anti-racism reappears in Wieviorka's characterisation of anti-racist actors (Wieviorka 1993b: 426).

Wieviorka does not discuss how anti-racism operates in practice. Empirical research suggests that Wievorka's two types of anti-racist actor are rarely found separately from one another. While the problems he highlights may be present in organisations, they are often found in more complex forms than he suggests. Furthermore, this defensive model of anti-racism does not fully acknowledge the positive social project which he sees as central to anti-racism as a social movement.

Catherine Neveu recognises the complexity of anti-racist mobilising as placing different organisations on a continuum between the poles of universalism and particularism (Neveu 1994: 103). Empirical research reveals a much more complex picture over time, with sometimes the same organisation articulating discourses which at different moments veer more or less to one or the other position (Lloyd 1998b). Anti-racists operate in an ambivalent field, caught between the universal and the particular: at one level they appeal to universal values of human equality and the application of social justice; at the other, in opposing discrimination, in representing or practising solidarity towards certain groups of people, they are also working within a particularist agenda (Lloyd 1994).

During the 1980s there was a great deal of proactive mobilisation by young people from immigrant families who established defensive networks against the 'double peine'.[4] Adil Jazouli highlights the failure of established 'left' organisations or existing 'immigrant' associations to respond to the changing articulation of their demands in the late 1970s (Jazouli 1986). They developed their own collective identity with a strong grass-roots orientation, and they were anti-institutional and highly critical of the role of the organised left.

The March for Equality of 1983 fitted this social movement paradigm of anti-authority, anti-institutional grass-roots activity, articulating broad, universalist demands and protesting against the social exclusion of young people from immigrant families in the call for equality. For Jazouli this identification of grass-roots demands with universal aspirations epitomises the ethical nature of the mobilisation (Jazouli 1992: 53). While the March was the 'founding historical act' of a movement of suburban youth, its very success enabled well-funded and more institutionalised anti-racist organisations such as SOS-Racisme and France-Plus to emerge. Their success marked the political defeat of the more radical grass-roots activists who were replaced by people with experience of 'left' organisation who managed spectacular youth mobilisations around concerts against racism. Jazouli argues that the grass-roots mobilisation found it difficult to move from the local to the national level, and that in doing so it was co-opted, even aborted. He implies a rather stark dichotomy between the social corporatist organisations operating at a policy and associational level and the broader grass-roots social movement.

Etienne Balibar argues that in order to be broad-based an anti-racist strategy should promote the autonomous organisation of immigrants and mobilise communal traditions of resistance to exploitation. Pointing to the increasing fragmentation of working-class identity and politico-ideological systems of beliefs, he identifies the challenge to anti-racists to prevent sections of the working class and petite bourgeoisie from drifting towards a defensive, xenophobic ideology. Important anti-racist mobilisations by young people from North African back-grounds in the 1980s could, he suggests, form the backbone of a broad movement of associations, organised groups, parties, churches and trade unions, which could join the struggle against segregation and racism and for the recognition of the multiracial pluralist France (Balibar 1984).

As we have seen, some aspects of anti-racist campaigning involve elements of ethnic mobilisation, since ethnic minorities form an important constituency and their organisations may play a leading role in defining the issues, in demonstrating in public, negotiating and debating. In many ways anti-racists depend on them in claiming legitimately to represent a constituency. Groups from the 'dominant culture' may also be involved in anti-racist mobilisation but their action is often dependent in important ways on the first, 'ethnic' form of mobilisation. In a sense, and in some circumstances, anti-racist activity can be a transmission belt between ethnic minority groups and the wider political arena.

A central weakness of the writings of the Touraine school, which has been so influential in the French debate about anti-racism, is that they find it difficult to conceptualise an anti-racism which might operate simultaneously on several different levels, at grass-roots, in the associations of civil society and with allies in government. This approach obstructs any exploration of the connection between anti-racist social movements, anti-racist associations and policy initiatives, and closes off an important area of work on anti-racism in the labour movement (Castells 1975; Gorz 1970; Phizacklea and Miles 1980; Wrench 1995). At the same time, the Tourainian social movement analysis makes a number of valuable contributions to the study of anti-racism. It emphasises the change in conscious-ness which comes about with participation in such movements and draws attention to the issues of racialisation, and of who is mobilised and represented. The question of power relations in alliances and the danger of co-optation is a central problem for anti-racists.

Balibar sees anti-racism as intervening where the nation-state 'reflects racism back' to society (Balibar 1992: 85). This is a 'virtual' transaction which only becomes tangible when the mechanism is challenged, as when North African families were introduced into social housing, Habitations à Loyer Modéré (HLM), or when the Socialist Party discussed extending the right to vote to migrants with residence qualifications. If the 'virtual' process of delegation seems to fail, citizens may take it upon themselves to force racialised groups back 'into their place', or pressure the state to do so. Because racism is located in relations of domination and oppression and operates through mutually reinforcing relations between public opinion and the political class, it follows that anti-racism must intervene in both arenas and articulate a discourse of democratic rights.

Balibar argues that anti-racist politics is still in its infancy and that 'anti-racist movements of opinion will become genuinely political only when they organise or co-ordinate their efforts at a European level' (Balibar 1991: 18). Minorities experiencing discrimination will need to find a political voice and pose the question of a wider citizenship in Europe, thereby raising issues of democratic control and cultural equality (Balibar 1991a: 19).

There are many differences between anti-racism in Britain and France. Leadership has been less of a contentious issue in France, and anti-racist activity tends to be more centralised on Paris (although grass-roots campaigns are important). This centralisation has made it easier for major political parties to co-opt anti-racist organisations, as was the case with SOS-Racisme and the Socialist Party. During the 1980s reform to the law made it much easier to form associations and there was an enormous growth in what has been described as the 'associational movement' which mobilised large numbers of young people against racism (Barthelemy 2000; Lloyd 2000; Wihtol de Wenden 1997).

Inherent to the anti-racist project is some concept of international action and relatedness. It is not surprising then that anti-racism has been deeply affected by the processes associated with globalisation. European unification has been of particular concern to campaigners since the late 1980s through campaigns connected to the harmonisation of immigration laws and to the growth of the extreme right in Europe.

European anti-racist activity

The central aim of the Single European Act of 1986 (SEA) was free movement of capital and labour for nationals of states of the European Union. 'Third country nationals' were not included in these measures, which therefore involved the establishment of tighter external frontier controls (Geddes 1995). Immigration controls (along with issues like national security, terrorism and crime) were discussed by intergovernmental structures and were not subject to democratic debate or control. The Schengen agreement of 1985 was initially signed by France, Germany and the Benelux countries, but has had a much wider impact on the rest of Europe.

Many of the measures introduced since the mid-1980s by national governments actually originated from these meetings. The Ford report of the European Parliament argued that by defining immigrants as a special kind of problem, associated with a threat to national security, European governments served to legitimise the racist discourses of the extreme right (Ford 1992). Following the Palma document (1990) on the crossing of external frontiers, a uniform visa and carriers liability legislation was introduced for all European countries.

In an associated development, the rights of asylum have been restricted: in Germany and France this involved changes to constitutional law, in other countries (such as the UK) restrictive legislation. This gave rise to changes in the rights of many third country residents, including their claims to social benefits to work, and an increase in the power of the police to control identities in public places.

At different levels and in different ways anti-racist movements have protested against these new restrictions and the undemocratic way in which they have been planned and introduced. Some protests have focused on immigration controls and particularly the plight of undocumented migrants and asylum-seekers, while others have concentrated on the need to stop the growth of racism which is seen as a by-product of this new Europe.

In the context of the new Europe, as in globalisation more generally, there has been an increase in interest in civil society. The European Commission (DGV) has been attempting to stimulate a European civil society, acknowledging the need for voluntary and other representative organisations to have a role in a wide range of social issues at European level (*Social Europe* 1997: 17). In March 1996 the European Forum on Social Policy brought together a range of organisations to develop 'mutual understanding about the respective roles, responsibilities and capacities of the various actors in civil society in developing a strong civil dialogue, involving both social partners and NGOs' (ibid.).

The efforts to build anti-racist co-operation is an example of the construction of this international civil society. At one level it may make sense to understand the developing consciousness of the European dimension of the problem of racism and of the existence of a common anti-racist agenda in terms of a pan-European social movement of shared values and objectives. Anti-racists are faced with two broad and related problems: first, how to work together and second how to gain access to the relevant power structures in order to make their case heard.

Issues of identification and representation, key aspects of social movements, are crucial to anti-racism where matters of one's identity are at stake. Differences between analyses of racism and anti-racism can lead to more intractable problems, especially when they impinge strongly upon group identity which may be tied up with national differences as in France and Britain. As I suggested earlier, we may understand the different ways in which this is expressed in terms of a continuum between groups with a strongly universalist orientation through to those who are highly particularist.

Attempts by anti-racist groups to establish the Anti-racist Network for Equality in Europe in 1991 foundered over these kinds of difficulties. There was a debate, led by the British-based Anti Racist Alliance (ARA) and the Standing Conference on Racism in Europe (SCORE), over the priority to be given to black leadership in the organisation. This revealed very different analyses of the causes and extent of racism. It illustrated the uniqueness of the British analysis of anti-racism and of 'race relations' in Europe at the time. In the context of meetings between French and British anti-racist activists it became clear that the British had difficulties in accepting that there could be a situation where (according to Catherine Neveu) 'the dominant terminology is not a racialised one, . . . [and] groups most subjected to racism and discrimination are hardly (physically) distinguishable from the indigenous population' (1994: 99). While the British framed the debate in highly racialised terms, the French tended to think in what they saw as more 'universal' categories of equality and rights. Furthermore, it was argued that the black/white race relations paradigm was inadequate for explaining a situation where there are multiple sites of racism, for instance against African migrant workers but also Yugoslavs, Chinese, Turks, and Muslims in general. This meant that there could be different criteria for the establishment of anti-racist alliances: the British focusing on identity based on phenotype and ethnic identity rather than experience and similar political economic and social position in forming anti-racist alliances, which tended to be the basis of other European groupings (Neveu 1994: 98).

Other difficulties were involved in the formulation of the Migrants Forum, a DGV-funded organisation to represent all migrants (King 1995). The term 'migrant' was unacceptable to ethnic minority citizens, who nevertheless wanted to be represented at European level. Protracted negotiations drew attention to the British exception, where ethnic minority citizens' access to political rights does not end discrimination. For the majority of 'migrants' in other European countries who enjoyed second-class citizenship at best, the British case was hard to understand. Yet for British anti-racists this problem was crucial. 'Citizenship may open Europe's borders to black people and allow them free movement, but racism cannot tell one black from another, a citizen from an immigrant, an immigrant from a refugee and classes all third world people as immigrants and refugees and all immigrants and refugees as terrorists and drug dealers' (Sivanandan 1995).

To the extent that anti-racists recognise a similar agenda and share parallel concerns and approaches to their work, there may be no need to construct a formal set of anti-racist institutions at European level. After all, informal co-operation has already given rise to spontaneous and joint demonstrations as for instance in co-ordinating campaigns or opposing European meetings of the extreme right. The European Commission and Parliament does however find it useful to have organised interlocutors and has continued to attempt to create anti-racist structures.

During the European Year against Racism DGV moved to set up the European Union Network Against Racism. This arises from the Union's own need to have some sort of organised lobby to which the bureaucracy can relate (for instance in co-operating with the European Commission Against Racism and Intolerance in the run up to the European Conference Against Racism, itself preparatory for the UN World Conference Against Racism in 2001). In debating how to respond to these developments, anti-racists were caught between the reluctance to compromise dearly held positions and the danger that the European bureaucracy would promote a structure with its own chosen groups and its own programme which would make it more difficult for anti-racist groups to determine their own agenda.

Co-operation is less problematic when organisations work in similar ways. Relatively well organised groups who can develop professional exchanges of information are well placed to take advantage of these opportunities. The dissemination of information and legal advice can be rapidly adapted to use fast means of electronic data transmission (GISTI, JCWI and United are good examples). They may however experience some difficulty in maintaining their own priorities and activity agendas, especially when responding to domestic developments.

Other groups may take advantage of new technology to improve the reach and effectiveness of their communications, with the help of other organisations. The *sanspapiers* movement has established links throughout Europe by means of a website and discussion list through which they make available the texts of the most recent ministerial circulars and exchange advice and experience.[5] Similarly at European and international level the 'United' initiative in Amsterdam funded by DGV operates largely through a website, exchanging and co-ordinating information about anti-racist activities.[6]

Co-operation is more difficult for the more protest-oriented, reactive types of anti-racist group, which share many of the characteristics of social movements. They nearly all suffer from a lack of resources, and their supporters identify strongly, even emotionally, with the goals of the movement, which raises the question of representation, and a tendency to define themselves in terms of what they oppose rather than what they support. Let us examine these questions one by one.

Informal, voluntary, militant types of anti-racist groups or coalitions such as the British-based Assembly against Racism, the MRAX (Movement against Racism and Xenophobia) in Belgium, the MRAP (Movement against Racism and for Friendship Between Peoples) in France and Nero e no solo in Italy have relatively few resources and rely heavily on members' contributions and small project grants for their functioning. Such organisations have few resources to fund travel to meetings, time and personnel, people with the necessary pluri-language skills. Organisations with meagre resources are at a disadvantage in competing for funding, co-operating with well-endowed partners and insisting upon their priorities.

The second major problem is access to institutions. The structures of the EU have been frequently criticised in terms of their opaqueness and emphasis on control measures rather than actions against racism. The important difference is between the intergovernmental structures (such as the Council of Ministers) and the European Commission and Parliament. Key individuals in both the latter institutions have sought to expand their roles in developing anti-racist initiatives.

Following the Vienna Conference in October 1993, the Council of Europe set up the European Commission Against Racism and Intolerance (ECRI) to formulate general policy recommendations for member states on issues of racism. ECRI's responsibilities encompass the collection and publication of data, the publicising of examples of good practice and the analysis of legal measures against racism.[7]

The European Parliament's Evregenis (1985) and Ford (1992) reports established that the rhetoric by which immigration controls are introduced and their content have helped to legitimise racism, and may partly account for the electoral success of the far right (Ford 1992). The European Parliament called for EU ratification of the European Convention on Human Rights and the Geneva Convention on Refugees, and criticised the control of movements of third country nationals by unaccountable intergovernmental groups. However, its call for the establishment of a European body against racism on the lines of the CRE and a European residents' charter was rejected by the Social Affairs commissioner Vasso Papandreou, who argued in 1992 that the Commission had no influence over the criminal law of its members.

Member governments of the EU have resisted the establishment of European policies against racism despite their endorsement of international statements condemning racism, such as the European Convention on Human Rights or the preamble to the Social Charter which acknowledges the need to combat all forms of discrimination 'on the grounds of sex, colour, race, opinions and belief'. National provisions against racism vary considerably across Europe (Costa-Lascoux 1990; Geddes 1995: 211; MacEwen 1995). Faced with mounting evidence of the growth of the extreme right, and pressure from the European Parliament and the Commission, the Council of Ministers set up a Consultative Commission on Racism and Xenophobia in 1994, charged with 'making recommendations, geared as far as possible to national and local circumstances, on co-operation between governments and the various social bodies in favour of encouraging tolerance, understanding and harmony with foreigners' (Kahn 1995).

The Kahn Commission argued that the Treaty of Rome should be amended to cover racial discrimination. The European Parliament and Commission have taken up its proposals in taking initiatives against racism and xenophobia at European level. At the forefront, exerting pressure is the Starting Line Group which includes the CRE, the Churches Committee for Migrants in Europe, the Dutch National Bureau Against Racism and the Commissioner for Foreign Affairs of the Senate of Berlin, supported by over thirty national and European organisations. They argue for unambiguous legal competence in the Treaty of Rome and an EU directive for the elimination of racial discrimination. The group organises among other NGOs and targets the Commission and political parties in the European Parliament. This is an important development in that it illustrates how groups can pool resources, expertise and their access to decision-makers, through forming an 'advocacy coalition' (Kingdon 1984; Sabatier 1988; Stedward 1997).

The Unit on Freedom of Movement and Migration Policy in DGV has taken anti-racist initiatives under its social policy remit, through the white paper on social policy (1994) which focused on racism, xenophobia, anti-Semitism and integration (Stedward 1997: 196). The unit offered financial assistance to NGOs intervening on issues involving migrants and on measures to combat racism, xenophobia and anti-Semitism such as educational packs, practitioner conferences, training sessions and the establishment of the Migrants Forum and the EUMC (Stedward 1997: 196).[8] This tactic of negotiating around the denial of community competence against racism has been used to include racism and xenophobia in most of the main statements about social exclusion (Robbins 1994).[9]

Conclusion

This chapter has focused on a set of issues with both general and specific implications. In general terms, I have addressed some of the problems of establishing democratic structures within civil society at a supra-national level. European unification and globalisation may increase precariousness among migrants and ethnic minority populations. Providing they have the resources, groups can exploit the enhanced opportunities presented for rapid communications by means of the internet and e-mail. While globalisation has not closed off political action either within civil society or at the level of the nation-state, it does pose problems of scale and structures in alliance-building. Who should be driving the formation of alliances? How can small, under-resourced organisations ensure that they are not sidelined? The establishment of European policies and structures on migration and asylum have produced new problems and new interlocutors for anti-racists, whilst also opening up new opportunities for intervention. This chapter has examined some of the difficulties which under-resourced organisations may experience in responding to political opportunities at the transnational level. This raises a problem inherent in globalisation, which while creating uniformity also stimulates particularist agendas, for example identity politics, but also racism and extreme forms of nationalism. This is a difficult problem for anti-racists because they are not outside the dynamics they are trying to control.

The factors which prevent anti-racists from responding to the opportunities for co-operation in the new Europe are inseparable from the political dynamics of globalisation itself. Anti-racism is multifaceted and various. It cannot be wholly separated from ethnic mobilisation because in some instances the two are closely intertwined, and depend on one another. If we separate out different levels of mobilisation (European, national, civil society, grass-roots), we can distinguish some of the factors which divide groups from one another. For instance, organisations vary in terms of their distance from policy-makers. Groups with close relationships to centres of power benefit from funding and may find some of their priorities taken up by decision-makers. This may, however, be at the expense of their credibility with the grass-roots sections of the anti-racist movement who may suspect that their concerns are being diluted. This question of co-option is important for anti-racists because of the centrality of their claims to legitimately represent their constituency.

A central feature of the problem is its imbalance. Decisions about immigration have been taken away from democratic fora and made behind closed doors. There is a widely perceived link between the harmonisation of immigration and asylum controls and the rise of racism and xenophobia These problems are not outweighed by the scope of opportunities presented to anti-racists by the European Parliament and the European Commission. The opportunities also contain the danger that the anti-racist agenda could be co-opted by these powerful organisations and that groups could become dependent on European funding and lose touch with their grass-roots support, which is a crucial resource.

Even if anti-racist organisations accept the need to form pan-European structures, they still face a number of problems. Racism takes a multiplicity of forms, depending on historical, political, social, cultural and economic contexts: for similar reasons (not simply because it is a response to racism) anti-racism is also multifaceted. Serious study of anti-racism does reveal common themes: anti-racists all work with changing perceptions of discrimination, attempt to represent people who experience racism and develop solidarity actions. Underpinning these themes is a wider social project about social justice, equality and social cohesion. In different ways at different moments and in different contexts, anti-racists have sought to build consent for their ideas by promoting an anti-racist common sense, through broad campaigning, legislation and education.

If instead of focusing on the issues which divide them, anti-racists look at what they have in common, it may become clearer that some joint projects at European level may be possible. There are often as many difficult divisions between groups within countries as between countries. We know surprisingly little about these features of anti-racism in Europe, and this is an important theme for future research. There is a need for detailed study of the main organisations and also of the way in which they co-operate with other groups in civil society like political parties, trade unions and religious organisations. How do they co-operate within specific political campaigns for the defence of public services and welfare for example?

A central issue is that of understanding alliances and how they work. My study of the way in which anti-racist groups have worked together within France has shown that in spite of cultural and generational differences, a 'transversal' way of working was sometimes possible, based on recognition of common aims and respect for the positions of different participants. As a system of 'alliances' transversal collectives are unstable over a long period of time, but they also offer a more open, tolerant and pluralist way for pressure groups and social movement type organisations to work together (Foucault 1977; Yuval-Davis 1997c). This is the sort of loose, perhaps *ad hoc* co-operation which may be most effective at European level and points to forms which global civil society may take in the future.

Notes

1 There was regular contact with anti-racists elsewhere, however. For instance there were attempts to co-ordinate lobbying for legislation against racism between Fenner Brockway and the MRAP in France. See Lloyd 1998b.
2 The Ligue des Droits de l'Homme (LDH) was established in 1898. The Ligue contre l'Anti-Semitisme et Racisme (LICRA) was set up under a different name (Ligue contre les pogroms) in 1928, while the Mouvement Contre le Racisme et Pour l'Amitié entre les Peuples (MRAP) was formed in 1949 from Resistance organisations. All three are still active.
3 This is the state of aimless existence of the unemployed poor and marginalised in contemporary France: 'the extreme point of domination, an experience of survival which is wholly dominated by the convergences of the forces of domination and exclusion'. See Dubet 1987, p. 13.
4 The 'double peine' or double penalty was used against mainly young men from migrant backgrounds. A criminal conviction (sometimes very minor) would be punished by imprisonment compounded by a deportation order.
5 The sanspapiers' web address is: http://bok.net/pajol/
6 United's web address is http://www.united.non-profit.nl
7 ECRI's web address is http://www.ecri.coe.int
8 The European Monitoring Centre on Racism and Xenophobia, established by the European Union in 1997. See www.eumc.at
9 This rather ramshackle approach was seriously disrupted in May 1998 by a ruling of the European Court of Justice that there was no legal basis for expenditure on a wide range of budget lines related to civil society and humanitarian actions. This temporary freeze was unblocked, but it underlines the precarious and vulnerable nature of this expenditure, and has reinforced the campaign to establish a firm legal basis for these measures.

5 Germans into foreigners

How anti-nationalism turns into racism[1]

Nora Räthzel

In this chapter I consider not only the flexibility and fluidity of notions of the nation and its respective Other, but also the stability of these constructions, the relations between flexibility and stability, and between homogeneity and heterogeneity. I also debate aspects we usually discuss only in passing, when talking about the nation-state and ethnicity, such as social antagonisms, class relations, social justice and their relation to self-determination on ethnic grounds. Finally, I consider how these relationships and the way they are disarticulated have some impact for anti-racist strategies. My view is that ethnic formation holds both a promise and a danger in terms of the achievement of anti-racism and social justice.

In the first part of this chapter I use some political events in Germany in order to develop some questions about the relationships between the nation, ethnicity, social justice and anti-racism. In the second part I discuss what I consider to be the dialectics of the homogeneity and heterogeneity of the nation-state, the relationship between ethnicity and nation, and, finally, what this could mean for politics which combine the struggle for social justice with the struggle against racism. I also show how anti-nationalism can turn into racism. It provides a critical evaluation of ethnicity as a mode of fighting for social justice.

Germans into foreigners

In March 1996 we witnessed in Germany a puzzling discussion about international solidarity, the dangers of racism and populism. Commentators, from both right-wing and left-wing newspapers, agreed that it was dangerous to play the numbers game with immigrants in order to win elections. What had happened? Had all our dreams come true? Had the harsh critique articulated by many scholars during the peak of racist aggressions in 1992 finally convinced the press and they were now trying to educate politicians? Perhaps one might start to believe in the practical use of social sciences. And yet, the overall effect was to turn the arguments upside down.

Just before the elections in three German Länder, Oscar Lafontaine, the leader of the Social Democrats, demanded that the migration of *Aussiedler* (ethnic Germans) into Germany should be restricted. He argued that they were too costly, given the crisis of the state's budget and the high numbers of unemployed (over four million). Lafontaine had already made the same point in 1989, when large numbers of ethnic Germans had migrated into West Germany due to the opening of the borders in Eastern Europe, mainly from Poland and the Soviet Union. He gave different reasons for his statement and public reactions were also different. In 1989 Lafontaine had argued that it was a sign of narrow patriotism to prefer *Aussiedler* before other immigrants. All those who wanted to enter the country should be judged by their needs, rather than by their nationality, or their ancestors. This view was opposed at the time, particularly by conservative politicians, who argued that it was 'natural' to prefer one's 'own kind' before anyone else. This was referred to as a human and indeed even a trait exhibited by any living being, as animals behaved in the same way. Only Germans, it was said, because of their notoriously disturbed national identity, were unable to feel in this natural way.

It is important to note that in 1989 immigrants coming from Eastern Europe were defined as Germans. Lafontaine, who wanted to restrict their entry, was accused of the typical German 'disease', the inability to show a 'normal national feeling'. By 1996, things were quite different. Lafontaine, and with him the Social Democratic Party, were accused of giving up their old international perspective. They were exchanging international solidarity for national chauvinism, it was said. In short, they were losing their identity. Another criticism was that in raising the question of the numbers of *Aussiedler* in public, the Social Democrats were likely to provoke feelings of racism and *Ausländerfeindlichkeit*. If there was a problem, it should not be debated in public, but dealt with confidentially. It was concluded that the Social Democrats had merely revealed that they had no idea how to solve the economic crisis and therefore had to resort to scapegoating. It was a new experience in Germany to see a claim to restrict immigration so unanimously rejected. If we remember the years 1990–3, when the right to asylum in Germany was practically abolished, almost all social actors, except for the Green Party, argued in favour of restricting the entrance of asylum-seekers. It is astonishing too to see how Aussiedler suddenly became 'foreigners', for otherwise it would have been senseless to speak about international solidarity in this context.

I want to suggest that one underlying reason for the rejection of Lafontaine's proposal is the fact that in spite of their implicit exclusion from the German nation, *Aussiedler* are still seen as the more desirable immigrants. Otherwise, one could not imagine such a reaction in favour of them. As I have argued elsewhere (Räthzel 1995), the arguments concerning *Aussiedler* have been contrary to those concerning *Ausländer*, even when referring to the same issues. I want to give some examples:

Aussiedler

> If Aussiedler and Übersiedler realise that what they have to offer is needed, that we want them as fellow human beings, but also as citizens, who are ready to take up responsibilities for society, then this is the best presupposition we can offer them for a good integration.[2]
>
> (*Informationen zur politischen Bildung*, 222, 1989: 9,
> magazine from the Ministry for Political Education)

Ausländer

> Integration – for foreigners who have been living here for a long time – is desirable as far as they want it themselves. . . . But first they have to insert themselves into our social relations and when they have done this properly they may ask for citizenship . . .[3]
>
> (*Frankfurter Allgemeine Zeitung*, 28 June 1990, quoting a member of the CDU)

Aussiedler

> There has always been a lack of housing. The arrival of Aussiedler is not its cause, it only makes this lack visible. Many people think that our country is over-populated and is unable to host hundreds and thousands of Aussiedler. The facts are: The German population fell between 1970 and 1987 by 1.3 million. Even if the number of Aussiedler and Übersiedler amounted to 300,000–400,000 every year, this would not pose a problem.[4]
>
> (Ihre Heimat sind WIR, *Aktion Gemeinsinn*, 1989: 27)

Ausländer

> It is obvious that in a country so densely populated as the Federal Republic of Germany all efforts towards integration are destined to fail if incoming numbers stay as high as they are today (650,000 during the last three years). The main problem is not even the labour market, but the rejection of foreigners by the population. It occurs inevitably, when the threshold of tolerance is transgressed.[5]
>
> (*Die Zeit*, 1 January 1982, quoted in Räthzel 1995: 274–5)

As *Aussiedler* have always been considered to be Germans, and therefore more desirable immigrants than those considered as alien, there is an unwillingness to discuss them as a 'problem'. This does not mean, though, that the government does not impose restrictions on them. In 1996, a law was passed, decreeing that *Aussiedler* who do not settle where the government has sent them but choose to live with their relatives (for example) would have their social security money cut. This could be interpreted as a violation of the Basic Law, which secures the right of free movement for all Germans. To impose restrictions is one thing, to discuss them in public is another.[6]

Whatever the reasons for such a shift in viewing *Aussiedler*, one wonders if it does have an effect on the way in which Germanness is conceived in general. Is the German nation seen as a civic unit today? And does this make it more inclusive and more open to something like 'international solidarity'? To answer this, I want to report on another discussion that took place at the same time. Its subject was contract workers on German building sites.

Contract workers and transnational consciousness

Such workers are employed by contracts between Eastern European governments and the German government, partly as the result of European unification which gives EU-citizens the right to work in any of the member states under the same conditions as in their own country. While contract workers from Eastern Europe have to be paid the same wage officially (social security is paid according to the procedures in the sending countries), EU-workers can be officially paid less, at the same levels they are paid in their own country. In reality both groups of workers are employed for wages ranging between 2 and 5 DM per hour, while the minimum German wage for the same work is 19 DM per hour. In 1996 trade unions were fighting for a law that guarantees the same minimum wage for all workers. On the one hand, a general minimum wage for all workers is highly desirable. On the other hand, the way this claim is put forward involves not just equal pay for all, but the exclusion of non-German workers from those building sites. This becomes clear when it is argued that the demand for equal pay is necessary, because so many German construction workers are unemployed as foreign workers can be paid lower wages.[7] In other words: if there were no wage differentials, there would be no foreign workers – or not as many – and German workers would be re-employed. International solidarity seems to have disappeared in these arguments.

On the one hand, one does not want to argue in favour of super-exploitation of foreigners or any other group of workers. After all, one indication of racism in Germany, which is never operationalised in opinion polls, is the continuing low position of migrant workers in the labour market (see Räthzel 1999). On the other hand, contract workers are able to get work only if they accept lower wages. Demanding equal pay means, in the last instance, playing the national card and results in unemployment for large groups of non-nationals. Leaving things as they are means unemployment for large groups of nationals (and also long-term non-nationals) and over-exploitation of newer non-nationals. It seems as if fighting for social justice on a national level is bound to (re)produce social injustice between nationals and non-nationals. Or to put it more sharply, it seems as if the fight for social justice is based on racism. Is there a way out of this quandary?

I shall return to this central question about the relationship between social justice and the fight for anti-racism after re-examining some basic assumptions about the character of the nation, of ethnic groups and interest groups, such as the workers' movement or the women's movement. First, however, I want to look at three different stages of German constructions of Self (the nation) and Other (not belonging to the nation), which I shall then use to give flesh to the points I want to make on a more general level.

Three stages of German constructions of the nation and the other

Stage I

As I have argued before (Räthzel 1995), the West German 'Self' was constructed against the East German 'Other'. I have overlooked, however, what I now think of as the central point on which this opposition focused: the construction of West Germany as a democratic country. In other words, construction of the East German as the Other was part of the programme of promoting in West Germany the notion of German democracy and democratic attitudes. It was in opposition to East Germany and East Germans that Western democracy could be shown as the successful means for a good life. As the point has often been made before, a good life meant an economically secure life. By comparing West Germans to their 'brothers and sisters', who had in theory the same abilities, precisely by being part of the same 'family', one could show how Western democracy unleashed all the 'German virtues' and how Communism suppressed them. To prove the qualities of democracy, one had only to look at the reversed mirror image of the undemocratic part of Germany.

But there was also another 'Other': when economic security was threatened, unemployment rose, housing for people with an average income became a problem and the school system did not secure the right qualifications for the world of labour. In such periods, the social security that was provided for East Germans (no unemployment, low housing rents) could become something to aim for. In such periods, the *Ausländer* 'problem' surfaced. Discussions about there being too many of 'them', taking 'our' jobs, houses and exams, which had been marginal, became central. And indeed, in times of economic crisis repatriation programmes *rückkehrhilfe*[8] were discussed and realised.

I would suggest that during the 1960s the political consensus in West Germany, particularly the approval given to the West German nation-state, was secured in two ways. On the one hand, it was secured by the reversed mirror image of the undemocratic East German Other, which one did not want to become. On the other hand, it was secured by the image of the *Ausländer*, who was seen as the cause of internal social crisis. This image secured consent to the system in so far as the internal conflicts could be shown to come from 'outside'.

Stage II

This stability was first broken by the so-called 'generation of 1968'. The economic/ social security aspect of Western democracy did not appeal to our generation who had not experienced the war and who did not know what poverty or social insecurity meant. But the discourse of democracy had put down roots in our thinking. We were to demand the realisation of this promise of freedom and justice. The reversed mirror image of the East German brothers and sisters suffering under Communist dictatorship did not work for us in the same way for a number of reasons. First, they were not 'brothers and sisters' for us, only inhabitants of another country. Second, we did not believe in the necessary connection between Communism and dictatorship, because we saw the deep injustices within the capitalist system and the way it supported right-wing dictatorships and conducted imperialist wars (particularly in Vietnam). On the one hand, the image of democracy was central. It was the lack of democracy in the West and the violation of its professed values (found in Germany especially in 'anti-terrorist' politics) that led to the radical dissention of a great part of our generation. This found expression in the founding of a new party, the Greens. It was to represent those who did not find any political voice within the existing political landscape. This break with the system was also a break with the construction of the German nation as a Western democracy, providing social and economic security through the mechanisms of the 'social market-society'. The new party was also strongly anti-nationalist at the beginning with the exception of a small group around Peter Brandt, who wanted to rearticulate the concept of the nation from a left position. The founding of the party institutionalised a fundamental opposition to the present construction of the nation-state and, because of this, the first step of re-integration into the system.

The beginning of the 1980s also marked a new phase concerning the image of the *Ausländer*. It was now clear, at least for the majority of those who thought politically, that the guestworkers had ceased to be guests and were largely here to stay. Discussions about integration and intercultural education began. The Greens were the first to demand a right to 'settlement', *niederlassungsrecht*. This meant the right to have full citizenship without becoming a German national, something many migrants did not want.[9] This unwillingness to give up their nationality of origin for German nationality coincided with ideas on the left and among the Greens who were suspicious of the nation-state in general and therefore opposed the idea that the rights of citizenship should be connected to people's nationality.

Stage III

In spite of contestations from the new left, the image of the East German and the *Ausländer* as the Other continued within the dominant discourse in West Germany. In fact, the new left strengthened these constructions to some extent. They did this implicitly by pitching the idea of 'the new left' against 'the old left' of Eastern Germany, and by being only interested in *Ausländer* as far as they belonged to some revolutionary movement, e.g. in Vietnam, Chile or Mozambique, etc. This construction came to a head and faltered with the arrival of about 300–400 *Aussiedler* and *Ubersideler* annually (since 1988), and finally with the breaking down of the Berlin Wall (1990). Clearly, as the East German Other now became part of the nation, s/he could not be the Other any more, in the same sense. But at the same time, there was no further need to prove the superiority of Western democracy given that the Eastern system, against which it had had to be defended, had vanished (or yielded to the 'superior system' as often claimed). It became rapidly clear, however, that an opposition that had been constructed for forty years could not disappear over night. On the contrary, being 'one people' led to the surfacing of differences and contradictions making unification a rather contradictory and ongoing process.

In the light of these conflicts, it can come as no surprise that the other Other gained 'value', at the risk of sounding rather cynical. The debate about the numbers of asylum-seekers which was taking place during the second half of the 1980s escalated in 1989 and 1990 into racist violence, costing the lives of more than twenty people, mainly of Turkish origin. In 1993 the right to asylum was practically abolished, partly as a result of the public concern about the numbers of asylum-seekers and racist violence. Nobody, except Lafontaine, discussed the even higher numbers of *Aussiedler* as a problem.

Another result of the crisis of unification was the final incorporation of the Green Party into the national consensus.[10] The first aspect of this, although it appeared to be the opposite, was the strong objection voiced against German unification, on the basis of a conviction that 'they' (East Germans) would undermine Western democracy which had been constructed, it was now said, to a large extent by the 'generation of 1968'. Another aspect was the self-critique that followed the rejection of unification by the Green Party. Internal conflicts about this and other questions led to the 'fundamentalist' fraction, which opposed integration into the national project, leaving the party. On the question of *Ausländer*, the Green Party finally abolished its demand for 'open borders'. This did not mean, though, that it accepted the construction of migrants as the source of unemployment, bad housing, etc. On the contrary, a great campaign was launched in 1993 in favour of dual citizenship during which one million signatures were collected. However, the politics around migrants and the anti-racist position of the party have lost considerable strength as a result partly of the Green Party merging with an alliance of civil movements from East Germany (Bündnis 90).

What emerges as a new consensus of the nation-state is something more divided, more complex but no less stable than the pre-1989 consensus. One could best describe the situation by saying that each social group and each social conflict has its Other. The contract workers from Eastern Europe and the new workers from the EU are blamed for unemployment in different areas. Concerning internal security (or insecurity rather), there are the 'Rumanian gangs', the Russian Mafia, or Kurdish drug dealers. Where the loss of Western values is a concern, Islamic fundamentalists serve as a unifying Other, against whom those values have to be preserved. To prove that Germany is not a racist country, but a country that is 'friendly to foreigners' (this expression comes from former chancellor Helmut Kohl), there are the 'good Turks' who are not Islamic fundamentalists, who have assimilated, and who are therefore accepted as 'our neighbours and colleagues'. The Green Party and many on the left in general used to have their Other represented by *Aussiedler*, criticising the privileges they have in relation to those migrants who are defined as non-Germans, but also constructing them as German nationalists and racists. But this has changed since it is clear that they are nevertheless discriminated against and since the Social Democrats have chosen them as their Other.

Finally, there are the former 'brothers and sisters', now *Ossis*. This is an abbreviated nickname for *Ostdeutsche*, and *Wessis*, is the respective name for West Germans, invented long before anyone could think about the breaking down of the wall, by the alternative scene in West Berlin. A constant cause of discussion was the problem of unification, what would be the values of the new Germany, how to teach the *Ossis* to live in a meritocratic society where initiative and achievement count. In other words, the East German Other and the difficulty of integrating him and particularly her (as women were losing much more in the new state) serve as a means to re-construct the German nation.[11] Instead of seeing them as a threat to unification, these discussions should be understood as the process through which a new consensus was being shaped, a consensus that will not be as homogeneous as before, but will consist of different images of the nation each with their own Other. It will be, or already is, a consensus that is more postmodern.[12]

Almost all the different images of the Self and the Other that coexist and fight each other in the new unified Germany find a common denominator in the term *Standort Deutschland* (literally 'Germany as a location'). It refers to Germany as a location for capital investment which is threatened, particularly according to a managerial class, by wages that are too high, or, as trade unions and managers say, by competition from former 'third world countries'. The general Other results from globalisation and the threat that arises from the developing Asian countries, the flexibility of capital, which can, given the possibilities of communication technology, produce whatever it wants in any part of the world under any condition it wants. This is the image reproduced time and again by the press and by politicians, claiming that they cannot really influence the economy any more. To show how this threat constitutes political decisions and gives them a national orientation, the trade union research foundation finally decided to set up a research programme on discrimination in 1993. Until then it had claimed that research on migration or discrimination against migrant populations was not its task because it had nothing to do with workers' interests. This decision was taken in 1993, in order to set up a research programme on *Standort Deutschland*. Thus, one could say that the unity of the different constructions of the German nation and its respective Others is constructed through the unifying force of the right of access to the German labour market.

Homogeneity and heterogeneity of the nation-state

This short discussion, despite lacking detail and ignoring many contradictory developments as well as economic and political events that played a part in shaping the specific constructions of Self and Other, serves to illustrate some factors for rethinking the concept of the nation-state.

It shows that homogeneity and heterogeneity of the nation-state are two sides of the same coin. There would be no need constantly to construct a homogeneity if there was no heterogeneity. Moreover heterogeneity, far from being an impediment for homogeneity, is the means by which it is constructed.[13] So, the construction of a homogenous nation-state is not necessarily challenged by positing the existence of heterogeneity. First, in stressing historical heterogeneity, we only stress the capacity of the nation-state to integrate different ethnic groups. Sometimes, the existence of different ethnic groups can only be recognised by the people's names. Sometimes though, different regional groups still claim their own identity. But most groups, at least in Western Europe, do not make claims to build their own state. Second, stressing ethnic heterogeneity within the nation-state means accepting the definition of the 'problem' as being one of ethnicity. But why should the fact that a nation-state comprises groups which define themselves as different in ethnic terms constitute a problem? For example, Switzerland is composed of four different ethnic groups. This may lead to tensions, to different political perspectives which sometimes overlap with different ethnicities, but these tensions are not seen as a threat to the cohesion of the Swiss nation-state. Despite this, although Switzerland is constructed as a multicultural nation-state, with a great autonomy for the different ethnic groups and Cantons, there is the construction of an alien Other which unites these differences.[14]

The 'problem', therefore, is not the existence of different ethnic groups within one nation-state, but the construction of one or more ethnic groups as not belonging to the nation. The construction of the Other (which I want to call 'othering' in the following) is an inherent feature of the nation-state. Balibar (1991a) has explained this as the necessity to construct one ethnicity as the basis of the nation. As no nation-state is based on one ethnic group, the unity has to be constructed through the construction of an Other, who shows, like a reversed mirror-image, the image of the nation: 'We' is defined by not being like this 'Other'. This is one aspect, which still refers to the level of ethnicity. But there is another level in which there is no homogeneity of the nation-state and this is the vertical split of our societies into rulers and ruled, work and capital, men and women. This is not an ethnic but rather a social heterogeneity, for these are social hierarchies. I have indicated above how German constructions of Self and Other were always related to ways of securing a national unity, where it was threatened by growing social contradictions. By constructing an ethnically defined unity social hierarchies are made secondary. They are bridged by constructing two opposing ethnic groups constituted through the category of the nation, the Self, and the non-national, the Other. This unity has to be constructed through a 'myth of origin', be it ethnic, racial or political. It cannot be constructed as a social unity because it is precisely these social antagonisms that have to be bridged. Images of the Other are therefore always articulated with social conflicts, social injustice and social tensions (criminality), by which a given society is haunted. Constructions of the Other function as explanations for internal contradictions, thus aiming at constructing these internal contradictions as conflicts between the external (the Other, that does not belong) and the internal.[15]

I would suggest that no matter how the nation-state is constructed in the dominant national ideology, as homogeneous by descent or by political will, as plural by descent or by political will, any construction of a nation-state is necessarily constructed through an alien Other threatening social cohesion. This structure reproduces itself through space and time, through all the innumerable variations, models and different actual empirical forms of nation-states.

In the past this has led some Marxists to think that national belonging was not 'real' or 'important', that it was only something that existed on the surface, while the deeper and real belongings were belongings to a class and the real contra-dictions were the social ones, and that therefore the worker had 'no fatherland'. This notion was repeated for the women's movement by Virginia Woolf. I want to argue that it is precisely because national belonging and/or ethnic belonging have or develop their own life, their own history, mechanisms and emotions, that they have the power to render social antagonisms secondary. But I also believe that we cannot understand the way in which national/ethnic belonging works, if we do not examine the way it is intertwined with and related to social antagonisms and social belongings.

The nation-state and the imaginary subject position

Very often, nationalisms and racisms are seen as the result of the social position of individuals, as a result of poverty and unemployment.[16] People, it is said, who are unemployed search for somebody to bear responsibility for it and they find

Ausländer, *Aussiedler*, blacks, Algerians, etc. The state, which needs to divert attention from itself, or better from the economic system it is reproducing, also needs a scapegoat and finds the same people, those not of and yet existing within the nation. But why is it that those who are defined as non-nationals are those who are singled out as scapegoats? Why is there a need to construct a national unity in the face of an internal crisis? Why do people not turn against the state, join the opposition parties? Sometimes this happens of course, but more often a social crisis results in a shift to the right, to a demand for a 'strong hand'.

In fact, what the nation-state provides for its members, or what it is asked to provide, is the feeling of being master of its own fate and feeling that it is a subject. To say that those who do not belong to the nation are the cause of a social crisis, of social injustice, is to constitute a social actor with the ability to put an end to this external threat: it constitutes us, the nationals, as a powerful social actor and it constitutes the problem (social crisis) as one which can be solved by social control, that is by controlling the numbers of immigrants. The power of the powerless (nationals) derives from an identification with the state to whom this power is handed over. In identifying with a powerful nation-state, the powerless individuals gain what I want to call an 'imaginary subject position', as opposed to a subject position. A subject position would be one where individuals act within a horizontally structured collectivity, or community. One could call this self-determination and in turn term the 'imaginary subject-position' a subordinated or alienated subjectivity.[17]

In other words, the weakness of the individual is the strength of the nation-state. In so far as individuals are unable to build horizontal organisations which enable them to act as subjects, to take control over their lives, control is handed over to the nation-state. This explains, in my view, the strength of national belongings through different political conjunctures, different specific definitions of the nation, competing belongings to regions, and opposing social movements, that is, in heterogeneous contexts. In an age where nation-states are political subjects, there is no other entity that promises such a powerful (imaginary) subject position.[18]

I would therefore suggest that national belongings, the construction of a national Self and a non-national Other, relate to the quest for self-determination and social justice. But the encapsulation of these within the form of the nation transforms self-determination into an imaginary subject position and social justice into social injustices on the grounds of ethnic/national belonging.[19]

As an example we can come back to the case of German trade unions and contract workers. We can see that the trade unions' position assumes an imaginary subject position. Instead of acting as a horizontally organised collective of all workers against different forms of exploitation, it identifies with the state and demands action from this dominant power in the form of a law for a minimum equal wage. This does not ask the state to act against those who have the power to employ, but against those who are more powerless than those workers represented by the trade unions. Such a demand hands over a power to the state which it can then also use against workers in general, with or without German nationality. It transforms self-determination into determination from above, a subject position into an imaginary subject position. Social justice is thus impeded by reproducing ethnic hierarchies.

Such processes in almost all spheres of social and daily life have led individuals to organise as ethnic minorities or ethnic groups fighting for their rights and against discrimination and racism resulting from the ethnic majority. Are such organisations more likely to secure social justice? Or are they more likely to secure self-determination, as this is one of the core demands of ethnic minorities? I suggest that ethnic minorities are structured in a similar way to nations. In order to explain this I want to turn to the issue of dominant and subordinated ethnic groups. It is precisely because the dominant ethnic group (or groups) is defined as representing the nation that it ceases to be seen as ethnic. In the following, those ethnic groups seen as representing the nation are called the dominant ethnic groups, and those seen as not belonging to the nation are called the subordinated ethnic groups.

Dominant and subordinated ethnic groups

I want to argue that subordinated ethnic groups, though they are not represented by the nation-state in which they live, are nonetheless structured in a similar way to a nation-state. First, they live within societies structured through dominance and hierarchies, and are shaped or influenced by these. Second, if they have migrated, they come from nation-states structured through dominance and hierarchies. Much of what is called 'culture' is the ways in which these structures have become part of daily life or ways of resisting these structures. The difference between subordinated ethnic groups and the dominant ones that are represented within the national project lies in the fact that the hierarchies structuring the first are not institutionalised in the same way.

As with the working class or women, there is a tendency to believe that those who are oppressed are different from (or better than) their oppressors, by virtue of their oppression. Moreover, there is a tendency to see such groups as homogeneous, as if oppression automatically unites a group. Of course we are well aware that this is not the case and yet a tendency to homogenise and to depict subordinated ethnic groups as something nice and perhaps exotic is enshrined in the use of the term 'cultures' for ethnic groups (as implied in the term multiculturalism). We associate culture with a refinement of attitudes, or alternatively with forms of resistance which develop in daily life (see for instance Willis 1979 and Hall 1981) by subordinated groups/classes. On the other hand, the term culture is used to name any kind of habit, attitude, idea or tradition of a given population (see the famous definition by Raymond Williams (1958) of culture as a 'whole way of life'). This fluidity of the term obscures the difference between practices of liberation and resistance, and practices of domination and oppression. All of these are labelled as 'their culture' where subordinated ethnic groups are concerned. I cannot remember having heard anybody say that unequal payment for men and women, for instance, was just part of the German culture and therefore necessary to preserve.[20]

I want to argue that subordinated as well as dominating ethnic groups are structured by:

- social hierarchies
- gender hierarchies – patriarchal domination
- a homogenising myth of origin
- emotional attachment to the group
- internal contradictions/oppositions
- liberation forces
- necessity of othering.

As subordinated ethnic groups do not have possibilities for achieving an imaginary subject position by identifying with the state, patriarchal forces of domination can become important. They are the ones that can, in some way, replace the power of the state. This is one of the reasons why we sometimes find stronger or more overt sexism in subordinated groups compared to dominating groups. Juri'c-Pahor (1993) has shown, with reference to the Slovenes in Austria, that repression by the dominant ethnic group placed women of the subordinated ethnic group into the position of having to reproduce not only the members of the ethnic group, but also their values and mores. Women are held responsible for the maintenance and reproduction of family ties, while men are positioned as those who fight repression politically. The refusal of this role by women is seen as a betrayal of ethnic unity.

The patriarchal organisation of a subordinated ethnic group provides an imaginary subject position for its members. This is the case when organisations are structured hierarchically and power is handed over to leaders instead of being delegated to speakers. A delegation can be called off and others can take the position of speakers. Leaders who see themselves and are seen as being leaders because they represent a higher (patriarchal) order (often formulated in religious terms) cannot be removed from their posts by ordinary members. They can of course be opposed and delegitimated. This was the case when Muslim women in Britain refused to be spoken for by religious leaders of their community and organised a demonstration under the heading: 'religious leaders do not speak for us' (see the chapter by Pragna Patel on the work of Southall Black Sisters and Women Against Fundamentalism in this book). Subordinated ethnic groups can also provide subject positions, if structured horizontally, allowing equality for all their members. This becomes more difficult the more social hierarchies develop within a subordinated group. With the integration of a greater number of its members into higher positions within the dominant nation, the social coherence of the subordinated group loosens. This is the other side of the power gained by such a development.

Writing about African-Americans in the USA, Manning Marable describes the situation thus:

> We calculated the gains of the movement by the percentage of black Americans represented in the political system, as well as in professional, managerial and

legal positions of authority. This model of symbolic representation clearly broke down in the 1980s. Blacks were elected as mayors of major cities, who aggressively pursued policies, such as increasing sales tax on the public and reducing taxes on corporations, which directly went against the best interests of black working-class communities. The elevation of Clarence Thomas to the US Supreme Court dramatically revealed the inherent contradictions and limitations of simplistic, racial-identity politics.

(Marable 1995: xii)

The nation-state has the potential, by being in power, of managing social antagonisms and gender hierarchies through the incorporation of some of their interests into the national project. However, this is not the case for subordinated ethnic groups because their power is limited. Therefore members who gain some success within the social hierarchy are usually incorporated into the national project. They may become alienated from their own ethnic group unless they subscribe consciously to a political project of civil rights. A case in point is that of Clarence Thomas in the USA, the black judge who was elected to the Supreme Court who declared that he objected to equal opportunities policies because they were a case of positive discrimination and therefore unjust.

On the other hand, the more subordinated groups find themselves in a defensive position, the more they tend to build a homogeneity that excludes heterogeneity, instead of using the latter as a means by which a flexible homogeneity can be constructed. Under such circumstances, they can become essentialist and define their myth of origin in fixed ways (as in the case of the Rushdie affair). This results in making the category 'ethnic' the master category of social identification. As in certain forms of Marxism every social belonging was reduced to or seen as secondary to belonging to a class, here everything is seen as secondary to belonging to the ethnic group. These tendencies may diminish in as much as members of subordinated ethnic groups are able to build powerful institutions of their own and to gain access to the state institutions of the nation-state. When this happens, differences within the groups resulting from different positions within the structures of dominance (women, gays and lesbians, workers) surface and threaten unity on the one hand, but also provide more powerful and complex representations of different subject positions within the ethnic group and to a transgressing and transforming of its identities. This may be one way to explain the richness and diversity and also the power of subordinated ethnic groups (or some of their members) in the USA, in Great Britain and in France, and the very slow and hesitant development of political power and political and cultural consciousness of subordinated ethnic groups in Germany.

If we see dominant and subordinated ethnic groups as being structured in a similar way, we can also see that they perpetually reproduce each other. The nation-state, as I have argued, needs the Other. This Other, in trying to fight for its equality, for its recognition, is forced into reproducing structures of domination in an even more rigid way within its own groups. Forms of resistance are often just the reversed mirror image of forms of domination; this is true for all groups opposing structures of domination. Also, the more a group gains power and achieves its aims, the more it will be absorbed into the nation-state and its institutions, losing its organising force. Social hierarchies may override ethnic solidarity.

While some subordinated ethnic groups may integrate into the national project, other ethnic groups may enter the nation-state and take their place as the subordinated, powerless Other. But we should not forget the lessons of history: German fascism taught us that even the most assimilated/integrated Other can be singled out again and become the alien and made responsible for all evil.

Dominant and subordinated ethnic groups seem to me, in spite of all the different ways in which they are constituted and constitute themselves, according to place and time, very solid entities, reproducing themselves endlessly over time. One prosaic way of observing this is to look at unemployment statistics in different nation-states. Despite different policies and the fact that particular groups occupy the lower parts of the social hierarchy, one will always find groups not defined as belonging to the nation (subordinated ethnic groups) being over-represented amongst the unemployed, or amongst those with the worse jobs, housing and wages. The dynamic nature and flexibility of ethnic groups and nations may be precisely their way of surviving. Their instability does not stand in contradiction to their stability, but is the way in which it is achieved.[21] Just as you can never swim in the same river twice, there is, nevertheless, always a river to swim in.[22]

Does this mean that a nation-state, within which ethnic minorities have citizenship and the possibility to fight racism with the support of an anti-discrimination legislation, is just the same as a nation-state where there are none of these possibilities? This is certainly not what I want to say. Otherwise we could just stop analysing specific situations and specific conjunctures and stop proposing any politics of multiculturalism, anti-racism, or whatever. The point I want to make is perhaps not so much a point but a series of questions for which I have no answers.

If it is true that the relations of the nation and the Other reproduce themselves as relations of domination and subordination through the different modes in which they progress/develop in time and space, do we have to consent to this? Do we have to accept that this is just how things are, that there cannot be a society without such forms of domination, social injustice and gender hierarchies, and the only way we can progress is to improve things as much as possible?[23] Alternatively, as society is not governed by iron natural laws, can we find ways out of this circle by analysing the ways in which stability and instability feed on each other?

Multiculturalism and the politics of recognition – ways to social justice and self-determination?

All the above concepts hold the promise of equality, of justice for different (ethnic) groups in spite of, or through valuing their differences. But what we have seen over the last ten years or more is not a tendency to more social justice, to more equal rights, but on the contrary, a deepening of the social contradictions, a spreading of new racisms and nationalisms. Where members of one subordinated ethnic group have gained access to better social positions, other members of the same group or members of other groups have done worse, or at best held their low positions. If what I suggest about the way in which dominant and sub-ordinated ethnic groups are structured is true, this is no surprise. In building a political perspective on ethnic identifications only, one is bound to reproduce internal hierarchies of gender and class.

Does this mean that we need to return to social movements, to the workers' and the women's movement in order to overcome social hierarchies and social injustice? We have learned in the past that these movements are themselves structured by gender and ethnic hierarchies, that they take part in the nation-state's practices of othering (see my example of the politics against contract workers in Germany). One of the reasons for reproducing these structures is the fact that these movements form part of their respective nation-states. They demand rights from the state, they are more or less incorporated by the state. The majority of their members are defined as belonging to the nation. In moments of crisis social movements tend to hand power over to the state, much the same as unorganised individuals. As we have seen in the example of the contract workers (and I am sure everybody can think of similar examples in their own country), it would seem 'unnatural' for a trade union not to protect the rights of their (national) members, but to care for workers coming from 'outside' instead.

I am convinced, though, that in the age of globalisation there is no way of securing social justice on a national level. This was also true in the past. But it might have been easier then to overlook the price that others had to pay for the progress achieved in the metropolis. Today, it seems as if any decision in favour of 'one's own members' has to be taken as a direct decision against those coming from 'outside'. The only legitimation for producing this injustice is the assumed 'natural' necessity to secure the well-being of those belonging to the nation-state.

Multiculturalism and a politics of recognition (as promoted for instance by Charles Taylor 1994a, 1994b) are no solution to this problem, because they do not tackle social hierarchies within the different ethnic groups (dominant or subordinated). These politics assume that subordinated ethnic groups are a homo-geneous group, culturally as well as socially. One example was the Rushdie affair, where some fractions of the British Labour Party argued in favour of banning Salman Rushdie's book *The Satanic Verses* in order to protect the cultural rights of the Muslim minority. Some members of this Muslim minority, mainly women, stood up in defence of Rushdie, and against such an act. Those who advocated the banning of the book did not see Rushdie as part of this Muslim minority and articulating a certain perspective about these minorities as 'mongrel selves'. Moreover, the politics of multiculturalism only apply to those who are already 'inside' the borders of a nation-state.

From the perspective of ethnic belonging/national belonging, whether to a dominant or a subordinated group, there is a solution neither to the question of social justice, nor to the question of subjectivity (self-determination). At the same time, there is no such thing as an individual or a collective social actor whose view is not ethnically or culturally given, even if some ways of thinking are transethnic, given that ethnic groups may share histories of thought and practice (the Enlightenment, for instance). Perspectives are always contextual and particular.[24]

One could say that identifying with ethnic belonging (including national belong-ings) or belonging to political groups and movements are ways of making 'arbitrary cuts' through the complex and multi-layered realities of our different belongings. According to the way in which these cuts are made, different alliances or adversaries are developed. The challenge lies in keeping the different, often contradictory, belongings 'in the game' (see also Hall and du Gay 1996).

From the perspective of political groups, like the workers' or the women's movement, there is no solution to social justice or self-determination either, because they tend to reproduce ethnic hierarchies and to fall back on positions where they identify with 'their' state. Interest groups operate on a national level even if they sometimes meet and try to discuss politics on an international level. These international meetings are only an addition to national politics and have no essentially different quality in comparison to national politics. At the same time, social injustices (including gender hierarchies, age hierarchies, etc.) can only be fought by organising across ethnic boundaries. It is precisely because they affect different ethnic groups in different ways that social hierarchies reproduce themselves. Consequently, only actions taken across ethnic/national boundaries could break through this circle of reproduction.

Transnational ethnicities, transnational social movements?

First I want to summarise my suggestions to make them clearer and more open to criticism:

1   Heterogeneity of nation-states is no solution to the problem of othering because heterogeneity is no contradiction to the homogeneity of nation-states, but one means through which it is achieved.
2   The fluidity of ethnic identifications (dominant and subordinated), the ever changing way in which they are constructed and construct themselves and others, constitutes the ways through which stability and a 'static repro-duction' of dominant and subordinated ethnic groups is achieved.
3   Groups organising around social interests to achieve social justice, equal rights for men and women, etc. tend to reproduce ethnic hierarchies, when they fall back on identifying with the state. Equally, subordinated ethnic groups reproduce social hierarchies and gender hierarchies as long as they do not take into consideration that their structure mirrors that of the dominant ethnic group.
4   Any policy attempting to achieve social justice and self-determination on a purely national level is doomed to failure.

The title of this section attempts to suggest some existing tendencies that may show a way out of this closed system. I want to use the term transnational as a concept marking a distance from the old term international.[25] An international solidarity sets out from a national perspective. National parties unite (or try to do so) on an international level. A transnational association would have to take ethnic belongings more and less into account than an international one. It would have to take ethnic (national) belonging more seriously because of the power relations that are related to those belongings. To take another German example, which can be generalised, parts of the German left refuse to think of themselves as German. Some of those who criticise nationalistic politics believe that any construction of 'us' on national grounds is exclusionary and should be avoided. But in refusing to be associated with the German nation-state one is also rejecting accountability for German politics. One is denying the fact that in being a German citizen one is part of a privileged population that benefits from global power relations. This is what members of those nations/ethnic groups claim who are subjected to these politics. But here we find a mirror construction. We find that members of dominating ethnic groups (nationally and internationally) are reduced to this membership and not only made accountable but guilty of global power relations. These mechanisms often paralyse international organisations/associations (for instance women's associations), because they fail to see the complexity of belonging to a dominant group (e.g. in terms of nationality) and at the same time to a dominated group (e.g. in terms of class and gender).

In order to be accountable for politics of domination and in order to understand the subordinated position of others it will be necessary to take national/ethnic belongings into account. But in order to form associations which seek social justice and self-determination such belongings must be transcended.

Let me exemplify this by coming back yet again to contract workers and the trade unions. A transnational worker's politics would be one that asks: how can the situation of all workers, irrespective of their nationality or ethnic origin, be improved? How is it possible to formulate a politics that would secure jobs for the German workers and the contract workers as well? I cannot give the answer to this question, because the answer could only be the result of a political process starting from this point of view. But it is obvious that to pose the question in this way implies a different politics. German trade unions would have to try to speak to contract workers, to discover their interests and needs, would have to communicate not only with trade unions in the respective countries, but also perhaps with other organisations who work in the interest of those workers. For a number of reasons (national traditions, the urge of unemployment, patriarchal structures, national co-option of trade unions, etc.) upon which I do not want to dwell here, it is difficult to imagine that this could happen. But to pose the question in such a way would be a step towards combining the struggle for social justice with the struggle for anti-racism.

The women's movement has some experiences with transnational associations. This is perhaps the only social movement that is trying to reconcile ethnic/national belonging and an overarching interest as an oppressed group: in other words differences and similarities (see Räthzel 1996 and Yuval-Davis 1997c). One organisation that could be called transnational was the European Forum of Left Feminists. It was not intended to bring together different national organisations on an international level. There was no representation on the grounds of belonging to an organisation in one's respective countries. Women became part of the Forum on an individual basis. At the same time there was an attempt to ensure that women from all countries received all information. The Forum dealt intensively with questions of nationalism, racisms and ethnic belongings from the point of view of women. But it is perhaps an indication of the difficulty of such a transnational structure that the Forum had practically no political power and no political significance and has in the meantime, as far as I know, vanished all together! It has been unable to take any political decisions or launch political campaigns in Europe. One reason is that women see their work within national organisations and structures as more important. And indeed, in the short run it is much more effective to work on a national level.

Other, more effective women's organisations organise around the women's world conferences. The fact that they often disagree and have to solve conflicts arising from different positions of power between women from the metropolis and women from the so-called third world is a good rather than a bad sign, as it shows that these issues are dealt with.

NGOs are another example of associations acting on a transnational level, for they do not aim at national, but at international politics from the beginning (e.g. human rights organisations, ecological organisations). But, although not all are as rigidly structured as Greenpeace, they understand themselves more as pressure groups than as mass movements, and they are one-issue groups, not dealing with the complexities of subordination and exploitation.

Stuart Hall has argued that individuals have different identities and position-alities in fighting different oppositions:

> The point is not simply that, since our racial differences do not constitute all of us, we are always different, negotiating different kinds of differences – of gender, of sexuality, of class. It is also that these antagonisms refuse to be neatly aligned; they are simply not reducible to one another; they refuse to coalesce around a single axis of differentiation. We are always in negotiation, not with a single set of oppositions that place us always in the same relation to others, but with a series of different positionalities. Each has for us its point of profound subjective identification. And that is the most difficult thing about this proliferation of the field of identities and antagonisms: they are often dislocating in relation to one another.
>
> (Hall and du Gay 1996: 473)

I would add that if no way is found to unite these different negotiations, to find a unity without reducing these different identifications to one another, the relations of domination which define these different oppositions will reproduce themselves.

The question is whether associations or alignments can be formed or are already emerging which try to account for these different positionalities of individuals. Or is this perhaps too conservative a question? Can we do without transnational associations, without associations at all, because they will always tend to reduce internal complexity and therefore tackle only one or two hierarchies, reproducing others? On the other hand, if we look at the way in which the processes of globalisation produce new and perhaps even deeper splits between the 'winners and the losers' of these processes, can we imagine how these processes could be fought without very strong associations?

Or are we to see the dissolution of nation-states (perhaps we are already witnessing such a process) through globalisation of the capitalist market economy and will this in itself lead to an end of nation-states and the Other? But if these processes unfold without any counter-politics from those who care for social justice, anti-racism and self-determination, will they not lead to different and perhaps even more serious forms of oppression and exploitation?

Irrespective of the value of what I have tried to say in this chapter, one issue is important for further research and for discussions of questions of ethnic/national belonging. It is the issue of examining the relationships between these belongings and belongings to other political or interest groups, the way they are constituted and how this impedes or facilitates the struggles for social justice, anti-racism and self-determination.

Notes

1 An earlier version of this paper was published in French in Rea 1997. An earlier version was prepared for the conference: 'Ètat, Nation, multiethnicité et droits à la citoyenneté/State, Nation, Multi-Ethnicity and Citizenship in Montreal, 30 May–2 June 1996. I am very grateful to Cathie Lloyd and Floya Anthias for their comments and proposals for amendments. Thanks also to Sedef Gümen, who read the paper at an earlier stage.

2 'Denn, wenn die *Aussiedler* und *Aussiedlerinnen* merken, daß das, was sie zu geben haben, hier erwünscht ist, und daß sie bei uns gebraucht werden – als Mitmenschen, aber auch als mündige Bürger, die zum Beispiel bereit sind, staatsbürgerliche und gesellschaftliche Verantwortung zu übernehmen – so ist das wohl die beste Voraussetzung für eine gelungene Eingliederung, die wir ihnen bieten können' (*Informationen zur politischen Bildung*, 222, 1989: 9, Magazine from the Ministry for Political Education).

3 ' "Integration" der hier seit längerem lebenden Ausländer – soweit sie das anstreben – ist wünschenswert. Die Reihenfolge gehe aber umgekehrt . . . zuerst Einfügen in die hiesigen Lebensverhältnisse, dann die . . . Bewerbung um die deutsche Staatsangehörigkeit, mit der das Wahlrecht verbunden sei' (*Frankfurter Allgemeine Zeitung*, 28 June 1990, einen CDU Abgeordneten zitierend).

4 'Ein Mangel an preiswertem Wohnraum bestand in den Ballungsgegenden schon früher. Durch den *Aussiedlerzustrom* ist er jedoch stärker bewußt geworden. Es gibt die generelle Befürchtung: Unser Land ist ohnenhin schon zu voll. Und wenn jetzt noch Hunderttausende von *Aussiedlern* kommen, wird es noch enger... Die Tatsachen: Von 1970 bis 1987 ist die Zahl der Deutschen bei uns von 58,2 auf 56,9 Millionen zurückgegangen – um 1,3 Millionen also. Selbst wenn in den nächsten Jahren jeweils 3 bis 400 000 Deutsche aus dem Osten und der DDR neu zu uns kämen, drohte von daher keine Übervölkerung' (Ihre Heimat sind WIR. Aktion Gemeinsinn, 1989: 27).

5 'Es leuchtet ein, daß in einem ohnenhin so dicht besiedelten Land alle Integrationsbemühungen scheitern müßten, wenn es bei den heutigen Zuwachsraten bliebe. . . . in den letzten drei Jahren eine Zunahme der Ausländerbevölkerung um 650 000 Menschen . . . Dabei spielt die jeder sicheren Voraussage sich entziehende Lage auf dem Arbeitsmarkt nicht einmal die entscheidende Rolle. Wesentlicher ist die Duldungsschwelle in der eigenen Bevölkerung' (*Die Zeit*, 1 January 1982).

6 It might be that the newly implicit construction of *Aussiedler* as *Ausländer* was only used to accuse the Social Democrats of abandoning international solidarity. But why not accuse them of a lack of national thinking, as it was done in 1989? Perhaps because one does not want to encourage national feelings after having seen the results in the form of young right extremist movements and a growing right extremist party? Or

perhaps because one has the impression that a majority of Germans do not regard *Aussiedler* as Germans? Or perhaps because it is not appropriate to talk about who belongs to the German nation, when even those who have always been defined as Germans (always meaning since 1871) regard each other sometimes with more resentment than they regard non-Germans (I refer to the *Ossi–Wessi* opposition)? One can only speculate. But the result is that those formerly defined as Germans have been made into foreigners and that Lafontaine's anti-nationalist attitude of 1989 has become a form of racism.

7 To the accusation of being racist, the trade unions answer, that they are not against foreigners in general. Their best colleagues are Turks and the other non-Germans, who have lived in the country for a long time and don't work for dumping wages. It is clear that a hierarchy is constructed between the 'old immigrants' that are more or less accepted as colleagues and the 'newcomers' whom one wants to keep out.

8 Non-nationals who decided to leave Germany were given a certain amount of money as an incentive. This money was supposed to help them start a living in their country of origin by starting a small business, etc. For reasons that have not been analysed, this 'help' was not used a lot. One reason might have been that the amount of money was small and that in taking it and leaving Germany, non-nationals would have also given up a part of their pension-rights.

9 The naturalisation rate of non-Germans is still below 2 per cent annually, mainly because there are so many demands to be met in order to get German nationality. The attempt of the new 'red-green' government to change this has been stopped by the Christian Democrats for the time being, as they brought an appeal against the law to the Constitutional Court (in 1999).

10 The result of which we now see in the way the Green party is abandoning almost every element of its former political aims in order to stay in power. I mention only the support for the bombing of Yugoslavia of the majority of the party and its leaders and the inability to get one of their most basic goals, the closing down of nuclear power plants, seriously on the agenda.

11 One of the first gains of state socialism that was cut were nurseries and kindergardens (both public and private). As a result, it became impossible for some women, especially for single mothers, to continue their jobs in the same way as before. Also, women's unemployment rate rose more than that of men.

12 It was Zygmunt Bauman's work which taught me to use the term in a non-ironic way as his analysis of the specificity of 'postmodern times' convinced me. Nevertheless, I do not agree with his point that in postmodernity social cohesion is no longer managed by the (nation-)state, but entirely through the market, through consumption (see Bauman 1992). In my opinion the (nation-)state is still vital for building social cohesion, though not by organising it top down (which was perhaps never true for capitalist democratic nation-states, in an absolute way), but in the way it serves as the reference point for social belongings. (I shall elaborate on this in the next section.)

13 This is especially true for Germany, where one prominent definition of the pecularities of the German nation is the differences (between regions) it encompasses. The heterogeneity of the German nation is seen as its strength. Of course, it is then defined who belongs to this heterogeneity and who doesn't.

14 Whereas Swiss Italians are part of the nation, Italian migrants from Italy are 'aliens'.

15 This also to be seen by the fact that minorities, defined as not belonging to the nation, are more often than not found in the lowest social positions. They make social injustice more bearable for the nationals, by having to take these lowest positions, *and* this makes it possible to explain social injustices away, by blaming the deficits of these minorities for their positions: lack of language, lack of skills, certain characteristics, that make them want these positions.

16 This is especially true for theories trying to understand right extremists' racism in Germany: see for instance Heitmeyer 1988. A brilliant summary and criticism of different ways of explaining racism can be found in Phil Cohen 1992.

17 In earlier texts I used to call the subject position the ability to act, but this was not understood very well in an English context. I am not sure, whether this way of putting it is more understandable.

18 In an article on *Heimat* (homeland) (Räthzel 1994) I have given an example of how a woman, a militant of a group combatting sexism and racism, argues that foreign men should be expatriated, if they become a threat, for instance by using her favourite café. I also discussed some ways in which feelings for the homeland can be articulated against *Ausländer* and how this leads to an articulation of homeland and nation. National belonging also takes it strength and organising power from the way it is articulated, sometimes even identified with homeland, childhood, the daily habits. But we must bear in mind that these articulations are the *result* of ideological work, they are by no means natural or to be taken for granted. In some scholarly work this cultural, everyday aspect of belonging is too easily confused or equated with the nation. I wonder now if that is not even the case in Benedict Anderson's excellent book and in his definition of an imagined community. The question is, when and under which circumstances does this imagined community organise itself as a community following the political perspective of the nation-*state*. And must we not make a difference between an identification with, for example, a German community and a German nation? Moreover, would it not be necessary for a movement trying to gain social justice and self-determination to dis-articulate these cultural belongings from the notion of the nation and re-articulate them with such a movment? I guess that this is what the notion of hegemony in Gramsci is about. But because of the time he lived in and the specific situation in Italy, Gramsci conceived of the hegemony of the subordinated class as one of unifying the nation. I think for his time this was a necessary perspective. But we might reformulate it these days where the nation can no longer be seen as a progressive social entity.

19 This might sound odd, regarding the claims to an end of the nation state as a result of globalisation processes, both from above (the movement of capital across the globe, the way in which the US acts as an international police force by bombing whatever country it wants, without caring much about international organisations and treatises) and from below (namely processes of migration and the establishment of transnational communities). Without wanting to minimise these processes, I would want to suggest that the nation-state is still the main source for constructions of belonging: first, because it is the political subject on the international political scene; second, even if migrant populations can be seen as transitive subjects, the way they transcend national borders is by relating to different nation-states, not to none; third, if nation-states have less power in relation to capital (though one might argue if they do not choose to have less power using their assumed powerlessness as a legitimation for letting market forces rule) they try to put themselves back on the scene through the way they tighten their borders against unwanted individuals. See the restrictions on migration in all European countries, the moving of borders into the different nation-states within the Schengen countries as an example. Here, as a reaction of loosening border-controls between the countries, it is now possible to control peoples passports in any underground or railway station. Fourth, even if people construct their belongings on the basis of regions or (subordinated) ethnic belongings they have to refer to nation-states when demanding rights. There is no other entity to grant them – or to deny them for that matter. International juridical institutions can normally only intervene after all measures have been tried in the respective nation-states; institutions below the level of the nation-state can grant only very restricted rights. The construction of super-nations like the European Community weakens the sovereignity of nation-states but it also strengthens it, because the negotiaters are nation-states and their members feel empowered or disempowered every time 'their' nation has won or lost a battle.

20 I have no space to discuss this any further, but have looked at the different ways of using the term culture and proposed a more restricted use in Räthzel (1997).

21 I have only a very prelimary insight into the theory labelled chaos in different disciplines of natural sciences (physics, mathematics, biology). But as far as I can see by now, the way in which this theory has come to understand non-linear processes as reproducing themselves through instability, provides a very useful model for understanding social processes and the relation between fluidity, flexibility and stability (see Gleick 1990).

22 For the individual Oliver Sacks has described the relation of flexibility and stability in the following way. Talking about the return to health of patients who have been profoundly ill (sleeping illness or post-encephalitic symptoms) for almost half a century, he says: 'the work of Lashley, in particular, has conclusively shown how individual skills and memories may survive massive and varied extirpations of the brain. Such experimental observations, like careful and thoughtful clinical observation . . ., indicate that one's *persona* is in no way "localisable" in the classical sense, that it cannot be equated with a given "centre", "system", "nexus", etc., but only with intricate totality of the whole organism, in its ever-changing, continuously modulated, afferent-efferent relation with the world. They show, instead, that one's ontological organisation, one's entire being – for all its multiplicity, all its shimmering, ever-shifting succession of patterns . . . – is nevertheless a coherent and continuing entity, with a historical, stylistic, and imaginative continuity, with the unity of a life-long symphony or poem.' (Sacks 1990: 239). However, one would not like to compare the continuity of Nation and Other with such a beautiful thing as a poem.

23 As for instance a Canadian colleague very much in favour of multiculturalism said to me, when I argued that bilingual or multilingual schools would be one way of overcoming a mono-national structure: 'It will never happen, because it costs too much. You cannot fight reality.'

24 Even those who stress that they do not belong either to a nation or to any subordinated ethnic group cannot but speak a certain language best, hold certain views for self-evident, judge the world from the point of view (or points of view) they have learned in a given time at a given place. As Danielle Jutteau has pointed out in an unpublished paper ethnicity is the way we grow up (and are educated by our mothers, foremost) to do things, to feel and think about things. A lot of this becomes so self-evident that we do not know it to be something specific, before we see different ways of thinking, feeling and judging. But even if we learn different ways of thinking, speaking and making sense of the world, they are still specific, limited ways. The human being as such, with no ethnic shape, the citizen of the world, does not exist. Already the notion of a citizen of the world is a particular, specific notion, developed by a specific 'culture', the Enlightenment.

25 The term transverssal, made prominent in Britain by Nira Yuval-Davis, is another way of formulating new politics that transcends identity politics (Yuval-Davis 1997b).

6 The modern world racial system in transition[1]

Howard Winant

As the world lurches forward into the twenty-first century, there is widespread confusion and anxiety about the political significance, and even the meaning, of race. In this chapter I argue that far from becoming less politically central, race defines and organises the world's future, as it has done for centuries. I challenge the idea that the world, or the national societies I briefly consider in comparative light, is moving beyond race. I suggest that the future of democracy itself depends on the outcomes of racial politics and policies, as they develop both in various national societies and in the world at large. This means that the future of democracy also depends on the *concept* of race, the meaning that is attached to race. Contemporary threats to human rights and social well-being – including the resurgent dangers of fascism, increasing impoverishment, and massive social polarisation – can be managed or even understood without paying new and better attention to issues of race. Thus this chapter is a preliminary effort to provide a set of conceptual tools that can facilitate this task.

The present moment is unique in the history of race. Starting after the Second World War and culminating in the 1960s, there was a global shift, a break, in the world-wide racial order that had endured for centuries. The shift occurred because many challenges to the old forms of racial hierarchy converged after the war: anti-colonialism, anti-apartheid, world-wide revulsion at fascism, and perhaps most important, the US civil rights movement and US–USSR competition in the world's 'South', all called white supremacy into question to an extent unparalleled in modern history. These events and conflicts linked anti-racism to democratic political development more strongly than ever before.

The rise of a world-wide, anti-racist, democratising tendency, from the late 1940s on, was but the first phase, the initiation of the shift or break in the old world racial order. A second phase was to come after several decades of fierce struggles: this was the containment of the anti-racist challenge, which had largely occurred by about 1970. Thus, despite all the political reforms and cultural transformations wrought by social movements and democratic politics around the world, despite the real amelioration of the most degrading features of the old world racial system, the centuries-old and deeply entrenched system of racial inequality and injustice was hardly eliminated. Rather, in a post-war social order faced with an unprecedented set of democratic and egalitarian demands, racism had to be adapted. Thus a new racial politics developed, a reformed variety that was able to concede much to racially-based democratic and egalitarian movements, yet that could still maintain a certain continuity with the legacies of imperial rule, conquest, enslavement, etc.

So, all around the world, a centuries-old pattern of white supremacy has been more fiercely contested, more thoroughly challenged, *in our lifetimes*, than has ever before. As a result, for the first time in modern history, there is widespread, indeed world-wide, support for what had until recently been a *dream*, Dr King's dream let us say, of racial equality.

Yet white supremacy is hardly dead. It has proven itself capable of absorbing and adapting much of the dream, repackaging itself as colour blind, non-racialist and meritocratic. Paradoxically, in this reformed version racial inequality can live on, still battening on all sorts of stereotypes and fears, still resorting to exclusionism and scapegoating when politically necessary, still invoking the supposed superiority of mainstream (aka white) values, cheerfully maintaining that equality has been largely achieved. It is rather ironic that this new, colour blind racial order may be more effective in containing the challenges posed over the past few decades by movements for racial justice than any intransigent, overtly racist backlash could possibly have been.

Although the reformed and officially non-racial version of white supremacy has succeeded in curtailing progress toward the dream in many dubious battles – over immigration and citizenship, income redistribution and poverty, and above all in respect to the compensatory programmes commonly called affirmative action – non-racialism has hardly won the day. It has certainly not eliminated the movement for racial justice that spawned it. Rather, the racial politics that results from this synthesis of challenge and incorporation, racial conflict and racial reform, has proved neither stable nor certain. It is a strange brew, often appearing more inclusive, more pluralistic than ever before, yet also filled with threats: of ethnic cleansing, resurgent neo-fascism, and perhaps equally insidious, a renewed racial complacency.

The global racial situation, then, is fluid, contradictory, contentious. No longer unabashedly white supremacist, for the most part, the world is, so to speak, abashedly white supremacist. The conflicts generated by the powerful movements for racial justice that succeeded the Second World War have been contained, but not resolved. Thus no new world racial system has yet been created; instead the problems of the old system have come to a head, and the outlines of what will succeed it can at least be glimpsed, if not securely foreseen.

What does such a glimpse, however preliminary, reveal? The new world racial system will struggle to adapt the rhetoric of egalitarian social movements to the exigencies of a post-imperial, post-Cold War, post-apartheid reality. To some extent, this system has succeeded in reinventing itself along non-racist lines; in fact, its capacity to redefine itself as beyond race is in many ways a crucial index of its stability. Yet there is also a widespread recognition that the reforms undertaken in the 1950s and 1960s have ossified, that they have not gone far enough, that indeed they may be providing a kind of cover for a reassertion of white privilege, white rule, northern cultural norms, all under the banner of post-racial societies, now officially colour blind and pluralist.

Adequately to investigate the *fin de siècle* dynamics of race on a global scale is, of course, a rather daunting project. Here I merely survey the task, focusing on the historical and comparative dimensions of the world racial system. I discuss that system's origins and precedents, examine its contemporary national (and trans-national) manifestations, and draw some political conclusions.

The latter point is perhaps most important to us. I want to focus critical attention on the emerging new racial system's democratic commitments, for racism has historically proven one of democracy's most formidable antagonists. Here I both evaluate the equilibrium of this racial system, and seek out its likely sources of destabilization and opposition at the outset of the twenty-first century. This chapter offers, necessarily in schematic form, a historical account of the emergence of the modern world racial system; a group of national case studies; and a concluding meditation on the contemporary dynamics of race.

The modern world racial system

This is obviously not the first global racial system. The racial dimensions of modernity itself have been widely acknowledged. The Enlightenment's recognition of a unified, intelligible world, the construction of an international economy, and the emergence of a global culture, were all deeply racialised processes. To understand how race was fundamental to the construction of modernity is of more than historical interest: it also explains much about the present. Notably, it puts in context the idea that after the Second World War there occurred a break from the long-established verities of race.

The early modern history of race is full of precedents for the horrors of our own age. The tension between slavery on the one hand, and nascent democracy on the other, structured the lengthy transition to the modern world. Resistance against slavery contributed crucially to the broader redefinition of political rights for which early advocates of democracy yearned and fought. Indeed the violence and genocide of earlier racial phenomena prefigured contemporary atrocities like the Holocaust, 'ethnic cleansing', and totalitarianism.

How racial was nascent capitalism? Were the politics and cultural groundwork of modernity premised on racial distinctions? Did the generally limited democracy of the 'North' (or the 'West') consist in part of an application of the principles of colonial rule to the 'mother countries'? In what ways did early forms of resistance to racialised forms of rule – as seen in abolitionism and slave revolts for example – dynamise the world-wide impetus toward democratisation? In what ways did anti-racism itself become an archetypal democratic movement? Did the resistance to slavery, which grew into anti-racism, ultimately do more than fight-ing for the human, social, cultural and political rights of racially subordinated groups? Was it not also crucial in permitting the acquisition of those same rights by whites? In other words, is the modern, inclusive form of democracy, to which we have become accustomed, itself the product of global struggles against racism?

The abolition of African slavery was the great rehearsal for the break with white supremacy that took place in our own time. Abolition was made possible by three momentous social changes: the triumph of industrial capitalism, the upsurge of democratic movements, and the mobilisation of slaves themselves in search of freedom. Abolition was not completed with the triumph of the Union in the American Civil War and the passage of the Reconstruction amendments to the Constitution. Only when Brazil, the last country to free its slaves, did so in 1888, did the first crucial battle in the centuries-long war against white supremacy draw to a close.

But abolition left many emancipatory tasks unfinished. New forms of racial inequality succeeded slavery. Even after slavery ended, democracy was still partial. Racialisation continued to define the mechanisms of authoritarian rule and to distribute resources on a global scale. Racial thought and practices associated subordinated status almost irrevocably with distinct types of human bodies. This ranking of human society by race still enabled and justified world systemic rule. Generalised processes of racial stratification continued to support enormous and oppressive systems of commercial agriculture and mining. Thus until the mid-twentieth century the unfulfilled dreams of human rights and equality were still tied up with the logic of race.

Although there was always resistance to racist rule, it was only in the period after the Second World War that opposition to racial stratification and racial exclusion once again become major political conflicts. Civil rights and anti-racist movements, as well as nationalist and indigenous ones, fiercely contested the racial limitations on democracy. These movements challenged the conditions under which racialised labour was available for exploitation in the former colonies as well as the metropoles. They extended the anti-racist legacy of the Second World War and articulated comprehensively with the geopolitical conflicts of the Cold War. They rendered old forms of political exclusion problematic, and revealed a panoply of mainstream cultural icons – artistic, linguistic, scientific, even philosophical – to be deeply conflictual. They drew on the experience of millions who had undergone military mobilisation followed by an embittering return to a segregated or colonised homeland. Such movements recognised anew their international character, as massive post-war labour demand sparked international migration from the world's South to its North, from areas of peasant agriculture to industrial areas. These enormous transformations manifested themselves in a vast demand to complete the work begun a century before with slavery's abolition. They sparked the world-wide break with the tradition of white supremacy.

As the tumultuous 1960s drew to a close, the descendants of slaves and ex-colonials had forced at least the partial dismantling of most official forms of discrimination and empire. But with these developments – the enactment of a new series of civil rights laws, decolonisation, and the adoption of cultural policies of a universalistic character – the global racial order entered a new period of instability and tension. The immediate result of the break was an uneven series of racial reforms that had the general effect of ameliorating racial injustice and inequality, but also worked to contain social protest. Thus the widespread demands of the racially subordinated and their supporters were at best answered in a limited fashion; in this way a new period of racial instability and uncertainty was in-augurated.

Some national cases

Although the break was a world-wide phenomenon, it obviously took very different forms in particular national settings. Racial conditions are generally understood to vary dramatically in distinct political, economic and cultural contexts. In this chapter I comment, necessarily briefly, on four national case studies: the United States, South Africa, Brazil and the European Union (considered as a whole). Examined in greater detail in other work (Winant 2001), these cases were chosen not only because they are central national stages on which the world's racial drama is being played out, but also because they are also crucial variants, important laboratories, where new racial dynamics are being developed.

Throughout these comparative case studies, I argue that the post-Second World War break is a global backdrop, an economic, political and cultural context in which national racial conflicts are being worked out. To carry out each national case study, I employ a comparative political sociological model. In this model four dimensions of social and political change that have occurred in the latter half of this century are systematically examined: demographic change, the rise of movements for racial equality and democracy, reform of state racial policies, and interaction with global racial networks. I suggest that in each dimension there has been an undermining of the previous racial formation, creating new tensions in the countries studied about the significance of race and the persistence of racial inequality.

Changing demographic patterns – internal and international migration, as well as urbanisation and limited but real social mobility – have reconfigured national populations. These changes created new awarenesses – of racial difference and diversity, of shifting national identity. They signalled the arrival of new actors on the political stage, whose very presence facilitated the growth of anti-racist social movements.

Thus the emergence of newly mobilised groups. In the post-Second World War period such groups often brought new political demands for inclusion, sometimes inducing serious crises in national political systems. Democratic instrumentalities that tended to be limited by discriminatory or exclusionist traditions were pressured to innovate and reform themselves.

Over the post-war years national political systems responded to these pressures with alterations in state racial policies. These ranged from coercion and repression to adaptation and reform. New developments in policy studies allow greater empirical exploration of the trajectories of incorporation that have proved so crucial to racial reforms.

These national cases, however, cannot be understood in isolation. Anti-racist movements often drew on international resources, ideas, and political leverage. Thus, for example, movements and states were deeply affected by international pressures for democracy and universalism, preventing a full return to the racial dynamics of a previous era. Diasporic perspectives on race; new insights on the dynamics of political communication and discourse; new perspectives on migration and citizenship studies; and new research on the impact of NGOs in human rights as well as other fields, all provide important avenues through which contemporary perceptions of anti-racism can be reframed, placing it once again in an international context (as it was in the earlier, anti-colonial decades of the twentieth century).

Interacting in complex ways, these four key dynamics – demography, mobilisation, reform and globalisation – have undermined the logic of the previous racial system in each of these four national cases. They have sparked new tensions and debates about the significance of race and the persistence of racial inequality. The interplay of these four variables can and should be compared in depth as it occurred in these case study settings, and elsewhere as well. Here I can offer only a limited overview of this effort, focusing chiefly on a few key questions.

The United States

How permanent is the 'colour line'? The activities of the civil rights movement and related anti-racist initiatives achieved substantial, if partial, democratic reforms in earlier post-war decades. These innovations continue to coexist, however, with a weighty legacy of white supremacy whose origins lie in the colonial and slavery era. How do these two currents combine and conflict today?

Massive migration, both internal and international, has reshaped the US population, both numerically and geographically. A multipolar racial system has largely supplanted the old bipolar black–white system, leading to new varieties of inter-minority competition, as well as new awareness of the international embeddedness of racial identity. Racial stratification varies substantially by class, region, and indeed among groups, although substantial racial inequality certainly endures. Racial reform policies are under attack in many spheres of social policy and law, where the claim is forcefully made that the demands of the civil rights movement have largely been met, and that the US has entered a post-racial stage of its history.

To assess this range of contentious issues is to examine the crisis in participatory democracy first revealed in the US by the social movements of the 1960s, and now endemic to most dimensions of political life. The limited incorporation of the egalitarian and inclusionist demands lodged in the early post-war decades by the black movement and its allies is often noted. It is not commonly recognised, however, that the adoption of civil rights reforms also had the effect of discrediting and delegitimating autonomous (i.e. civil society-based) mobilisation on racial grounds. Nor are current concerns about globalisation (in the economic and cultural spheres, for example) usually recognised to have racial dimensions.

South Africa

In the mid-1990s, South Africa – the most explicitly racialised society in the late twentieth century – entered a difficult but promising transition. The apartheid state had of course been committed to a racialised framework of citizenship, civic inclusion, and law in general; the post-apartheid constitution incorporates the principle of non-racialism originally articulated in the African National Congress-based Freedom Charter of 1955. Yet the country still bears the terrible burden of apartheid's sequelae: racial inequality persists across every level of society. The legacy of segregated residential areas, combined with a highly racialised distribution of resources of every sort, urges moderation on political leadership. White fears must be placated in order to sustain the country's economic base and minimise capital flight. Whites continue to hold controlling positions throughout the economy; the handful of blacks who have made their way into the corporate and state elites understand very well the price the country would pay for a radical turn in policy.

Yet this is a state committed to racial equality, and to promoting black advancement, individually and collectively. Can the post-apartheid state stabilise the process of political, social and economic integration of the black majority? Can it maintain an official non-racialism in the face of such comprehensive racial inequality? How can the vast majority of citizens – excluded until so recently not only from access to Africa's wealthiest economy, and denied the most elementary civic and political rights – garner the economic access they so desperately need, without reinforcing white paranoia and fear? How can the post-apartheid state facilitate the reform of racial attitudes and practices, challenging inequality, supremacism, and the legacy of racial separatism without engendering white flight and subversion?

Both the anti-apartheid movement and the new government's policies were shaped by global concerns as well as by local ones. Internal political debates reflect changing global discussions around race and politics. Just as the South African Black Consciousness Movement drew on the speeches of Malcolm X and Aimé Cesaire in its understanding of racial oppression, just as the anti-apartheid movement used international anti-racist sentiment to build momentum for sanctions on the old regime, so too the current government is both guided and constrained by international pressures and issues.

Moreover, internal politics too bring international resources to bear: through the post-war era, the anti-apartheid movement drew much of its resources and ideas from an international anti-racist movement, largely linked to an international trend to support decolonisation. Since the 1994 election, however, international constraints have limited the sphere of action of the new democratic government. Critics of affirmative action policies, for example, emphasise the danger of undermining efficiency in the name of redistribution, much as critics of redistributive policies deploy neo-liberal economic arguments to reject nationalisation; in each case, they invoke international discourses that are non-racial in form, yet have racial implications in practice. The South African state continues to face a considerable challenge from both left and right: will it be possible to reconstruct South Africa by building not only a democracy but a greater degree of consensus, of citizenship and belonging? To what degree can a policy of class compromise forestall the dangers of social upheaval and capital flight (Webster and Adler 1999).

Understanding these processes requires viewing South African racial debates in global perspective, and exploring the ways in which local actors seek to change the terms of engagement as they restructure national politics. The 1994 elections changed the racial character of the state, although many white civil servants remain in place; affirmative action policies, to which the ANC-led government is committed, could reorganise racial distribution of incomes, if not wealth. Yet in the context of a global debate over affirmative action, and in the face of the threat of the flight of white capital and skills, the process of reform has been far slower than many South Africans, white and black, expected. This dilemma remains unresolved: how can democratic non-racial institutions be constructed in a society where most attributes of socio-economic position and identity remain highly racialised?

Brazil

Brazil presents significant parallels, both historical and contemporary, to other American nations, including the US. These similarities include Brazil's history of slavery and black inequality, its displacement and neglect of a large indigenous population, its intermittent and ambiguous commitment to immigration, its incomplete democracy, and its vast and increasingly urban underclass (disproportionately black). Brazilian racial dynamics have traditionally received little attention, either from scholars or policy-makers, despite the fact that the country has the second largest black population in the world (after Nigeria). Its post-emancipation adoption of a policy of 'whitening', which was to be achieved by concerted recruitment of European immigrants, owed much to the US example, and also drew on nineteenth-century French racial theorising (Skidmore 1993).

Amazingly, the 'myth of racial democracy' still flourishes in Brazil, even though it has been amply demonstrated to be little more than a fig leaf covering widespread racial inequality, injustice and prejudice (Hasenbalg and Silva 1992; Hanchard 1994; Andrews 1991). The Brazilian racial system, with its 'colour continuum' (as opposed to the more familiar 'colour line' of North America), tends to dilute democratic demands. Indeed, Brazilian racial dynamics have made it difficult to promote policies that might address racial inequality. Public discourse resolutely discourages any attempt to define inequality along racial lines; the current President, Fernando Henrique Cardoso, is the first even to broach the subject seriously, although vociferous denials both official and informal persist. If politicians do point out racial inequalities, they challenge the myth of racial democracy, and are subject to charges that they are themselves provoking racial discrimination by stressing difference.

Reliable research on racial stratification and racial attitudes in Brazil remains scarce (Telles 1992, 1994; Twine 1997; Datafolha 1995). A whole range of political questions thus remains mysterious. Consider the example of voting rights: illiterates could not vote until 1985, but there is no reliable data on the proportion of illiterates who were black – and thus the extent to which black Brazilians have been disenfranchised through the twentieth century remains uncertain, though it is undoubtedly large.

The emergence of the *Movimento Negro Unificado* (MNU) as a force to be reckoned with – though by no means as strong as the 1960s US civil rights movement – represents a new development. The MNU used the 1988 centennial of the abolition of Brazilian slavery, as well as the 1990–1 census, to dramatise persistent racial inequalities. As in South Africa, this phase of the black movement takes its reference points partly from international anti-racist struggles, often drawing on examples, symbols and images from the civil rights and anti-apartheid movements.

In the 1990s, a range of racial reforms have been proposed in Brazil – largely in response to the increasingly visible *movimento negro*. To enact these reforms, to prompt the state to adopt anti-racist policies, however, will require far greater support for change than presently exists. The political dilemma is familiar: blacks need organised allies, in the party system, among other impoverished and disenfranchised groups, and on the international scene. Yet in order to mobilise, they must also begin to assert a racialised political identity, or there will be little collective support for racial reforms. How can blacks address this dualistic, if not contradictory, situation? How can Afro-Brazilians assert claims on the basis of group solidarity, without simultaneously undermining the fragile democratic consensus that has begun to emerge across many constituencies? How can democratic institutions be built alongside policies designed to address racial inequalities, without undermining a vision of common citizenship and equality?

The European Union

The last few decades have established that indeed, 'the empire strikes back'. Racially plural societies are in place throughout Europe, especially in former imperial powers like the UK, the Netherlands, France and Spain, but also in Germany, Italy, the Scandinavian countries, and to some extent in the East. The influx of substantial numbers of non-whites during the post-colonial period has deeply altered a dynamic in which the racial order and the imperial order had been one, and in which the 'other' was by and large kept outside the walls of the 'mother country'. As a stroll around London, Frankfurt, Paris or Madrid quickly reveals, those days are now gone forever. Yet the response to the new situation too often takes repressive and anti-democratic forms, focusing attention on the 'immigrant problem' (or the 'Islamic problem'), seeking not only to shut the gates to Maghrebines or sub-Saharan Africans, Turks or Slavs (including Balkan refugees), but often also to define those 'others' who are already present as enemies of the national culture and threats to the 'ordinary German' (or English, or French, etc.) way of life. This rationale for racial exclusion and restriction in Europe has been analysed as differentialist: its distinction from the meritocratic logic of discrimination in the US has been linked to a generally lower European interest in issues of individual equality, and a relatively greater concern with the integrity of national cultures (Taguieff 1999 [1990]; Wieviorka 1995).

Thus the particular racial issue that must be confronted in Europe is the newly heterogeneous situation, the multiplication of group identities. Currently anti-democratic tendencies are widely visible: new right and neo-fascist groups are widespread. At both the state and regional levels the agenda of restriction is gaining adherence, jeopardising mobility of employment or residence, and sometimes stigmatising religious or other cultural practices. Conflicts over immigration and citizenship have taken on new intensity, with crucial implications for the character of democracy.

The dynamics of integration raise a wide range of questions about future European racial logics. Conflicting principles of citizenship – *jus sanguinis* vs. *jus soli* – are deeply imbedded in the distinct European national makeups, and their resolution in a common cultural/political framework will not come easily (Brubaker 1992). Relations with ex-colonies vary, raising serious questions not only of immigrant access and economic ties between the old empires and the new Europe, but also giving rise to serious anxieties about security and terrorism. Popular anti-racist sentiments stimulated the formation of many multiculturalist and pluralist organisations, particularly in the early 1980s. But over the past decade they have largely ceased to function as mass mobilisation initiatives in support of democracy. So, while the slogan *Touche pas mon pôte* (Hands off my buddy) no longer summons tens of thousands into the street in defence of the democratic rights of racially defined minorities, the transition to racial pluralism is still very much under way.

Toward new racial dynamics

To understand the changing significance of race in the aftermath of the twentieth century, the century whose central malady was diagnosed by Du Bois as the problem of the colour-line, requires us to reconsider where the racialised world came from, and where it is going. In the settings studied, the break that began with movement activity after the Second World War, and that was contained from the late 1960s onward by political reforms, has not been consolidated. Just as earlier stages of modern racial history failed to resolve many issues, so too does the present epoch. At the end of the century the world as a whole, and our national cases as well, are far from overcoming the tenacious legacies of colonial rule, apartheid and segregation. All still experience continuing confusion, anxiety and contention about race. Yet the legacies of epochal struggles for freedom, democracy and human rights persist as well. To evaluate the transition to a new world racial system in comparative and historical perspective requires keeping in view the continuing tension that characterises the present.

Despite the enormous vicissitudes that demarcate and distinguish national conditions, historical developments, roles in the international market, political tendencies and cultural norms, racial differences often operate as they did in centuries past: as a way of restricting the political influence, not just of racially subordinated groups, but of all those at the bottom end of the system of social stratification. In the contemporary era, racial beliefs and practices have become far more contradictory and complex. The old world racial system has not disappeared, but it has been seriously challenged and changed. The legacy of democratic, racially oriented movements such as the US civil rights movement, anti-apartheid struggles, *SOS-Racisme* in France, the *Movimento Negro Unificado* in Brazil, and anti-colonialist initiatives throughout the world's South, is thus a force to be reckoned with. My aim in this chapter has been to trace the parameters of this situation.

It is impossible to address world-wide dilemmas of race and racism by ignoring or 'transcending' these themes, for example by adopting so-called 'colour blind' policies. In the past the centrality of race deeply determined the economic, political and cultural configuration of the modern world; although recent decades have seen a tremendous efflorescence of movements for racial equality and justice, the legacies of centuries of racial oppression have not been overcome. Nor is a vision of racial justice fully worked out. Certainly the idea that such justice has already been largely achieved – as seen in the 'colour blind' paradigm in the US, the non-racialist rhetoric of the South African Freedom Charter, the Brazilian rhetoric of racial democracy, the emerging racial differentialism of the European Union – remains problematic.

What would a more credible vision entail? The pressing task today is not to jettison the concept of race, but instead to come to terms with it as a form of flexible human variety.

What does this mean in respect to racism? Racism has been crucial to the global reproduction of capital for five hundred years; it remains so today, yet it has been changed, damaged, and forced to reorganise by the massive social movements which have taken place in recent decades. In the past these movements were international in scope and influence. They were deeply linked to democratising and egalitarian trends, such as labour politics and feminism. They were able both to mobilise around the injustices and exclusion experienced by racially subordinated groups, and simultaneously to sustain alliances across racial lines. This is background; such experiences cannot simply recur. Yet the massive mobilisations which created the global break that followed the Second World War have certainly reshaped our world. Were these movements fated to be the last popular upsurges, the last egalitarian challenges to elite supremacy, to racial hierarchy? Surely not. In all the countries we have studied, and in transnational anti-racist networks as well, these earlier precedents still wield their influence. They still spark new attempts to challenge racism.

At the same time, new political and intellectual leaders have come onto various national stages in recent years, arguing that the worst racial injustices (of the US, Brazil, South Africa, etc.) are now firmly relegated to the past, and that the problem of racism can now be viewed as essentially solved. So why maintain affirmative action policies? Why direct resources toward immigrants, victims of segregation and apartheid, the (disproportionately dark-skinned) poor? Don't we already have equality now?

Will race ever be transcended? Will the world ever get beyond race? Probably not. But the entire world still has a chance of overcoming the stratification, the hierarchy, the taken-for-granted injustice and inhumanity that so often accompanies the race concept. Like religion or language, race can be accepted as part of the spectrum of the human condition, while it is simultaneously and categorically resisted as a means of stratifying national or global societies. Nothing is more essential in the effort to reinforce democratic commitments, not to mention global survival and prosperity, as we enter a new millennium.

Note

1 An earlier version of this paper was presented at a 1997 conference on 'Economy, Ethnicity, and Social Change' at the University of Bristol. Thanks to Floya Anthias and Cathie Lloyd for comments.

7 Anti-racism in France, 1898–1962
Modernity and beyond

Jim House

Anti-racism, as this book implicitly suggests, is by definition a transnational movement. Political cultures differ greatly, however. Anti-racism within each Western European country has a separate if interconnected history, moulded and often channelled by the various aspects of a specific country's political culture and colonial legacies. One important intellectual task to undertake within the contemporary anti-racist project is therefore to rethink the wider political contexts within which anti-racism has had to work in the past. A similar process of historicisation thus needs to be undertaken for anti-racism as has been undertaken for racism (Birnbaum 1993; Taguieff 1990; Balibar 1992). Consequently, this chapter adopts a historical focus, looking to the lessons to be learnt for anti-racism today from both the inter-war period (1919–39) and the way in which anti-racism changed in the period of decolonisation (1945–62) to become more inclusive.

The history of anti-racism in France, a history of a broad range of movements, mobilisations, ideas and ideals, affords many perspectives on the question of occidental modernity. Nowhere in Western Europe did a political culture incarnate and embrace the modern project with such apparent fervour as republican France. Joan Scott has observed that we need to read 'the repetitions and conflicts of feminism as symptoms of contradictions in the political discourses that produced feminism and that it appealed to and challenged at the same time' (1996: 3). I will attempt to show how, not unlike elements of feminism in France, various strands of anti-racism have, in the French context, both appealed to and challenged the ideologies of the republican nation-state – that key political, social and cultural expression of modernity. This chapter will attempt to trace the many ways in which anti-racism in France related to modernity, and the conclusions to be drawn from this for a postmodern context.

Modernity acted as an inspiration to emancipation, in particular through the Revolution of 1789 and its varied ideological and social legacies. I will argue that this inspiration has been clearly reflected in the strand of republican political culture which I will call 'republican anti-racism', forged at the time of the Dreyfus 'affair' a century ago. Republican anti-racism became more widespread in the 1930s within an anti-fascist discourse, and was then reworked and revised only in the light of the independence struggles in the post-war period, and has again been reworked since the 1970s (see Lloyd 1998a; House 1997).[1] Through a short analysis of the LICA (International League against Anti-Semitism) in the 1930s, I will attempt to show how republican anti-racism worked from a set of assumptions which often limited its ability to challenge the diverse forms of racism which existed at given historical moments. This occurred, in particular, through the presentation of France as an essentially 'non-racist' country, the view that racism came almost uniquely from the far right, and the exclusion or marginalisation of the opposition to colonial racism.

As Ali Rattansi has remarked, if modernity in its rationalist, 'tolerant' guise was presented (for example by republican thinkers) as being the antithesis of racism, many modern projects such as colonialism were of course to inspire a huge expansion of ideological and practical forms of racism (1994: 3). Until the 1950s, republican anti-racism was therefore cut through with tension between a liberal rights discourse and overt or tacit support for the colonial project. Consequently, it was those on the margins of the republican tradition in France and elsewhere who most highlighted the contradictions inherent within the modern project (as regards racism in particular). This will be shown first through analyses of the challenge to racism which emerged within mobilisations of Algerian, West African and Antillean colonial subjects and citizens in France in the period from 1919 to 1939. Second, I will look at the campaigns of the predominantly Jewish republican anti-racist association the MRAP (Movement against Racism and for Peace, subsequently Movement against Racism and for Friendship Between Peoples), from its creation in 1949 to the end of decolonisation in 1962. This period has had important consequences for republican anti-racism: I will attempt to show how the experiences of the Holocaust, Occupation and Resistance brought a transformation in the conditions governing republican anti-racism's receptivity towards new perspectives on what racism was and how it should be fought. This change took place in the context of the exacerbated anti-North African racism of the Algerian War of Independence (1954–62). The War of Independence also served to question the idea of a 'non-racist' France, and the view that racism stemmed uniquely from the far right.

My conclusion will argue that the MRAP's action of the 1950s to early 1960s can act as a model for a more inclusive contemporary anti-racist politics, one which involves listening to the varied experiences of those subjected to racism. Throughout, I will argue that re-thinking anti-racism must include a re-evaluation of republican anti-racism's ambivalent relationship with the nation-state and the legacy of empire. Such a re-evaluation is not attempted by some of the most prominent theorists in France currently working on anti-racism. For example, in his influential work on the genealogies of contemporary anti-racism, Pierre-André Taguieff (1990, 1995) fails to engage at any depth with racialised groups' critiques of colonial racism. Taguieff's re-formulation of republican universalism is therefore conducted within a limiting framework which excludes the experiences of many racialised groups. Furthermore, Taguieff's attempt to re-formulate 'universalism' reveals a belief in supposed French cultural superiority, which is itself a central legacy of empire (Taguieff 1996). Lastly, Taguieff's view of anti-racism as the reactive, negative 'double' of racism arguably simplifies the complex political and social production and expression of anti-racism and racism, to which my discussion will now turn.

Interpreting anti-racism

Anti-racism is difficult to define, both conceptually and practically (Solomos and Back 1996: 102). We could perhaps adopt, for the study of anti-racism, Ali Rattansi's comments about racism. Rattansi suggests that we should avoid 'supposedly water-tight definitions . . . in favour of actually examining how racial logics and categories work in relation to specific events and social fields' (1994: 71). Such a flexible definitional approach to anti-racism is necessary because anti-racism is irreducible to specifically reactive, defensive forms against the ideological, practical and discursive manifestations of racism (Taguieff 1990, 1995; see House 1997; Lloyd 1998a). Anti-racist agency can have transformational features (Gilroy 1993b: 133) and form counter-cultures (Gilroy 1993a) which present values aimed at changing society and the way social relations are experienced and perceived. Moreover, the difficult negotiation of the passage from the reactive to the transformative is one of the key questions with which anti-racist activists are faced in any situation (Solomos and Back 1996: 111). Anti-racism in France has articulated values of equality, emancipation, solidarity, tolerance, social justice and the right to define contingent individual or group identities. Historically speaking, anti-racism has emanated from forms of political action such as anti-colonialism/ anti-imperialism, which, whilst admittedly being wider political projects, nevertheless contain important critiques of racism, hence their inclusion within my definition of anti-racism.

Interpreting anti-racism involves examining both the socio-economic, political and cultural factors which govern the emergence of anti-racism, and the forms anti-racism then takes. Anti-racism emanates from a variety of levels of production – social, political and cultural. I will also refer to vectors of both anti-racist discourse and action. These vectors are the channels through which anti-racism is expressed. Historically speaking, in addition to the declared anti-racist organisations, such vectors have been human rights organisations, associations for the defence of immigrants, anti-imperialist and anti-colonial groups, trade unions, intellectual and academic sources of anti-racism, as well as institutional, local or state-level initiatives.

There is always a plurality of definitions and experiences of racism within and across different racialised groups (Wieviorka 1993b: 418–19) and anti-racist movements more generally. Questions of class, generation and gender shape both how racism is experienced, and the forms anti-racism will take (see Anthias and Yuval-Davis 1992). Anti-racism contains both 'formal and informal oppositional trends' (Solomos and Back 1996: 112). Anti-racism in its organised, structured, associational form usually works on several different fronts at any given time – appealing to civil society (Cohen and Arato 1995) as much as to the state, in a mixture of short-term and long-term campaigns, whilst also directing its action to specific vectors of racism such as fascist groups and overtly racist politicians and political parties. Contemporary anti-racism's synthetic quality can be understood in terms of a number of politically oppositional traditions. These traditions developed (in particular) in the course of the twentieth century to fight anti-Semitism as well as colonial/post-colonial racism against (for example) North Africans (House 1997; Lloyd 1998a). Both racism and anti-racism need to be understood and studied in the plural. In what follows, the dialogues and silences between various forms of challenge to racism will be examined, starting with the legacy of republicanism for anti-racism until 1945.

Republican political culture and anti-racism

If republican anti-racism became a clearly definable concept only in the 1930s, it always refers back to its founding event, the Dreyfus 'affair', for legitimacy (Taguieff 1990: 20). The pre-history of republican anti-racism is therefore traceable to the moral protest at the unjust imprisonment and conviction of the Jewish army officer Alfred Dreyfus. This moral protest sought to defend justice and parliamentary democracy against the anti-republican coalition of the right and the far right (Winock 1992; Lloyd 1998a; Marrus 1971). The LDH (Human Rights League) formed in 1898 to defend Dreyfus, and the Dreyfusard movement more generally, constituted a broad alliance of the centre-right, centre and moderate left, and in many respects represented the wide and increasingly conservative, middle-class republicanism of the Third Republic (Jenkins 1990: 190; also Nord 1995). This republicanism significantly diluted the more radical revolutionary heritage of 1789 (and 1793): political and social rights potentially for all became rights for some (Noiriel 1991, 1992). For example, social citizenship (as it would be called today) became increasingly coupled with nationality in the period from the 1880s (Balibar 1992, 1997; Noiriel 1991, 1992). Henceforth, defending the Republic necessarily implied stressing the rights of the citizen as much as the rights of the 'abstract' individual.

The time of the Dreyfus affair saw the invention of the term 'republican tradition' (see Rudelle 1987) as part of the reinvention of the revolutionary heritage (Girardet 1987: also Hobsbawm and Ranger 1983). Republican political culture (the republican model) has never been static (Nord 1995; Nicolet 1994; Scott 1996; Hazareesingh 1994; Fentress and Wickham 1992: 135–7): there were and are specifically left-wing and right-wing 'sub-cultures' of republicanism (Jenkins 1990). The republican model, and the invocation of the republican tradition invoked to defend that model, both clearly state the importance of *liberté, égalité, fraternité*. However, the precise content of such values and the articulation between them are left wide open: this allows for a *rassemblement* around a series of broad objectives. The defence of republican values is therefore a malleable idiom always likely to draw a wide political base. The repertoire of republican symbols, discourse and imagery has been constantly reworked and appropriated for legitimacy in successive examples of political mobilisation (Agulhon 1989; Tartakowsky 1998; Lloyd 1998a; Geisser 1997).

This republican tradition, fashioned at the time of the Dreyfus 'affair', has formed the 'space' within which republican anti-racism was to evolve, whilst the vectors of republican anti-racism have stressed certain elements of that tradition in a particular way (Lloyd 1996). I will deal in turn with four main aspects of this republican tradition which have had a direct impact on anti-racism in France: the construction of the national republican state; the ambivalence of assimilation/ difference; the image of France as a 'non-racist' country; and the colonial legacy.

Ambivalent constructions of the nation

In France, the state constructed the modern nation. This 'nationalisation' of French society involved the forging of an 'imagined community' of republican nationhood (Anderson 1990), during which process a 'fictitious ethnicity' was developed (Balibar and Wallerstein 1988: 130; see Balibar 1992, 1998). This fictitious ethnicity was articulated within a discourse which carried a variety of possible meanings. For example, the influential religious historian Ernest Renan's apparently volontaristic, contractualist approach to joining the French nation is often seen as proof that French nationhood was not based on ethnicity, being open to anyone, of whatever 'origin', who adhered to republican values (Brubaker 1992). However, Renan also espoused a culturally essentialist vision of nationhood which defined French identity as the slow accumulation of the influences of successive generations (Silverman 1992: ch. 1). For Renan, French nationhood could not, therefore, be gained overnight. The republican model was thus a profoundly ambiguous source of identity. It promoted a 'republican Frenchness' theoretically antithetical to the racialised model of the anti-republican nationalists (such as Barrès, who argued that Jews could never be 'authentically French' (Sternhell 1985)). At the same time, the possession of nationality (and hence citizenship) rested on the individual's 'cultural conformity' (Silverman 1992: 33) with this fictitious French ethnicity. For example, republicanism of whatever hue maintained hostility to the expression, in the public sphere, of social identities such as Jewishness, even when such identities were used as a resource against anti-semitism.

The necessarily incomplete process of constructing the nation and forging nationhood often provoked forms of resistance which redefined existing social identities such as regionalism. In the colonies/mandates, colonial policy was not always assimilationist – with the intention of (eventually) applying the same legal and political framework and the same social and cultural values as in France. Associationist policies were also used, which cultivated existing social and cultural values within indigenous colonised societies to ensure the preservation of the colonial order, under the pretence of a more respectful attitude toward such societies (Amselle 1996; Conklin 1997).

The way in which the nation was constructed, and empire ruled, therefore involved hostility to certain differences, as well as processes that actively created new social identities, or reworked and revitalised those which already existed. In the light of this, it is perhaps worth reflecting on the false separation between the 'logics' of assimilation and difference: as Max Silverman has pointed out, the very process of dividing up, of categorising individuals and groups according to their supposed aptitude for assimilation into French 'civilisation', itself involves differentialism (1992: 32–3). In the French context, 'difference' was cloaked in the metaphor of cultural distance (inassimilability), or cultural proximity (assimilability) (Silverman 1992: 107). This metaphor of cultural distance is still very much in place today, as shown by official and media discourses in France which essentialise 'Muslims' as supposedly irretrievably 'different' from the 'French' norm (House 1996). Historically, cultural distance has designated a variety of characteristics which may depart from the French 'norm' constructed, as suggested earlier, within the nationalising republican discourses. These characteristics may be regional, national or transnational, cultural and/or religious, ethnic, linguistic or gender-based. The discourse of assimilation led to the inferiorisation of (amongst others) colonial subjects and women, both relegated to the status of 'children' until they could exercise (adult) 'reason'. This occurred as part of the Third Republic's shifting (and simultaneously inclusionary and exclusionary) juridical boundaries between the foreigner and the national, the metropolitan citizen and the colonial subject, the male 'active' and female 'passive' citizen (Pateman 1988b; Scott 1996; Rosanvallon 1992; Balibar 1992; Conklin 1997; Stoler 1995).

In parallel to this interrogation of the binary opposition between assimilation and difference, the distinction between the 'cultural' and the 'racial' in republican colonial discourses should also be re-examined. Theoretically, republican discourse claimed that the major interpretational distinction was whether this 'difference' (once designated) was viewed to be 'incommensurable' for ever, or whether modernity could work to reshape potentially malleable individuals (Bauman 1991). This has traditionally been the benchmark by which a racial discourse is distinguished from a cultural one. In practice, as Frantz Fanon pointed out in his 1956 essay 'Racisme et Culture', the two 'logics' (racial, cultural) would and did feed off each other: the concept of cultural (or civilisation) superiority was itself a racist concept (1956: 122). Historically speaking, the borders between the cultural and the racial in racist discourse and discourses of colonial governance have been fluid (Touraine 1993: 31–32). Attempts to justify colonisation through invoking the supposedly latent passivity of North Africans or Madagascans show how both racial and cultural concepts were interlinked and difficult to separate at a practical level (MacMaster 1997; Lorcin 1995; Fanon 1961). Indeed, many different groups have been subjected to such complex, hybrid and ambivalent forms of exclusionary discourses and practices.

Challenging racism has thus involved dealing with forms of discourse and practice which are simultaneously difference-denying and difference-creating, whether emanating from the colonial state, 'liberal' republicanism, or overtly racist political movements. To conceptualise anti-racism as either assimilationism or differentialism, as does Taguieff, is therefore simplistic (1990: ch. 1; 1995). Levels and vectors of anti-racist discourse and action, far from existing in a socio-political void, are the result of complex processes of historical determination. The criteria for judging 'assimilability' would change over time: what is judged as 'different' depends on historical contingency, as does the constantly revised 'universal' (Anthias and Yuval-Davis 1992; Brah 1996). If, as Paul Gilroy says, 'there can be no single or homogeneous strategy against racism because racism itself is never homogeneous' (1992: 60–1), we should perhaps use a more fully contextualised reading of the production of anti-racism.

Several examples will now be used to illustrate the following: anti-racism has had to deal with ambivalent forms of the discourses of modernity that both deny the expression of difference and create difference; the construction of political agency within anti-racism is contingent and results from complex processes of historical determination; anti-racism is not simply the 'double' of racism. Before turning to the opposition to colonial racism, a first example will be taken from the anti-racist association the LICA, the largest organisation fighting anti-Semitism in the 1930s. I will attempt to show how the LICA was able skilfully to mould republican assimilationism to avoid some of the potential limitations which the republican model placed on the mobilising of Jewish identities for political action. At the same time, we will see how the LICA shared republicanism's belief that racism could not be French, and the progessivist faith in modernity as regards France's supposed 'civilisation superiority'.

LICA: the limits of republican anti-racism

The LICA was formed out of rejection of the excessive moderation of the older French middle-class Jewish organisations such as the Consistory, which, referring back to the Dreyfusard movement, had interiorised republican prescriptions concerning the relegation of the expression of Jewishness to the 'private sphere'. Consequently, the Consistory refused to fight anti-Semitism on the political terrain (Schor 1992: 211; also Weinburg 1977; Hyman 1979). LICA activists, on the other hand (for example Bernard Lecache and Léon Blum), did not try to hide their Jewishness (Blum 1938; Birnbaum 1991), whilst their discourse stressed the importance of the revolutionary emancipation of the Jews as a key historical event (Birnbaum 1989). The LICA '. . . implied a Jewish commitment based upon the understanding that one could not escape one's Jewish identity' (Weinburg 1977: 50–1). The LICA was relatively successful both in forging unity within and across the diverse Jewish communities in 1930s France, and in arousing solidarity for Jews in the diaspora. Fears over seeing the importance of the fight against anti-Semitism being diluted within a more diffuse anti-fascist paradigm kept the LICA autonomous from, but supportive of, the mainstream left of the Popular Front (1936–8). The LICA used republican discourses to attract different ethnic groups, different classes, and different nationalities (Hyman 1979: 205) within an imprecise, non-aligned left-of-centre republican association which employed traditional methods of campaigning and a humanistic discourse. The association insisted it was not exclusively a Jewish-based organisation (Paraf 1931: 2). Pressure from the association ensured the first legal text in France banning racist abuse in 1939 (House 1997: 105–15). Elsewhere, the LICA went beyond the inherent legalism of the republican model, by claiming the right to self-defence against racist attacks in urban areas which targeted Jewish-owned or frequented premises (House 1997: 88).

The LICA had nevertheless interiorised an important aspect of the republican tradition in its way of thinking about the production of racism within society. The one long-term disadvantage of the Dreyfusard movement and its legacy into the 1930s, the Resistance, and beyond into the 1950s, was the tendency to reinforce an essentially dichotomous vision of the production of racism within society. This vision concentrated solely on the far right, portraying a binary contrast between an 'anti-racist' republic and a racist 'anti-republic' (Balibar in Balibar and Wallerstein 1988: 77). Republicanism has usually analysed racism as purely an emanation of those political forces declaredly hostile to republican values, rather than seeing the success of these movements as representing the widespread amounts of racism present throughout society (Taguieff 1996). For example, in the 1930s the LICA exaggerated the extent to which the French anti-Semitic fascist leagues were dependent on Germany for ideological inspiration, thus ignoring the specifically French tradition of fascism which had developed since the 1920s (Soucy 1986, 1995; Sternhell 1987). Indeed the LICA used the term 'anti-French racism' to infer that racism could not be French.[2]

Republican identity was therefore portrayed within the LICA's discourse as being 'non-racist' at the very height of the colonial period. Until the 1950s the LICA, its humanitarian counterpart the LDH and the mainstream left all shared the faith in the progressivist modernity which talked openly of 'superior civilisations' (Liauzu 1982: 78; Salomon 1948; Guillaumin 1972). The LICA only included a consideration of colonial racism in the context of anti-Semitism in colonial Algeria, Morocco and Tunisia.[3] Republican anti-racism generally proved incapable of understanding national liberation movements, equating their forms of nationalism with proto-fascist European nationalisms. With a few very small-scale exceptions during the short-lived Popular Front governments (1936–8) (see Pierre-Bloch 1936), no voices were heard to argue for a more pluralist vision of racism: republican anti-racism's inclusivism was generally limited to mobilisation against anti-Semitism. Republican anti-racism presupposed a certain mode of thinking about what racism was (principally anti-Semitism), and where it came from (anti-republicanism in its various guises).

These factors were to have important consequences for the way opposition to colonial racism was to develop within metropolitan France. In the next section, I examine opposition to colonial racism in France in the inter-war years by Algerian nationalist and black political and cultural movements. Such activists also had to deal with the ambivalence of modernity (Gilroy 1993a: 191), as did those fighting anti-Semitism, but black activists were of course differently positioned within such discourses and practices.

Colonial dissonance

Opposing colonial governance – the example of Algerians, West Africans and Antillians (1919–1939)

The anti-colonial political and counter-cultural movements of Algerian, West African and Antillian colonial subjects and citizens in France should not of course be seen uniquely through the prism of their opposition to racism, since their varied preoccupations went beyond this. However, the rejection of racism was an ever-present theme of their action. As with the LICA, mobilisations by Algerians, West Africans[4] and Antillians were faced with the difficult issues relating to the construction of political agency within their challenge to racism.

Autonomous action by colonised groups arose not only because of the restrictive paradigm within which republican anti-racism and the mainstream left were operating prior to the 1950s. As Michel Fabre has summarised, the diverse range of French anticolonialists 'attacked the colonial system through the principles of the rights of man and the workers' international, which made no allowance for racial specificity' (1991: 147). A diverse array of extra-parliamentary anti-imperialist movements in France rejected the mainstream left's reformism and offered potential allies to colonised workers in France. These anarchist, Trotskyist and anarcho-syndicalist organisations all recognised the existence of racism within the imperial order. However, these organisations' exclusive use of class-based analyses and mobilisation did not recognise the articulation of class with other social identities ('race', ethnicity, nation), both amongst colonial groups and the French working class (Stora 1987; Dewitte 1985; Liauzu 1982).[5]

The inter-war period saw the transferral from Algeria to France of many of the stereotypes and differentialist policies prevalent in colonial Algeria: there was a constant criss-crossing of the Mediterranean as regards differentialist colonial governance and its discourse. Fearing possible contact between colonial migrants and the far left or Algerian nationalists, the colonial state organised the surveillance and segregation of the Algerian communities in France (MacMaster 1997). Similar policies affected West African subjects (Dewitte 1985). The colonial lobby, meanwhile, considered emigration as an economic threat to the Algerian economy, and orchestrated media campaigns which presented Algerian men as sexually aggressive, mentally unstable and dishonest (MacMaster 1997; Berthelier 1994; Macey 1998; Fanon 1961). These racialised discourses went largely unchallenged by republican anti-racism. Such stereotypes became sedimented in official, popular and intellectual discourses and have been constantly reworked ever since.

The Algerian nationalist organisation, the North African Star (ENA), developed in France in the mid-1920s out of the need for some autonomy from a domineering Communist Party (PCF) (Stora 1986, 1987, 1992: 13–60). The ENA claimed the right to self-representation and self-determination, denouncing such negative stereotyping and segregationist policies. ENA meetings and rallies mocked the contradictions of the discourse of rights used to legitimate the segregationism of colonial conquest: 'it's in the capital of the Revolution, the city of human rights, what irony (!), that these despicable laws are being applied to us' (Imache 1934; see Stora 1986). Similar strategies were adopted by black writers such as the poet Léon-Gontrand Damas, who outlined the contradiction of 'a France which doesn't lose an opportunity to pronounce itself the black peoples' friend, whilst not losing an opportunity to keep them mercilessly in chains' (1939: 340). The Jamaican-born Claude Mackay's autobiography *A Long Way from Home*, first published in 1937, explained: '(I)t is hell to belong to a suppressed minority and outcast group. For to most members of the powerful majority, you are not a person; you are a problem' (1985: 153).

This dissonance over the exclusionary mechanisms of the colonial system came to disrupt the imperial triumphalism of the time, and the aforementioned republican leitmotif of a 'non-racist' France (Girardet 1968). For the metropolitan French, these new viewpoints from racialised groups on what racism was, where its roots lay, and what its practical effects were, raised sensitive questions about the consensual republican ideology of the colonial 'mission', and were hence suppressed. Racism, as defined by the ENA, as well as the various black political and cultural movements of the inter-war years, is all-pervasive, and is presented as an intrinsic component of the colonial system: racism affects the attitudes of the metropolitan French, consciously or unconsciously, as well as the colonial settlers and civil servants. This attempt in the 1930s to impose a different version of common-sense values about the nature of the colonial society therefore anticipated many of the themes that Albert Memmi (1957), Fanon (1952, 1961) and Jean-Paul Sartre (1964) (each in their own way) would subsequently develop.

Counter-cultures and agency

Colonised groups often appropriated the emancipatory revolutionary discourses for themselves. In other cases, as we have seen with the discourse of the ENA and Damas (above), mocking use was made of the human rights discourse of the coloniser (Stora 1992: 69). As Raoul Girardet has pointed out, attempts to justify the colonial order often invoked France's 'mission' to spread its model of human rights, the result being a denial of the agency and dignity of the colonised (Girardet 1972: 168). For anti-colonial and counter-cultural movements of the inter-war years, the difficult negotiation of agency in opposition to racism was often undertaken via a conscious strategy of hybridisation (Young 1995: 21–2) of the political ideologies and mobilisational repertoires available within (a) republican political culture and (b) Marxism. These references were blended with traditions of resistance from pre-colonial and anti-slavery movements, often articulated within a consciousness of diasporic belonging. Such multiple strategies came as a response to the complex mix of assimilationism and differentialism of colonial state governance (Conklin 1997; Prochaska 1990; Stoler 1995; Amselle 1996).

The above points illustrate how choice of (here) cultural and political identity comes from a repertoire governed by historical contingency (Turner 1993: 64). In practice, the forms of resistance to racism and oppression, whilst necessarily influenced by the dominant modes of thought or practices of exclusion at a given moment, will usually take shape in a space which is only partially determined by the dominant discursive paradigms. The extent and nature of this *partial* determination is nonetheless of obvious importance in the creation of political agency. Such an analytical approach, whilst recognising the unequal power relationships at play, nevertheless looks to the creation of new spaces and sites from which racism has been contested. Here I will adapt the use Paul Gilroy makes in *The Black Atlantic* of W.E.B. Du Bois's concept of 'double conscious-ness', referring to the positioning of black thinkers as 'both inside and outside the West' (1993a: 30). 'Double consciousness' will be employed heuristically to explain the repertoire 'of forms of action, discourse and identification at play within the opposition to racism from many colonised activists, and the 'antagonistic indebtedness' they expressed toward occidental modernity (Gilroy 1993a). These points can be illustrated in relation to the varied levels and vectors of opposition to colonial governance, and employed by West Africans and Antillians living in France in the inter-war period (Dewitte 1985).

The celebration of hybridisation undertaken by cultural journals in the 1920s and 1930s, such as *La Revue du Monde noir* and *La Dépêche africaine*, brought together black intellectuals from throughout the French-speaking colonies and mandates, as well as African-American writers such as Langstone Hughes (Dewitte 1985; Fabre 1991; Langley 1973). Such journals served to redefine the boundaries between the cultural and the political through the rediscovery, reworking and revitalisation of African and Antillian cultural tradition ignored and derided by colonialism. Black student cultures in 1920s–1930s Paris were informed by Marxism, Surrealism and French and German ethnography (Jack 1996: 39–44; Jules-Rosette 1998: 33–8; Lebovics 1992; Dewitte 1985). As Bennetta Jules-Rosette has said of the contributors to *La Revue du Monde noir*: '(T)he philosophies and ideologies that shaped their thinking, while confining, also offered them the tools with which to challenge the foundations of their education and the restrictions of the colonial predicament' (1998: 33).

The radical and diverse perspectives of the nascent négritude movement in the 1930s around Aimé Césaire and Léopold Sédar Senghor were certainly more avowedly anti-assimilationist than the cultural journals previously mentioned (Jack 1996: 50–1; Césaire 1956). However, anti-essentialist critiques of négritude often hide the complexity of this cultural and political project which 'embodies the reactions of African and Antillian writers to European cultural and colonial experiences' (Jules-Rosette 1998: 2). Paul Gilroy has pointed out the cross-fertilisation at play within the négritude movement between African-American, Haitian, Antillian, African and 'mainland' France-based thinkers (Gilroy 1993a: 211). Furthermore, négritude nonetheless reworked the black cultural tradition using elements 'adapted from the culture of the hegemonic country [i.e. France]' (Lebovics 1992: 124), as had *La Revue du Monde noir*. Other commentators have pointed out the structural limits placed on a counter-cultural project attempting to cease definition in relation to the dominant French model, whilst, '[g]iven that the negritude movement was created in France with French people as its primary audience, the poets had to use French discursive spaces (ethnology, literary canons, Marxism and Christianity) to speak about Blackness' (Diawara 1992: 386). Cultural activists in the 1930s and those associated with the Présence Africaine cultural project (1947–) have of course been acutely aware of the unequal power relations corrupting cultural production in a colonial and post-colonial setting (Césaire 1956; Fanon 1956; Jules-Rosette 1998).

Resistance to colonial oppression was not restricted to cultural levels. Radical pan-Africanist movements of the early to mid 1930s, such as the League for the Defence of the Negro Race (LDRN) and the Negro Workers' Association (UTN), argued that the cultural question could only be solved at a political level with the creation of a black African state (Dewitte 1985). The LDRN insisted on the importance of concrete socio-economic demands, calling for the 'same social and political rights for Negro workers living in France as for white workers'.[6] Both the LDRN and the UTN sought to provide an alternative source of focus for working-class blacks (mostly dockers, sailors and labourers) to the French trade unions. However, the LDRN and the UTN did not ignore the potential solidarity of left-wing organisations and argued for inter-class black unity (see Dewitte

1985; House 1997: 159–65). These associations also contested the cultural aspects of colonial domination. Both the UTN and the LDRN's interweaving of 'race', class and ethnicity in demands for more rights and dignity mirrored the complex situations in which the colonised found themselves in France.

Why has this opposition to the colonial experience, colonial racism and the discourse of 'civilisation superiority' tended to pass relatively unnoticed within the wider history of anti-racism in France? First, restrictive definitions of what constituted racism kept colonial racism from the republican anti-racist agenda. Second, the cultural and political mobilisations analysed above occupy a tangential place within the republican left's established memory sites, key dates and social imaginary (Tartakowsky 1998). Attempting to 'write in' the struggles of the colonised within mainland France is not only 'compensatory', inserting new trajectories into the history of anti-racism. These mobilisations also provide further evidence, after the example of the LICA given earlier, to suggest that talking of anti-racism as a 'double' of racism is an inadequate explanatory framework. The history of opposition to colonial racism discussed in this section has also shown the contingent construction of political agency, and the variety of social, cultural and political resources drawn on by colonised activists.

In the next section of the chapter we will see how the crisis of modernity exemplified in the Holocaust, a crisis in the French colonial order, and a wider process of modernisation combined to transform the way in which republican anti-racism approached racism in post-war France. The different 'traditions' of mobilising against anti-Jewish, anti-black and anti-North African racism would be brought closer together through the 'communities of suffering' formed by these fundamental historical processes (Werbner 1997: 242).

Rethinking anti-racist models, 1945–1962

The experiences of the Holocaust, Resistance and the Algerian War each in their own way served to transform the perception of republican ideology within republican anti-racism and broaden the anti-racist agenda. The MRAP, a left-wing, republican anti-racist organisation formed in 1949 by mostly Jewish former Resistance activists, helped to redefine republican anti-racism in the 1950s: it did so by looking closely at the forms racism took, how racism should be conceptualised, and how it should be fought.

At a first glance, the republican ideology that emerged from Occupation and Resistance was reaffirmed rather than weakened. The state racism of the defeated Vichy regime was seen as the antithesis of modernity in general and republicanism in particular. This tended to reinforce the aforementioned myth of a 'non-racist' France that exonerated republican France from considering 'as its own' the racism practised within state institutions such as the judiciary and security forces (see Rousso 1990; Conan and Rousso 1994). The rebuilding of the republican edifice on the basis of the false idea that the population in France had unanimously resisted Nazi occupation attempted to reintroduce republican 'universalism' where there had been *vichyssois* 'differentialism' (see Lloyd 1998a). In fact, the legacy of the Holocaust, Occupation and Resistance would have far-reaching effects on republican anti-racism, due to the increase in colonial racism from the late 1940s onwards. This racism was linked to the state repression of Algerian nationalism and involved arbitrary identity checks, mass arrests and gratuitous security force violence based on supposed phenotypic characteristics (MacMaster 1997; Einaudi 1991). Such events led to a demystification of the supposedly non-racist republican state within elements of republican anti-racism and the far left. The questioning of the state's role broadened out, from the late 1950s onwards, to include the wider left-wing via the question of state-sanctioned torture (Alleg 1958; Vidal-Naquet 1962). This eventually moved republican anti-racism away from the previous over-concentration on the far right as a vector of racism (without of course ignoring the far right). An ethical position evolved within the alternative left which stressed collective responsibility and accountability for what the French state did in the name of its citizens (Rancière 1998).

It was the MRAP activists who were the first to show solidarity with colonial citizens in France, along with very marginalised elements of the far left (Lloyd 1998a; M. Evans 1997; Hamon and Rotman 1979). This solidarity was largely a result of the activists' direct experience of racism under Vichy. An essential theme of the discourse of the mainly Jewish resistance groups such as the National Movement Against Racism (MNCR, founded 1941) had been the need for solidarity between Jews and non-Jews in the fight against Vichy/the Occupier (Rayski 1950; Lloyd 1998a; House 1997: 201–5). In the immediate post-war period, anti-racist activists realised that the end of the Vichy regime and the defeat of Nazism would not signal the end of an anti-Semitism which was widespread throughout society. This view was reinforced by the inadequacies of the post-war purge of collaborators (*l'épuration*) (Novick 1968). Anti-racist activists therefore promoted the anti-fascist logic of vigilance against a return of state racism.[7] The Anti-racist Alliance (AA) had already explicitly acknowledged that this solidarity would have to be between all racialised groups. Created in 1947 in order to bring together former LICA activists and those from the MNCR, the AA aimed for a more inclusive anti-racism both in terms of the ideological belonging of activists and the broader definitional approach to racism. As the AA's Gérard Rosenthal declared: 'anti-racism must extend its realm of action to include all manifestations of racism' (1948: 1).

The MRAP emerged in 1949 from the break-up of the AA (split over the Cold War) as a broad alliance of different elements of France's left-wing Jewish communities largely sympathetic to the PCF. The MRAP nevertheless sought to be inclusive, with a purposefully broad social and ethnic base, and included figures such as the poet Aimé Césaire. Whilst the MRAP worked with Présence Africaine against anti-black racism (House 1997: 216–17), it was against the state repression of Algerian nationalism and of Algerian emigrants more generally that the MRAP became more heavily involved. The MRAP continued actively to oppose anti-Semitism. In contrast to the MRAP, an older, more politically conservative generation of post-war LICA members prevented their association from opening out substantially to oppose the anti-North African racism of the 1950s–1960s. These activists ignored the LICA president Bernard Lecache's earlier advice that 'it's impossible to want to limit ourselves to destroying only one form of intolerance – anti-Semitism. It's all racism which needs to be fought' (1944: 3).

The MRAP's theoretical response to the increase in anti-North African racism was to realise that there was a plurality of racisms: there was a movement away from the centrality of anti-Semitism (all the more remarkable considering the proximity of the Holocaust), and the acceptance that a specifically colonial form of racism existed. The MRAP's use of socio-economic analyses of the exploitation of immigrant labour helped this formulation. Notwithstanding this plurality and diversity of forms of racism, the MRAP argued that, for the means of mobilisation, all racisms should be seen as inseparable (*indivisibles*). Albert Lévy refers to the MRAP's conception of the 'unity in diversity' of racism.[8] Solidarity between all racialised groups was therefore necessary (Blumel 1949). Jews should support other racialised groups and help anti-colonial movements. If forms of racism were inseparable, the MRAP argued, there was always the latent possibility that one form of racism would come to target other groups. This position proved accurate as the anti-Semitic Poujadist movement of 1953–58 increasingly adopted an anti-Algerian stance (Borne 1977).

Through the MRAP's discourse of the need for solidarity between groups targeted by racism, we can see the evolution of what Pnina Werbner describes as 'anti-racists as a community of suffering [who] can, potentially, evolve their own counter-discourses and self-identifications in the political arena. By doing so, they can transcend their particular ethnicities, class origin and gendered identities to forge new moral and aesthetic communities imaginatively' (1997: 242). For example, the return, from the late 1940s onwards, of state racism in France on a large scale, with repressive techniques imported from the colonies, brought direct parallels for many with police tactics under Vichy. One edition of the MRAP's newspaper gave the following, ironical example of such a parallel: 'one of our friends, a Jewish primary school teacher, told us the other day that he'd been stopped coming out of the Metro station during a police round-up of Algerians. The shape of his face had made him a 'suspect': the detective was probably acting a few years too late.'[9] We can see here an example of Paul Gilroy's suggestion to set histories of racism in relation to each other (1993a: 213–17).[10] Elsewhere, Gilroy quotes from Fredric Jameson's judgement on the need not to collapse forms of racism into each other, but rather to consider parallels between different experiences of racism on the level of 'a more primary experience, namely that of fear and vulnerability' (in Gilroy 1993a: 206). The above quote from the MRAP arguably echoes these experiential parallels between Jews and Arab/Berber Algerians in France. It also highlights the way in which exclusionary practices of the state come to affect different groups (Guidice 1992; Woodall 1993).

The MRAP's much wider definition of racism did however lead to some problems. The extent to which the treatment of Algerians in the 1950s–1960s could be equated with that of Jews under Vichy became a source of disagreement within the anti-colonialist left.[11] At times, the MRAP, and the wider alternative left, tended to use a form of 'archetypal thinking' (J. Young 1988: 95), where one event (the persecution of Algerians) was figured in the light of others (the persecution of Jews under Vichy). This figuring can arguably be explained by the absence of any previous tradition of republican anti-racist campaigning against colonial racism: the only historical model of state racism available to refer to within a republican repertoire was the Holocaust and Vichy's role therein, rather than repressive colonial governance. Furthermore, in terms of the campaigning repertoire, this paradoxically saw a retention of the increasingly outdated anti-fascist model with which to fight colonial and then post-colonial racism. This retention of the anti-fascist model of anti-racism into the 1980s has been severely criticised as failing to respond to post-colonial forms of racism having moved onto the terrain of 'cultural' rather than overtly 'racial' and fascistic discourses (Gallissot 1985; Taguieff 1990, 1995; Silverman 1992; Lloyd 1998a).

The MRAP's response to the exacerbation of existing forms of racism during the conflictual processes of decolonisation should nevertheless be measured in relation to what existed at the time. As Reinhardt Koselleck states: 'social and political conflicts of the past have to be opened up via the medium of their contemporary conceptual limits' (1982: 414). We have seen how the tradition of republican anti-racism had previously concentrated on anti-Semitism to the exclusion of other forms of racism, and how it had interiorised the discourse of a 'non-racist' France. The MRAP therefore instigated a significant move away from these restricting factors by establishing dialogues between different class and ethnic groups. In the 1950s–1960s, however, the MRAP was unable to rely on strong support from a mainstream (Communist/Socialist) left which was confused as to how to interpret the imperial crisis of the nation-state. Historically, it has been the alternative, not the mainstream, left which has shown the most practical solidarity with colonial groups. This solidarity has not been without its paternalism, hence the continuing search for autonomy and agency of post-1968 anti-racist and immigrant-rights activism (Guidice 1992; Wihtol de Wenden 1988; Polac 1994; Lloyd 1998a; Bouamama 1994).

Conclusion

In this chapter I have tried to show how anti-racist politics in France have developed in relation to the discourses of modernity, with reference to colonial and post-colonial history and anti-Semitism. I have argued that it is necessary to reassess the way in which nation and empire have been constituted and articulated within liberal rights discourse (such as republican anti-racism) and in more overtly racialising exclusionary discourses within colonial governance and racist political movements (Ross 1995). The enabling and restrictive influence of a discourse of rights in the French context (discussed for example by Joan Scott 1996) suggests the possibility of dialogue between feminism and anti-racism, as well as the need for further interdisciplinary work on anti-racism across history, politics and the history of ideas (Lloyd 1998b). I have argued that anti-racism is irreducible to interpretational frameworks based around assimilationism/differentialism and universalism/particularism, just as anti-racism is rarely the 'negative other' of racism.

My discussion has shown that the possibility of an effective, inclusive republican anti-racism before the 1950s was largely precluded by the discourse of 'civilisation superiority' and the way in which the causes of racism were understood. A limiting discursive framework, therefore, ensured the marginalisation of the oppositional voices around colonial racism. Whether from Algerians, Antillians, West Africans or the French working-class far left, a consideration of colonial racism was not possible within republican discourses (including republican anti-racism) until the period of decolonisation.[12] The forging of an experiential empathy between different racialised groups in the 1950s, as shown by the MRAP's actions, was the start of a long, as yet incomplete period of rethinking anti-racism (Lloyd 1998a). The ambivalence within modernity towards a wide range of groups subjected to racial subordination can suggest a more inclusive anti-racist agenda, whilst recognising the different positioning of individuals and groups within such forms of oppression. I have suggested that anti-racism can look to the dialogues between colonised and coloniser, between and across different forms of the colonial experiences, whilst integrating the history of opposition to anti-Semitism which has experienced similar, although not of course identical, problems over how to construct agency. This ties in with recent theoretical reflections that unity and solidarity do not presuppose sameness (Gibb 1995), thus widening the social base for anti-racism. It also reflects a 'transversal politics' based around the recognition and negotiation of the different positionings and preoccupations of those participating in collective action (Yuval-Davis 1997b: 203–6).

Autonomous social movements in France involving undocumented residents have recently provided eloquent examples of how such transversalism can unite oppressed groups and attract solidarity from throughout society, and hence force political change (IM'média/REFLEX 1997; Balibar 1998). Indeed, it could be argued that contesting racism in postmodern France will increasingly need to be based around such transversalism: both the targeting of those defined as 'non-European' by the far right and elements of the right, and the re-drawing and strengthening in France of discriminatory legislation concerning non-European Union citizens, affect extremely heterogeneous social groups. An anti-racist politics which is constructed on the basis of dialogue, bringing together different social, cultural and political trajectories and experiences, would reflect the historical evolution of many of the mobilisations against racism in France in the twentieth century, and be better placed to counter the hybrid contemporary forms of racism.

Notes

1 The term *anti-racisme* only appeared in the LICA's discourse in 1936, probably transposed from the American English (see House 1997: 90–8).

2 See for example 'Requête respectueuse à M. le Préfet de Police', *Le Droit de vivre*, 1939, 147, 22 April: 1. As Taguieff has shown, the term 'racism' had come into French political discourse in the 1920s to describe ideological developments in racial thought specific to Germany rather than France (Taguieff 1990: 130–8).

3 See LICA President's espousal of 'interracial fraternity' in the French colonies, which represents a classic example of assimilationist colonial discourse (speech 7 March 1936, reproduced in *Le Droit de vivre*, 1936, 18, 14 March: 6).

4 The majority of those people referred to here as 'West Africans' were from the current states of Senegal and Mali, subsumed in colonial times within the vast French West African Federation (see Conklin 1997).

5 Marxist-inspired discourses viewed racism as an instrument of bourgeois control, and hence tended to ignore the existence of racism within the French working class.

6 *Le Cri des Nègres* 1931, 4–5, November–December: 1. The term *Nègre* (Negro) was deliberately used by pan-Africanist organisations, as *Noir(e)* (Black) was considered too assimilationist a term: hence the retention here of the English equivalents in translation.

7 Author's interview with Albert Lévy, former MRAP general secretary, Paris, 18 September 1995.

8 Interview with author, Paris, 18 September 1995.

9 'Au faciès', *Droit et Liberté*, 1958, 169, January, p. 2.

10 Gilroy refers in particular to anti-Jewish racism and anti-black racism in the context of the history of slavery and forced displacement.

11 Compare the appeals dated 18 October 1961 in *Les Temps modernes* (1961), 186, November: 624–8 and 'Contre la barbarie', *Esprit* (1961), 11: 667–70.

12 Such considerations were not 'in the true', in the Foucaultian sense (Foucault 1971: 35–8; Balibar 1994: 174–8; Young 1995: 11).

8 Back to the future

Avoiding *déjà vu* in resisting racism

Pragna Patel

The Stephen Lawrence case has touched us all deeply. Institutionalised racism has finally been recognised, a direct consequence of the outstanding work undertaken by the family and supporters of Stephen Lawrence and Duwayne Brooks. But that victory in turn was built on fifty years or so of tireless campaigning against street level and institutional racism in Britain. The black presence in Britain has recently been celebrated in public spheres, noticeably through the anniversary of the arrival of the *Empire Windrush* and the fiftieth anniversary of Indian independence. Sadly, those celebrations have not been about the end of racism in Britain.

Southall Black Sisters (SBS), too, celebrated its twenty-first anniversary in the year 2000. Against the background of the Stephen Lawrence case, we feel compelled to ask ourselves some searching questions about how we seize the moment and build on the anti-racist work that we have been engaged in for the last twenty years without re-inventing the wheel. The Stephen Lawrence inquiry, which led to the Macpherson Report, has created a space within which to engage in an open and honest debate on the nature of institutionalised racism in all its manifestations in Britain and to develop effective strategies to combat such racism. The challenge is how to take advantage of this moment, how to redefine and formulate anti-racist strategies, recognising past limitations of anti-racist thinking, so that we create and not constrain a new politics of resistance.

Our aim at SBS is simple. We want to ensure that such strategies and politics are informed by and benefit from the wealth of experiences of struggles for self-determination by black women – Asian and African-Caribbean women – in particular. Discussions on race and gender inequality, and how they intersect to create powerlessness amongst black women in our society, continue to be woefully lacking, as the categories of race and gender tend to remain mutually exclusive in debates on both gender and racism. Whilst the feminist movement needs to examine the ways in which women can experience gender discrimination differently, for example in racialised forms, the focus of this chapter is on the silence on gender and other forms of inequality within anti-racist debates. Such a silence has a crippling impact on the more general struggles for social justice within black communities in Britain. More importantly, in our view, the silence has had a far-reaching impact on any attempt to build effective coalitions to end inequality and injustice. In the current climate of renewed official interest in tackling racism, it is significant to note that very little, if any, of attention is paid by many (male) anti-racist activists to the fact that racism is not experienced in the same way by black men and women. And yet, the state has been forced to take notice of the demands made by women within the minority communities in its response to the Macpherson Report. A flurry of initiatives on domestic violence and forced marriages are some ways in which the state is striving to show its anti-racist credentials.[1]

What follows is an account of some of the work of SBS, in particular the dilemmas, contradictions and tensions that we have encountered when we make demands for equality in relation to the family, community and the state. Our experiences challenge the orthodoxies of both the anti-racist movement, which continues to emphasise the primacy of racial equality above all else, and the social welfare policies of the state, predicated as they are on the much-vaunted notion of multiculturalism.

This chapter begins with a brief examination of the origins of SBS and the context in which the group has developed its politics, based on the need to challenge racism and patriarchal oppression simultaneously. I examine the Macpherson definition of institutionalised racism and show its limitations. I suggest that critiques of the definition do not go far enough, in so far as they fail to take account of black women's experiences of racism, and how it interlocks with patriarchal systems of power to reproduce and reinforce both racial inequality and gender inequality. By recounting some of the immigration, policing and domestic violence case work and campaigning experiences of SBS, I show how institutional racism operates at a number of different levels for black women, including the politics of multiculturalism.

With regard to the way forward, I point to the necessity and urgency of developing an anti-racist politics that takes account of the rise of religious fundamentalism which appropriates anti-racist and multicultural language to further its own agenda – the control of women. I point to the need to avoid some of the obvious pitfalls that lie ahead by emphasising the need to make connections between racism and sexism and to make central to our agenda the current racism towards refugees. I argue that in order to do this there must be a critical self-inspection of past anti-racist politics, built on the myth of a homogeneous black community lacking in internal divisions and conflict. The creation of effective alliances to overcome all forms of oppression can only be built on the principle of equality and human rights being guaranteed for all in our communities and the wider society.

SBS in the heart of the anti-racist struggle

SBS was born in the heart of anti-racist struggles against racial attacks and police thuggery and racism that culminated in the murder of Blair Peach in Southall in the late 1970s (CARF 1981). Those early struggles became the catalyst for the emergence of SBS. The same women who were active in such struggles also found the confidence to push at the boundaries of the anti-racist movements in which they were engaged.

The founders of SBS in 1979 were Asian and African-Caribbean women involved in the forging of a new black feminist, anti-racist, socialist, anti-communalist and secular identity, one based on a shared history of racism, and of religious and patriarchal control within the community. They challenged the absence of a recognition of gender power relations within anti-racist movements and the absence of an acknowledgement of racism within white feminist movements which had resulted in the invisibility and silencing of black and minority women (Carby 1982).

The term black[2] was consciously used by many radical black activists, including SBS, to signify the shared experiences of colonialism and racism. It served as a useful mobilising term, potentially expansive when underpinned by progressive socialist principles, by including the various black and minority communities. For example, many black delegations to Northern Ireland and to the mining communities in the 1980s (in attempts to forge wider alliances and express solidarity with other oppressed sections of society in their struggles against imperialism and state repression) included activists from Chinese and Iranian backgrounds. SBS, too, had founding members who were from diverse backgrounds, including the Middle East. The term black was by no means accepted readily by everyone in the Asian and Afro-Caribbean communities. But the term helped to build confidence, subverting the negative perceptions of Asians and African-Caribbeans amongst other minorities as second-class citizens to be excluded from the political, economic and social processes in Britain. Borrowing from both the civil rights movement and the black power movement in the US, the term black became a symbol of empowerment and resistance.

Whilst recognising that the term 'black' glosses over the various ethnic divisions in society, and can be vulnerable to the projection of a politics of black nationalism, SBS has nevertheless, out of necessity, retained the term for a number of reasons. First, it remains vital at a practical level, as a bridging device in the formation of progressive political alliances and unity between all groups who experience racism in British society. Second, the term indicates that we remain at the heart of the anti-racist struggles in which SBS was founded. Third, the term helps us to counter the increasing climate of intolerance brought about by the fragmentation of identities along religious lines within our communities, distorting the progressive socialist and secular sentiments and vision of earlier anti-racist projects and identities. This distortion has led to a paralysis of joint anti-racist action and weakened the possibility of alliances between different groups who experience racism and amongst feminists and anti-racists. This is especially so in the wake of another seminal moment in the history of race relations in this country, the Salman Rushdie affair, which acted as a catalyst in the rise and assertion of conservative if not fundamentalist identities within minority communities.[3]

SBS has operated a centre for black women since 1982. More recently the staff at the centre have moved from being a collective to a hierarchical organisation in recognition of the problems that were posed by, amongst other things, the need for more transparency of management which was otherwise masked under the guise of a collective. The ethos nevertheless remains collective and democratic as both workers and users of the centre are encouraged to participate in management committee meetings. The need to involve users in the running of the centre has been an urgent task and one that we have not yet managed successfully since many of the users are women who have child-care demands, have never stepped outside of the home and speak little or no English. Nevertheless the users remain pivotal to all our work and thinking, having brought important dimensions to our understanding of oppression both within and outside of the home. They remind us, on a daily basis, of the absolute necessity of being accountable to those whose interests we seek to articulate. At present all users are encouraged to be members of the organisation and to attend general meetings held regularly throughout the year. From such meetings representatives are nominated onto the management committee.

Our day-to-day work is predominantly with South Asian women, directly reflecting the demands made by local women. Women arrive at our centre with stories of domestic violence, rape, divorce, child abuse, forced marriages, immigration difficulties, homelessness and poverty. The response of the state and the community to these women has been largely indifferent, when not characterised by discrimination direct and indirect.[4] These experiences have demanded that we question the limitations of the anti-racist movement, which, with its central focus on state brutality and racial discrimination, has on the whole needed to rely on the myth of a united community in defence of itself.[5] In doing so, we have sought to emphasise the centrality of black women's experiences within debates on racism.

It did not and does not come easy to us to demand scrutiny within the anti-racist movement as pressure to remain loyal to the need to fight state racism has been intense. But challenging domestic violence and its patriarchal underpinnings has led us to question the call for anti-racist unity at all costs, a call which has demanded our silence and complicity in hiding other forms of oppressions experienced within our communities on the basis of class, gender and caste inequality. Yet from the outset, what we have sought to do when we wage campaigns around domestic violence, for example, is not so much to separate ourselves off from anti-racist struggles, but to seek to redefine the content and direction of those struggles. We have sought to forge a new inclusive politics drawing on the strengths and insights of the feminist as well as other progressive movements, without lapsing into a politics of resistance that is hierarchically ordered. Our aim therefore has been to find ways of engaging in the various struggles for racial and gender equality simultaneously. But re-defining the anti-racist movement has involved an honest and critical self-inspection of the internal divisions of power within black communities. By addressing those internal divisions we hope to create the space for the emergence of genuine coalitions involving all those who experience racism, discrimination and state repression – a space where empowerment is achieved but not on the backs of other vulnerable and disadvantaged sections of society such as women and more recently the new refugees.

Institutional racism: now you see it, now you don't

Critics[6] of the Macpherson definition of institutional racism have argued that it amounts to a denial of institutional racism.[7] The definition is notable for its series of absences: for example the absence of 'wit' as opposed to 'unwitting', 'thought' as opposed to 'thoughtlessness' and 'conscious' as opposed to unconscious. The

end result is that such a definition actually denies and so takes away state responsibility for institutional racism: the collective failures of the organisation are said to
arise as a result of individuals who cannot be blamed for racism because they are
unthinking and ignorant in their prejudice and racist stereotyping. It has been
suggested that the most significant absence of all within the Macpherson
definition of institutional racism is the absence of any mention of power, control
and subordination of racial groups, concepts which are central to the notion of
institutional racism as defined by black activists and social commentators.

Barnor Hesse stated that an acknowledgement of institutional racism as having
to do with power, control and subordination as well as with the elements of
concealment and denial is important in understanding how individual and
institutional racism can be connected and played out. Instead of a focus on the
simple questions of how and why racism comes to be institutionalised – a process
which is very much bound up with British colonial rule and post-war immigration
law – the Macpherson Report at one and the same time declares the existence of
institutional racism but then, in the same breath, actually denies its existence and
puts it down to unwitting prejudices. Immigration laws and policies provide the
example *par excellence* of how state racism is constructed and managed, albeit in
covert ways, under the camouflage of what has been euphemistically described as
maintaining 'good race relations' or 'racial harmony'.

The result is that the solutions aimed at eradicating institutional racism focus
only on cosmetic changes whilst leaving power imbalances between the majority
and minority communities intact. This is one reason why recruitment of blacks
and racial awareness training in the late 1980s did not succeed as effective anti-
racist strategies. They challenged individual prejudices but not the culture of
unaccountability of state institutions such as that of the police, with their practices
of discrimination, exclusion and even oppression (Sivanandan 1985).

Institutionalised racism: the experiences of black women

Critics of the Macpherson Report have argued that institutional racism is predicated
upon the need to subordinate, control and exercise power over those in our society
who are considered to be 'different' by virtue of their racial or ethnic background.
They also argue that any effective anti-racist strategies must first unmask and then
seek to challenge precisely how such power, control and subordination comes to be
expressed or practised. I would go further to suggest that any such analysis will be
incomplete unless it takes account of the experiences of black women. How
institutionalised racism can and does intersect with patriarchal power to the
detriment of black women, and to the detriment of racial equality, demands urgent
attention, since many black women are otherwise marginalised and disempowered
by such intersections of race, class and gender. It is on the terrain of the politics of
multiculturalism[8] that the intersection of race and gender domination is at its most
subtle but also most dangerous. Multiculturalism – as an aspect of institutionalised
racism which impacts on gender inequality – has not received the attention it
deserves from anti-racist activists. But on the ground it remains one of the most
pressing challenges in our day-to-day struggles for freedom.

Our experiences at SBS show us that when women faced with control and subjugation based on patriarchal relations make demands of the state for protection, they are likely to confront the racism of the state in the form of indifference and even hostility.[9] But we find another more insidious process also at work in keeping women powerless. Through the politics of 'multiculturalism', for instance (discussed below), the state more or less enters into an informal contract with the more powerful leaders in the minority community where individual autonomy (women) is exchanged in return for some guarantee of communal autonomy (black communities). In practice this means that self-appointed community leaders maintain power over family, cultural and religious affairs of the communities, with the effect of concealing power relations between men and women and legitimising women's subordination within minority communities. Without understanding how the process of such disempowerment occurs, our understanding of institutionalised racism in this country can only be partial, and the strategies which flow from such partial understandings can be seriously deficient and even dangerous.

Many of us have argued that if we are to learn the lessons from history, we urgently need to re-think state racism in relation to the subject who experiences that racism rather than in the terms of simplistic notions of the 'state versus the black community'. Within the existing parameters of anti-racist debates and perceptions, there often appears to be a focus upon a male view of racism, to the extent that the lives and experiences of women are rendered invisible. Often, the only experiences that are celebrated or even recognised are where black women are relatives of 'recognised' victims of racism. In this view, racism is experienced only by men, to be confronted by men, and the reality of the lives of black women who come into contact with the state is ignored.

However, when demanding that we need to be able to think in terms of gender, class and race simultaneously, we have often encountered the response that translating such abstractions into practice is difficult. But that is the point: to find new ways, however challenging, to translate the new thinking into practice in the form of guidelines and policies, with which to hold the state accountable in relation to the needs of all members of the various black communities. And to do so, one has to look at the concrete experiences of women as well as men.

Domestic violence and immigration policy

One important example of the overlap of institutional racism with patriarchal oppression is the operation of the so-called 'one-year rule' within British immigration law and policy.

Racism in immigration, nationality and asylum laws remains a major obstacle for all minority peoples seeking to assert their full citizenship rights in the UK. Historically, the imperative of all UK immigration laws and policy is to restrict immigration (especially from the Indian sub-continent). The justification – to maintain 'good race relations' – hides the fact that the legislative framework has been constructed to restrict some (blacks and more recently Eastern Europeans) but not others from entering the country.

Assumptions about Asian marriages as 'sham' and 'bogus', entered into for the purposes of immigration, have underpinned the direction of immigration laws and policy. Asian women have experienced racism within immigration laws in ways that are also common to men, for example when denied the right to family reunion. But there are also differences in the ways in which racist assumptions combine with sexist assumptions about the role of Asian women in the family to deny women the right to choose the mode of life they wish to live.[10]

SBS has grappled with the tensions arising from immigration policies which divide black families and those which prevent women from leaving violent relationships. Growing social awareness of domestic violence and the ensuing policies developed in the last two decades do not extend to include those women who are affected by such immigration policies.

Since 1988, immigration rules have contained a restriction (known as the one-year rule) on spouses entering this country for the purposes of marriage. The one-year rule demands that men or women who enter the UK for the purposes of marriage must remain in the marriage for a probationary period of twelve months before they are entitled to stay permanently. If the marriage breaks down during the one year, for whatever reasons, and the couples are no longer living together at the end of it, the spouse from abroad no longer has a right to remain in the UK because of the breakdown of the marriage. But women who experience violence and abuse in these circumstances find themselves trapped in the marriages for fear of deportation if they leave the marriage. Further, the existence of the 'no recourse to public funds' rule further ensures that such women are locked into violent and abusive relationships since they are not entitled to claim any public assistance in the form of welfare benefits or state housing. Resources such as refuges are on the whole out of bounds for such women since they cannot pay rent or claim housing benefit or meet other daily needs. Access to the welfare system is a prerequisite to most women leaving violent relationships, since in our experience many women are plunged into poverty when they leave a marriage.

Our campaign to abolish the one-year rule began in 1992 and was supported by many black and minority women's groups, individuals and some trade unions. The campaign's main goal was to highlight the plight of women who are effectively trapped in violent relationships by the immigration rules. We have sought to expose the double standards inherent in official rhetoric on domestic violence, which does not include all women's right to protection from male violence,[11] and to change government immigration policy based on such discrimination. As a result of a hard-fought campaign of direct action as well as continued dialogue with the Home Office, a concession for women or partners who leave violent relationships within the probationary period was granted by the Labour government in the Immigration and Asylum Act 1998. But the concession represents only a partial victory.

The Home Office acknowledged the existence of domestic violence in this context, and conceded that a partner can obtain indefinite leave to remain if they can prove that they suffered domestic violence within the probationary period. However, the problem lies with the standard of proof of domestic violence required to demonstrate domestic violence if a woman is to make a case to be allowed to stay following the breakdown of her marriage. Despite our protests, the government has adopted a stringent test. Only a criminal conviction, a police caution or a civil injunction against the violent partner will be acceptable. Few women are able to provide the level of evidence necessary to secure a conviction against a violent partner. This is partly due to the very private nature of domestic violence where witnesses are rare, and partly due to an entrenched racist and sexist police and prosecutorial culture in which there is a complete lack of will to respond to domestic violence. Even if a response is forthcoming it is usually inappropriate or at times even oppressive. Police cautions, too, are extremely rare since they require an admission of guilt by the offending party. Court orders in the form of injunctions are difficult to obtain due to lack of access to legal aid, competent immigration lawyers and adequate legal advice. Linguistic difficulties and cultural constraints are added obstacles in obtaining the required forms of evidence. Under the terms of the concession, medical evidence is unacceptable. This is based on an assumption made by the Home Office that doctors are corrupt and capable of manipulation by women intent on deceiving the Home Office and circumventing the immigration rules! By ignoring the reality of the lives of countless black women in this way, the state's response begs the question: is there a real will or commitment to remove the discriminatory consequences of the 'one-year rule' for black women?

The real impact of the 'one-year rule' lies in the way in which black women, and in particular women from impoverished backgrounds who need state assistance, are disempowered and marginalised. Whilst the rule is applied to men in equal measure, it is women who are the overwhelming victims of male violence and so it affects them disproportionately. Apart from being racist – the failure to recognise the right of all black women to protection from violence and abuse – the rule has the effect of reinforcing and distorting patriarchal relations within the black family. The rule distorts marital relations in that it gives the settled husband more power and control over his wife and constructs her as an economic and social appendage of her husband. The rule thus serves simultaneously to reinforce both patriarchal and racial domination.

It has to be said that as much as the 'one-year rule' can become a convenient weapon of control over women by men, a woman can also gain some power and status in the family in circumstances where the husband's immigration status is dependent on hers. Sometimes, a woman will come to SBS having experienced domestic violence from a man whose right to reside in the UK is dependent on his marriage to her. If the marriage breaks down, he is liable to deportation. Such a woman may ask us to write a letter to the Home Office requesting the man's deportation as a means of protection for herself. We do not accede to such requests, because in our view it would amount to legitimising racist immigration rules and practices, and the physical and mental brutality that often accompanies the implementation of these rules.

Instead our first priority would be to help the woman to seek protection by utilising the criminal and civil justice system and, if necessary, to refer her to a safe house or refuge. We would not consider pursuing deportation as a means of protection for any woman since this would, in effect, involve trading the rights of the individual woman for the collective rights of the community. Balancing the rights of the individual with that of the community is difficult to get right within the context of a racist society. Such tensions pervade much of our casework, but we consider that our practice avoids the pitfalls of lending conscious or unconscious support to institutionalised racism and at the same time ensures that there is maximum protection for the woman. We have tried to develop a practice that is simultaneously anti-racist and anti-sexist. The new thinking can be translated into practice. If we can stretch our thinking as feminists to understand how our practices can have consequences in perpetuating racism, it is also incumbent for anti-racist activists and policy makers to examine racist policies and practices for their effects on the control of women in our families and communities. Incorporating feminist insights in the formulation of strategies to combat institutionalised racism is essential for the advancement of racial equality for all in our communities.

Policing, black women and issues of accountability

As the Stephen Lawrence inquiry was drawing to a close, SBS was helping an Asian woman, Perkash Walia, in her contacts with the police. Her ex-boyfriend, who also happened to be a practising priest at a Southall Hindu temple, had assaulted her. Perkash suffered a near fatal knife attack to her neck and a deep six-inch knife cut to her thigh, as well as beatings, kicking and attempted strangulation. Neighbours and witnesses to the actual attack called the police, who failed to apprehend the perpetrator although his whereabouts were well known until he fled to India. The police failed to carry out essential investigations or obtain crucial forensic evidence or witness statements.

Following a period in hospital where she underwent emergency surgery, it was left to Perkash to carry out her own investigations over a period of fifteen months, in circumstances where it had became apparent to her that the police were not investigating the matter professionally with the thoroughness that it deserved. Working on the assumption that women who experience domestic violence 'waste police time', they merely went through the motions, while Perkash obtained photographic evidence of her injuries and collected crucial information on the whereabouts of her assailant and the witnesses. Three months after she was assaulted, she found herself retrieving her own blood-stained clothing from the scene of her assault and presented this to the police! Some twelve months later, when her ex-boyfriend returned to this country to resume his post at the Hindu temple, Perkash monitored his movements until she alerted the police and insisted on his arrest. To her dismay, she discovered that the police had no evidence against him except a cursory four-page statement that was taken some two months after the assault on her.

It was at this point that she contacted SBS to put pressure on the police to charge her assailant and ensure that they carried out the investigations properly. The case eventually went to trial, at which Perkash was made to shoulder the burden of the entire prosecution case due to a complete failure on the part of the police to investigate and retain crucial independent evidence. The trial depended simply on her word against that of her assailant. Fortunately the jury chose to believe her, and her assailant was found guilty of grievous bodily harm. He was given a lengthy sentence of imprisonment. Perkash felt vindicated, because she had persisted and achieved some degree of justice in the face of police intransigence, and because the presiding judge at the conclusion of the case raised concerns about the police investigation. But she achieved her vindication despite rather than because of the criminal justice system.

The case highlights how Perkash's experience of domestic violence was compounded by police racism and sexism in circumstances where it is difficult to see where sexism ends and racism begins. Her experiences highlight just how institutional racism operates to the detriment of black women, not in a crude or overtly thuggish way but in combination with gender discrimination. The police played on the myth that women in Perkash's circumstances do not pursue criminal charges and on stereotypical assumptions of Asian women as passive, ignorant and unable to articulate their needs and demands, such that they felt able to ignore her at will. They did not expect her to show courage and determination in pursuing justice, not only in pursuing the criminal charges against her assailant, but also in making a formal complaint against the police for their litany of failures in the investigation of the case. What they were unprepared for was an independent woman with an enquiring mind of her own who wants to ensure that the police are compelled to account for their neglect of duty.

In many ways, Perkash's case echoes the criticisms made of the police in the investigation of the Stephen Lawrence murder. Yet, her experiences do not sit very comfortably within the boundaries of orthodox debates on racism, since they expose not only state racism but also the interplay of racial and patriarchal power.

Driven by the experiences of Perkash and countless other black women, who are similarly 'underpoliced' as a result of the operation of multicultural 'culturally sensitive' approaches, SBS has attempted to develop the debate on policing and black people beyond the narrow confines of the policing of racial violence. Our aim is multifold: to show the connections between the policing of domestic violence and racial violence in respect of police failures; to show that racist policing needs to be measured not in terms of its impact on vague notions of the 'black community', but in terms of its impact on the most disadvantaged and vulnerable sections of the community; and to strengthen the demand for police accountability. We are witness to many cases where the police routinely fail black women, as does the mechanism for police accountability through the discredited police complaints system, which has proved itself to be unable or unwilling to discipline or charge officers for their misconduct. Perkash herself is now engaged in challenging the reluctance of the complaints system to look at her complaints by invoking her rights under the Human Rights Act.

Perkash Walia's case also illustrates how state and community relations function to undermine women's rights. Some of the trustees of the Hindu temple who shielded Prakash's assailant were leaders of the community, having served on the local authority. They sit with the police on a regular basis in consultative forums, but are just as likely to be consulted informally. Both the police and these so-called leaders are thus undemocratically and secretively in the business of delineating the boundaries of police involvement in the community. In the process they seek to define the community, who makes up its constituent parts and who or what is to be policed. Needless to say, women needing protection from the police against domestic violence do not figure in definitions of the 'community' or on the 'community' agenda.

The issue of 'police and community relations' needs to be re-framed in ways which make the process democratic and transparent to all members of the community, including women who are all too often excluded from consultation processes on community 'race relations'. Ultimately, any analysis of institutionalised racism should also be about demystifying how the power brokers within our communities are able to maintain their patriarchal power bases and sanction violence against women, and so prove to be unrepresentative of the community on the question of racial and social justice.

One important aspect of the post Lawrence policing landscape has been the way in which the police have attempted to address the central recommendations of the Macpherson Report. One solution that seems to be rearing its ugly head is racial awareness training, although this has been effectively discredited as a means of countering racism within institutions, largely due to its misguided focus on individual prejudices (Sivanandan 1985). Then, the police seem to be pursuing with some vigour a recruitment drive to employ more police officers from the ethnic minorities. But we are wary of this, since it does not go far in dismantling institutionalised racism. Institutionalised racism is to do with how racist processes, practices, and policies and outcomes are structurally embedded in the institution with little or no effective accountability in respect of abuse of power or neglect of duty. In such institutions black officers may be no different from white officers.

Since the Stephen Lawrence case, we have received increasing requests by the police to address police conferences and train senior and rank-and-file officers on the issues of race, domestic violence and forced marriages. This has led to heated internal debates within SBS as to how far we can or should work with the police. During the Tory years, we grew up skilled in the art of oppositional politics. There was no other space in which to engage with the state. It was a vast impenetrable edifice which we had to oppose relentlessly, since many of the civil and economic rights of the vast majority of working-class and minority people were being dismantled. But under New Labour a few doors have opened up – the Stephen Lawrence case itself being a case in point – providing an opportunity to enter into a dialogue and influence the various state institutions.

Within SBS, we are all too aware of the limitations of the New Labour institutions. It is not so much a question of whether it is better to be inside or outside institutions – change occurs at both levels – but a question of how we can avoid being co-opted, as we are discovering in our experiences with the forced and arranged marriage working party. Yet the dilemma is that without some kind of engagement, however ineffective, we close off even the remote possibility that we can affect police policy. One of the most dangerous outcomes of non-involvement is that groups with no track record on feminist or even anti-racist issues will be perceived as the 'experts' and the voices that are listened to, whilst at the same time feminist groups like ours are relegated into the margins. There are no easy answers here but we are still learning how to develop skills of negotiation with the state without compromising our autonomy.

We have seen that very little is achieved through training police officers because we have no means of holding the police accountable. Similarly, multi-agency or inter-agency policing – a means by which all manner of state and voluntary agencies come together to develop common strategies for combating a number of social problems including domestic violence – can be but a smokescreen, giving the illusion that something is done in partnership. In the absence of more resources and accountability, there is little if any redistribution of power.

Anti-racist strategies have a lot to gain by drawing on the insights developed by black feminist perspectives on policing. Most important of all, our insights can help to create alliances between anti-racists and feminists. Such an alliance can do more than just expose the lack of democratic and adequate policing; it may also help the anti-racist movement to undertake a long-overdue introspection. By doing so, we would all be able to challenge more effectively the reactionary developments and prejudices that exist towards other minorities within our communities for example, or the emergent sexist black masculine identity which many youths (Asian and African-Caribbean) have embraced either in cultural or political religious forms.

The case of Zoora Shah: the politics of multiculturalism and religious identity

Since the Salman Rushdie affair, in a climate where religion has become the main mark of identity, what counts as anti-racism is often sometimes nothing more that a battle to preserve religious identity. This has posed problems for feminists and progressive anti-racists alike. The ongoing SBS case of Zoora Shah highlights the problems that we face when religious fundamentalists with their patriarchal and authoritarian agendas also use the anti-racist and multiculturalist language for specific ends: to police the boundaries of community and to maintain hegemonic control over local resources and institutions. Religious fundamentalist movements, in this country as elsewhere, have a political agenda that involves at its heart control over women's sexuality by maintaining traditional structures of the family at all costs (Sahgal and Yuval-Davis 1992). The interplay of anti-racism and religious fundamentalism therefore poses a serious and urgent question for all progressive anti-racists: what do we mean by anti-racism and what alliances are possible in the struggle against racism?

Zoora Shah is a Pakistani Muslim woman from Bradford who, following divorce from her first husband, killed a man after years of experiencing sexual and economic exploitation at his hands. She was convicted of murder and jailed for life in 1993, and thereafter SBS initiated a campaign to free her. The aim of the campaign was to expose the criminal justice system and the law for its male bias and for its failure to acknowledge or understand the desperate and powerless contexts in which abused women kill. In 1998 Zoora Shah lost her fight to overturn her conviction for murder at the Court of Appeal. She had chosen to remain silent at her original trial due to the powerful cultural codes of honour and shame that bind Asian women to silence. The court's response was to reject the cultural constraints she experienced by suggesting that she was an 'undeserving woman' who had 'no honour left to salvage'! Despite substantial contemporaneous medical evidence and witnesses who could testify that Zoora Shah was a depressed and destitute woman, the court delivered a profoundly racist and sexist judgement in which it betrayed a complete unwillingness to grapple with the reality of sexual abuse and domestic violence. Instead the court condemned Zoora for having had the misfortune to be thrown onto the margins of society following divorce and left to fend for herself and her young children.

In a desperate attempt to reduce her twenty-year tariff – the minimum period she was required to serve in prison under a life sentence – we felt that we had no choice but to seek the support of religious leaders in Bradford and elsewhere. We were only too aware that the reality of multicultural politics means that the state is more likely to heed the demands of Muslim community leaders than those of a feminist group such as ourselves who are perceived to be 'inauthentic' and somehow outside the 'natural' community. Such perceptions highlight the limits of our power, even when organised collectively as women. We found ourselves having to adopt a different language in order to obtain the support of a wide range of Muslim organisations. We took on a language of human rights and humanity, in place of our accustomed feminist language of autonomy and choice, arguing that Islam is not incompatible with compassion and tolerance. We chose to emphasise the need for the state and community to show compassion and mercy to women like Zoora Shah, rather than focus on our demand for justice for women who kill in self-defence or provocation in response to male violence.[12]

The response of these community leaders and organisations to our request for support for Zoora Shah has been interesting. Out of some six hundred Muslim organisations (including mosques) that we have contacted only a bare handful has given total unqualified support. Most Muslim leaders, ranging from fundamentalists to those who would view themselves as moderate liberals, have been silent or have refused to support the campaign. One reason is that, among fundamentalists and liberals alike, to be seen to support Zoora Shah is tantamount to acknowledging the patriarchal power relations that exist within our communities. That would upset their goal: to introduce Sharia law (Muslim personal law) or variations of it, as an alternative to the present civil law in the UK as a means of controlling Muslim women.

Yet more interesting has been the response of some Muslim organisations that have supported Zoora Shah, not on the basis that she is a woman who has the right to defend herself against male violence, but on a different basis: the need to oppose the British state as racist. According to them, Zoora Shah is discriminated against as a Muslim woman. The barbarity of the British state exhibited in the long-term prison sentence is, they argue, tantamount to a slow and tortuous death. Yet these same Muslim organisations unequivocally accept that if Zoora Shah lived in an Islamic state, subject to Sharia laws, the proper punishment for her 'crimes' would be death. (A quick death under Sharia laws is considered more humane than a long-term prison sentence.) They argue that strict adherence to the Koran would find her as sinning because she has killed, and furthermore as sinning because she did not take steps to end the abuse. They remain wilfully blind to the fact that there are many obstacles, including those placed by religious and community leaders, preventing women like Zoora Shah from escaping male violence. The message of such sentiments is clear. Domestic violence and other forms of male violence in areas such as Bradford are to remain taboo subjects.

The chilling nature of this response aside, it is curious to note that one reason sometimes given by these leaders for the need to temper Sharia justice is that 'we are British and will abide by the laws of this country'. This assertion of 'Britishness' may appear bewildering, given the fact that Islamic revivalism in this country has fostered a Muslim identity precisely in opposition to the British state and to the 'West' in general. It is also ironical that this 'Britishness' extends to Muslim women only insofar as they conform to traditional roles and norms. Any attempts by Muslim women to assert their 'Britishness', for example by determining their own sexuality, would be met with severe punishment for being a 'Western' practice. What is noteworthy is how these voices determine women's roles and the boundaries of the community, and how the agenda of those who claim to represent the community changes according to their bid for power within the family and within the state.

In Bradford, for instance, an Asian lesbian woman was hounded out of town by religious fundamentalists who had made an issue of her sexuality when contesting power locally in the last elections. In other cases, many Asian women have been dragged back to their violent and abusive families by so called 'bounty hunters', who are in fact networks of criminal gangs, businesses and often religious institutions whose aim is to police women and to impose traditional roles upon them.

The support we have had from some Muslim organisations/leaders in the Zoora Shah case should not deflect attention from the underlying patriarchal, and even misogynist, trends within all religious fundamentalist movements. What the response of some Muslim leaders to the case illustrates is the complex ways in which newly formed religious identities have become enmeshed with anti-racist identities, and also how religious fundamentalists use the language of multiculturalism or anti-racism to wield power and control over territories and resources.

In the recent past, we have seen an attempt by some Muslim fundamentalist groups to inject a religious dimension to the phenomenon of racist attacks and racial violence. In an unprecedented front-page piece devoted to predominantly African-Caribbean and Asian victims of racial attacks and murder, the *Guardian* newspaper crossed a threshold. It was a historical moment, recognition of the suffering and courage of many black people in the face of racial violence. And yet the very next day, in the *Guardian* letters page, a representative of the Muslim (fundamentalist) organisation Al Nisa pointedly reminded us that many of the Asian victims of racial violence printed on the preceding day were in fact Muslim.

Whilst it is undeniably true that in some instances Islamaphobia may result in Muslims being targeted at specific moments, the attempt to assert and 'elevate' a 'Muslim' experience of racism as distinct from the racial violence experienced by other communities can only be divisive. What we therefore see unfolding is that whilst gender oppression is downplayed in debates on anti-racism, religious discrimination is being overplayed. Such an over-emphasis of ethnic and religious difference and identity appears to be the main goal of community/religious leaders and, sadly, some academics and intellectuals. But it elevates the experiences of one particular community and singles it out for some kind of preferential treatment at the expense of a unified set of demands for the benefit of all. We cannot help but feel that the aim of such commentators is not to root out an injustice but to further a hidden agenda by creating a climate whereby racism is defined and perceived as attacks on specific religious/cultural identities only. Those who seek power within our communities, and the state too, usually in consultation with community leaders, have attempted to create differences where none in fact exist. This has important political implications, not just for the anti-racist struggles, but also for the feminist movement, and particularly and specifically for Asian women's projects that struggle to maintain a feminist unity across the various religious and ethnic backgrounds.

Within the official language of multiculturalism, differences amongst Asians have been distorted. It is of course important to recognise new or even different variants of racism, but many of the differences that are being emphasised are absurd and exaggerated. Recent Home Office research on the needs of Pakistani (read Muslim) women in the face of domestic violence[13] highlighted the problems of the 'one-year rule' and the concept of *izzat* or honour as if these were exclusive to Pakistani women. There was nothing in the experiences cited by the research that could in fact be singled out as being exclusively 'Muslim'. Yet the signs are that social policy is heading towards this kind of spurious recognition of difference, which merely serves to legitimise the creation of new (fragmented) identities of Sikhs, Muslims and Hindus.

In some Asian women's groups, the transformation of identities from an inclusive Asian identity to exclusive religious ones has given rise to very real problems. For example, in one Asian woman's group in East London, Muslim women made demands for a separate space within the centre in which to meet as Muslim women only. They did not make this demand because they faced dis-crimination and exclusion as a minority within the centre, but because their religious identity, formulated in opposition to 'others', would not permit them to seek out common and shared experiences as Asian women living in a racist society. This kind of dilemma is not easily resolved. But it does point towards the need to create a secular feminist space which can guarantee religious tolerance and diversity, allowing for constant negotiation as to the use of the space for all women, without fear of being straitjacketed into fixed identities.

So, in a climate where multiculturalism is here to stay, to whom should the state listen: those who argue that it is racist to intervene in the internal affairs of the community, or to those like us who argue that failure to intervene to protect women from domestic violence, forced marriages and other abuses amounts to a specific form of institutional racism? This is where the language of human rights can become a powerful tool for black women in their struggle for self-deter-mination. Indeed, the human rights discourse is the main discourse now available to us to counter the disturbing trends of multiculturalism which serve to reinforce patriarchal power relations within the family and undemocratic political representation within our communities. The human rights discourse can help us to avoid the pitfalls inherent when the language of anti-racism is appropriated by religious fundamentalists, conservatives and bigots. But even on the terrain of human rights, the path is not straightforward. The challenge that we will face in the coming years is to make our voices prevail, as the political battles between feminists and conservative and fundamentalist forces in our communities are played out in the legal arena under the terms of the newly created Human Rights Act.

It is precisely the language of human rights to which we turned, to assist us to force the state to formulate policies to protect Asian and other minority women from forced marriages. The Home Office, through a working party, of which we are members, is at present involved in a nation-wide consultation exercise within the various Asian communities to examine the extent of the problem of forced marriages and to force the various Asian community leaders to take overall responsibility. The consultation exercise is largely with religious and conservative leaders and institutions, and not with many of the feminist Asian women's organisations with a track record in providing alternatives and choices to a life free from violence and other constrictions to women's freedom. The dangers are obvious. On the one hand, the suspicion remains that, in classic multicultural mould, the state will want to be seen to be 'culturally sensitive' and so will allow community leaders to determine the solutions rather than be led by the women who experience forced marriages. At the same time this will allow the state to abrogate from its own responsibility to protect and enforce the human rights of Asian women and girls.

Paradoxically, whilst the Home Office has stated that 'mature multiculturalism should not be an excuse for moral blindness', it has paved the way to ensuring that the outcome is as flawed as the process by the very way in which the working party is constituted. It is drawn from so called 'representatives' of the various Asian communities, Muslim, Sikhs and Hindus. There was even an attempt to re-invent the SBS representative on the working party – Hannana Siddiqui – so that she is perceived to be a representative of the Muslim community rather than as a representative of SBS which has consistently organised across the ethnic and religious divides. But the process of engagement with the state at this level (which is new to us) does point to the dangers of co-option, particularly when members of the working party (including its figurehead Lord Ahmed) have demanded absolute loyalty to the working party.

At present, we are therefore involved in the highly difficult exercise of influenc-ing the agenda and outcome of the working party. Our aim is to include the voices of women at every stage of the consultation process and to prevent co-option by ensuring that there is a strong, independent and critical movement of black progressive feminist voices on the outside which will hold us and the state accountable. It remains to be seen how far the state will go in enforcing the human rights of women and how far it will go in ensuring that the issue is not linked to demands for more immigration controls.[14]

Multicultural policies and perceptions are an important dimension of the many-faceted nature of institutional racism. They must be challenged because of the devastating effect they have in perpetuating patriarchal power within minority communities. Respect for diversity and the right to equality are important concepts. But whilst much is made by community leaders about both, in reality recognition of 'diversity' is invoked as a means of controlling women within minority communities, whilst 'equality' has come to mean, in the gift of the state, a limited right to be different and nothing more. The result is that equality based on race and gender is not guaranteed between communities and even within them.[15]

Making connections between anti-racism and anti-sexism

One of the key recommendations of the Macpherson Report is the need to tackle racism through education. Education has always been one of central targets of much anti-racist activity.

It was therefore a surprise when we received an invitation from a local school – Villiers Secondary School – to work with fourteen-year-old boys and girls, not on the issue of racism, but on the use of sexist language in schools, which has become a particular problem. We saw the invitation not just as an opportunity to challenge the use of sexist language, sexual harassment in the workplace and violence against women in general, but also to make the connections between racism and sexism.

For us, the use of sexist language amongst youth in our communities is in part the result of the influence of deeply misogynist and often violent rap music within popular black culture. Such music, which mythologises the likes of Mike Tyson, finds followers amongst boys and girls alike. In our work with them it was clear that they saw different forms of offensive language and behaviour as hierarchically ordered – sexism was not as offensive as racism. But for many boys in particular, what was deemed to be entirely out of bounds and intolerable was any slur directed at their religion. A new black machismo politics is prevalent in black youth culture, one that succeeds in constructing black masculinity by denigrating women, perceiving them to be responsible for the emasculation of black men. In some of the rap music that we heard, women were placed on a par with the state as the enemy. If women are so grossly violated by the new forms of cultural resistance against racism, the development of progressive anti-racist strategies is a challenge indeed. Whilst we have attempted to confront such challenges it is clear to us that our struggles would be more effective if black male anti-racist activists also began to address sexism in a systematic way in their anti-racist work.

Refugees and anti-racism

One of the most instructive aspects of the entire Lawrence debate has been the role and involvement of the media. Across the political spectrum the media lined up in support of the Lawrence campaign. But much of the media coverage could not mention the Lawrence family without also adding the word 'dignity' or 'respectability'. It seemed as if the right-wing papers, and possibly even the liberal ones, were embracing the Lawrence family because they were the embodiment of aspiring middle England values who had been grievously let down by the state. A closer examination of the *Daily Mail*'s 'outrage', for instance, reveals not so much a concern with racial justice but a preoccupation with class values. The silence surrounding the appalling police harassment and persecution of the other main victim of the case – Duwayne Brooks – was very significant. It is noteworthy that while the *Daily Mail* spearheaded the campaign for the killers of Stephen Lawrence to be brought to justice, it also consistently demonised refugees in this country.

In our view, the treatment of refugees – at a legislative and socio-economic level – has become one of the most urgent tasks confronting anti-racist groups. Refugees are without question the most vulnerable section of society, stripped of even the most basic rights and relegated to not even second- but third-class status. The dehumanisation of refugees continues unabated with the introduction of detention, dispersal and voucher policies.

At SBS, we witness with increasing frustration and anger the ways in which asylum-seekers are made to depend for their survival on charity, to live in sub-standard accommodation isolated from any community of friends they may have and denied access to effective legal representation. We have already witnessed black women subjected to domestic violence and to the 'one year rule', who when attempting to apply for housing under the National Assistance Act are dispersed to isolated places such as Great Yarmouth! But one of the most worrying aspects of the forced dispersal of refugees is that it will increase their vulnerability to racial attacks. They have no ready-made community to which to appeal in times of trouble, so the task of mobilising around cases of racial attacks becomes even more difficult, even in situations which attract national attention.

Refugees are marginalised and subject to intense racism and hostility, not only from the British state, but also from the various settled black communities where a 'pecking order' politics prevails. It is precisely on the question of internal conflict and prejudice within black communities that much anti-racist work needs to concentrate.

Hostility and prejudice amongst the Asian community in Southall against new refugees from Somalia and Eastern Europe is rife. Somalian refugees make up the largest group of refugees in Southall and they are viewed in the same way that many white inhabitants of Southall viewed Asians in the 1950s, 1960s and 1970s. Many Asians can be heard commenting about how Somalians are 'taking over our jobs, housing and entitlements'. Such comments are frequently heard from those who fought for racial justice on the streets, in education and at the workplace, and marched on demonstrations in memory of Blair Peach in 1979. There are cases of Somalians being attacked by Asian youths. In such circumstances it is not hard to imagine that those victims would not be able to rely on the Southall community to support them in the face of racial violence from white or Asian youths or, indeed, the police.

Our work in the local Southall schools has also revealed that the very word 'refugee' has become a derogatory term. Many Asian school children use the term as a form of abuse and insult. They mimic the women refugees of Eastern European and Roma origin who can sometimes be seen begging in the main shopping thoroughfares of Southall. It is disheartening to know that despite the Blair Peach years, the forging of a radical politics of resistance against racism in Southall has been short-lived as far as the majority of the community is concerned.

When we asked teachers why the youth failed to see the parallels between their own parent's history of early migration and those of the new refugees, the startling answer was not that were unable to see the connections, but that they did not want to see them.

Conclusion: building bridges

We need to be wary of the ways in which the current reduction of the black progressive identities of the 1970s to ethnic and religious identities of the 1990s affects unity of struggle in defeating racism. This also means that we have to be careful about what anti-racist struggles constitute, whether or not waged under the term 'black'.

The reality is that at this particular juncture we can't really speak of any solid movements, be they feminist or anti-racist. We can only speak of fragmentation of movements. A united movement in this context will be unachievable, if imposed from above as opposed to taking root at community level. Current weaknesses in our engagement with resistance politics may be due to lack of vision, but are also the reality of the context in which we find ourselves. We have seen a shift in many of our struggles for equality and justice away from the political arena into the legal arena. Victories ranging from the Sara Thornton and Kiranjit Ahluwalia campaigns to those of Joan Fransisco and Stephen Lawrence have been achieved by the creative use of the law. The implementation of the Human Rights Act has also added another legal weapon to our armoury, which must be deployed. But such legal initiatives are occurring in a political vacuum.

Many silences resulting in the marginalisation and invisibility of black women have been broken by black feminist activism in this country. The survival of SBS into the twenty-first century is indeed a matter to be celebrated because it represents the resilience and courage of many black women in this country who have tried to make the transition from passive subjects to active political agents of change. Many of the women who visit our centre are political. The demands they make are political. The insights and critiques they have into their own predicament are profoundly political. Their experiences illuminate not just how women experience oppression, but how racism and other systems of oppression connect and relate to each other, which in turn challenges us to think of new ways of resisting state and community oppression.

Those with power in the community and within the state find new means of silencing us all the time. Our aim in SBS is to find ways of trying to stay one step ahead. We can only do that by building bridges across each other's experiences and insights in order first to understand and then to tear down the walls of state power and privilege. We will need allies within the wider feminist, anti-racist, trade union, gay and lesbian and other progressive forums/movements. Moreover, in the midst of our celebrations of survival and resistance, if we fail to critically examine our pasts in order to imagine our futures, we run the risk of being afflicted by a cyclical *déjà vu* condition. Standing on the threshold of the twenty-first century, every one of us involved in anti-racist struggles bears the responsibility of finding a cure.

Notes

1 See below for further discussion on the limitations of such state-led anti-racist initiatives.

2 The term black is not without its problems. As long ago as 1983, Floya Anthias and Nira Yuval-Davies cautioned against the use of the term. They argued that the term was problematic since it perpetuates the myth that racism is only applicable to those of a different colour and fails to take account of the diversity of ethnic experiences and the political and economic positions of different ethnic groups in relation to each other. Their arguments are particularly pertinent in the wake of the racism we have seen unleashed in the UK against refugees from the Balkan states.

3 In 1989, the Ayatollah Khomeni issued a *fatwa* against the writer Salman Rushdie for committing the sin of blasphemy in writing *The Satanic Verses*. The affair had the effect of giving an increasingly reactionary but militant section of Muslims within the Asian communities the confidence to make a number of demands based on a new-found religious identity. Many of those demands were made in response to real or perceived racism and had much to do with the need to maintain cultural and religious autonomy in the affairs of the community, especially over the family. SBS reacted by founding the organisation Women Against Fundamentalism with other women from across a range of religious and ethnic divides. The focus of our work was on British state racism, the rise of religious fundamentalism in all religions, and the control of women which lies at the heart of all religious fundamentalist movements. What was unique about the group was that women came together not on the basis of their identity, although differences amongst ourselves were recognised, but on the basis of a shared common agenda for confronting racism, sexism and religious fundamentalism simultaneously

4 See for example SBS (1990), in which we document in some detail the failure of the state and indigenous community institutions to address the needs of women.

5 See for example publications such as CARF 1981 and 1991.

6 Dr Barnor Hesse (Senior Lecturer, Department of Sociology and Anthropology, University of East London) addressing a conference on the Macpherson Report and its implication for local government, organised by the London Borough of Islington, November 1999.

7 Institutional racism is defined in the Macpherson Report as follows: 'The collective failure of an organisation to provide appropriate and professional services to people because of their colour, culture or ethnic origin. It can be seen or detected in processes, attitudes and behaviour which amount to discrimination through unwitting prejudice, thoughtlessness and racist stereotyping which disadvantage minority ethnic people.'

8 Multiculturalism is the process by which the state mediates relations between itself and minority communities. Its precedents lie in British colonial policies. Multiculturalism constructs minority communities as monolithic or homogeneous entities with no internal divisions. In its most progressive sense, the multicultural project does recognise difference and diversity as the basis for encouraging positive race relations, as opposed to previous notions of assimilation and integration. But the problem is that the acknowledgement of diversity does not translate into providing equality of opportunity or choice either to minority communities as whole or to the less powerful within such communities. Indeed, by creating a layer of community representatives (usually unelected and representing conservative and religious agendas) who claim to be the 'authentic' voice of the community and with whom the state consults, the principles of accountability and local democracy are bypassed by both the state and by the power brokers. Needless to say, multiculturalism does not address state racism but actually strengthens other systems of power relations within the community.

9 Our casework on police response to domestic violence, for instance, shows how black women and even their assailants often find themselves overpoliced – subject to excessive state responses! Often the police will ask them to produce their passports as evidence of their right to stay in the country. In some cases, women are themselves arrested and subject to harassment and even violence from the police.

10 One glaring example of how women in British immigration law experienced racial discrimination differently concerned the notorious practice of virginity testing of Asian women from India which came to light in 1979. The aim of the practice was to ascertain whether Asian women who came to the UK to join their husbands were bona fide financees. Underlining this test was that the assumption that Asian women are virgins before they marry, so if they were not virgins at the point of entry then they were ineligible to enter the country. This was one example of racial and sexual abuse that was officially sanctioned by the operation of immigration rules. An outcry led to the practice being stopped. Those who were appalled by the practice decried it as racist, but few within the wider anti-racist movement articulated the ways in which it also amounted to a violation of Asian women's bodies.

11 The rule is discriminatory in that it denies black women their rights when compared to women in the majority community who have been promised 'a life without fear' (see Cabinet Office, Women's Unit 1999).

12 In other contexts we have similarly addressed many Hindus in this country who have, since the destruction of the Babri Masjid, a fifteenth-century mosque in India in 1992, taken on a right-wing, nationalist and often fundamentalist Hindu identity. For more details of our campaigns against Hindu fundamentalism see Patel 1995.

13 See for example Choudry 1996.

14 Some people, including Asian men and women, have stated that the way to deal with forced arranged marriage is to bring back the so-called 'primary purpose' rule. The rule was a draconian and racist piece of immigration legislation which brought about untold misery and suffering for many Asian families who wished to be united. The rule was finally abolished in 1997. So far the state has resisted the temptation to link the issue of forced arranged marriage to immigration control.

15 Hananna Siddiqui resigned from the Home Office working party in June 2000, at around the same time that it published its report *A Choice by Right*. Her resignation was brought about by the inclusion of the option of mediation (essentially a process by which women are reconciled with their families who have forced them into the marriage) as a legitimate strategy of action for state agencies to adopt. The failure to condemn mediation as a strategy undermines the entire ethos of the report, which is to recognise that forced marriage is an abuse of women's human rights. The report therefore reiterates the multicultural approach to minority women, ensuring that differential human rights standards apply to them. This approach leaves women who are forced into marriage at risk of further violence and abuse and without state protection. The approach is also racist since mediation has been discarded as a valid option in official policy on domestic violence for women in the majority community.

9 Anti-deportation campaigning in the West Midlands

Gargi Bhattacharyya and John Gabriel

In recent years, academic writing on issues of race and identity has been characterised by a preoccupation with notions of change. Echoing wider debates in social theory, the talk has been about the accelerating experiences of postmodernity and globalisation, with their attendant formations of hybridity, fragmentation, performative identities and strategic essentialisms – and, in many ways, these terms have helped to illuminate contemporary events. Clearly, there are changes in the shape of our world and in our relations to each other – no one doubts the significance of globalising capital in all our lives. However, this exclusive focus on the shifting determinants of identity formation has distracted from more everyday and less glamorous issues.

Sadly, for those trying to organise resistance, the issues troubling black communities[1] in Britain remain tediously familiar and unchanging. Poor housing and healthcare, inadequate access to education and training, high unemployment, low incomes – such ills are nothing new. These issues have preoccupied community-based organisations throughout the period of post-war settlement in Britain. Their continuing prevalence reveals the extent to which recent interest in global, epochal shifts fails to register these mundane non-shifting events. The growth in significance of transnational blocs including the European Union, the proliferation of new media and communications technologies, and the expansion of service industries and global production lines have collectively helped to shape new global alignments and divisions. Yet, despite the significance of such changes, for many the everyday concerns of gaining and keeping work, finding somewhere reasonable to live and seeking protection from abuse and injustice remain much the same.

Such has been the sea-change in writing and thinking about ethnicity and forms of racialisation that it is easy to forget the debates of just a few years ago. The move towards questions of culture and identity (see e.g. Hall 1992; Gilroy 1993a; Bhabha 1994; and Brah 1996) suggests that we have all learned the lessons of the 1970s and 1980s. The polarised debates characterising those decades – between 'radicals' who linked racism to wider socio-economic structures and processes and 'reformers' who saw solutions to problems in terms of legal reforms, and between 'anti-racists' who defined the problem in terms of racism against those 'multi-culturalists' who allegedly saw the solution in terms of promoting cultural diversity and those using black experience to challenge white sociology –

have largely been eclipsed. No longer do we accuse each other of being stooges of the race relations industry and/or of taking the state's blood money to be the sell-out gate-keeping buffer zone between disaffected black communities and the sources of power. In the late 1990s much academic debate within sociology and cultural studies has vacated the seemingly old-fashioned terrain of politics and policy, no doubt partly to avoid those angry exchanges and factionalism of yesteryear. Nowadays, the talk is of essential black or traditional ethnic identities versus new hybrid or syncretic identities and cultural forms (see e.g. Werbner and Modood 1997), of white ethnicities (see e.g. Hickman and Walter 1995) and racisms between black communities.

Despite these developments, the relationship between the academy and race relations industry remains fraught, albeit on somewhat different terms. These days, academics who want their work to be 'relevant' and who are under pressure to earn research funding are often forced to negotiate the neo-liberal framework of contract consultancy and competitive tendering and the murky, compromise-inducing world of local authorities, quangos and government. Moreover, this post-Thatcherite climate has encouraged particular ties between government and the more public-sector-oriented academic fields of social and public policy, ties compounded by the retreat of more radical, critical and, some would say, head-in-the-clouds, social science approaches to the study of 'race' and ethnicity with all their talk of third spaces, diasporic cultural forms and fragmented subjects.

However, contrary to current thinking, extreme versions of which write – off campaigns and movements in preference for a discourse without subjects and dominated instead by *new* technologies and other global forces, the emphasis in this chapter is on first-hand experiences of immigration control and campaign activity and the persistence of *old* forms of exclusion. Attempts to organise resistance to the everyday hardships of poverty and state violence rarely figure in discussions which emphasise, instead, changing ethnic alignments and diverse forms of representation. Important though these developments are, they have served to eclipse discussions of the more mundane, pragmatic, unsexy, everyday world of local politics. Admittedly, developments in Europe and beyond have changed the parameters of such work. But the overall aim of this chapter will be to highlight continuities rather than changes and to accentuate the negative rather than the more celebratory versions of ethnic diversity.

In fact, as far as grass-roots, black community organisations are concerned, many of the earlier warnings with regard to the race relations industry have indeed proved well founded. In many areas black communities have been ill served by their publicly appointed servants and representatives. All too often local authority initiatives have formed bodies with specific responsibility for black communities, particularly in areas such as housing, which have sooner more often than later met with wider resistance and operational difficulties. While the wider resistance to these initiatives seems to be a clear attempt to question black people's entitlement to 'special' (or any?) services, the operational difficulties have included a wide-spread sense that these are the new gatekeepers, structured to keep black people disenfranchised. The wide-scale disbanding of race equality councils across Britain, with little resistance from local communities or local bureaucrats, could be taken as an indication of the extent to which these initiatives failed to gain the trust and support of the communities they were designed to serve (Gabriel 1998).

In our intention to focus on community-based campaigns, our aim is not to romanticise 'the community' and its endless capacity to self-organise a true and organic resistance. We realise that we are in danger of performing this old trick of appealing to the powers of real people ourselves. However, we hope to avoid this fuzzy romance by paying attention to what is effective in certain situations. More than anything we want to salvage a sense that, despite all the bad experiences associated with public institutions and especially those concerned with immigration, community politics in its widest sense can make a difference when nothing else can.

With this in mind, we would like to turn to the work of West Midlands Anti-Deportation Campaign (WMADC). The chapter begins with a brief history of the background to the organisation, followed by two case studies of individual campaigns: Baba Bakhtaura and Prakash Chavrimootoo. The following section will focus on the knowledges which have served to underpin and support such campaigns, before we conclude by reviewing some of the key features of WMADC successes. Our decision to look at this particular organisation is not because it is perfect or because it offers a panacea for the much larger numbers of people caught up in immigration/asylum controls, but because it has worked for the handful of people whose cases it has supported and because without it those people's destinies, two of whose stories we tell, would undoubtedly have been very different.

We want to use this section to identify some features of the context within which WMADC campaigned, notably the changing legal and administrative framework within which immigration and asylum control is implemented and the growth in importance of Europe-wide institutions and practices. Whilst ideas of hybridity, cultural syncretism, ethnic diversity etc. do not play a direct role in conceptualising campaign practice, they do serve to remind us that the terms we use and assumptions underpinning our understanding of anti-racist campaigning around immigration control is not intended to exhaust or monopolise anti-racist discourse but only to add an important dimension to it.

The changing legal framework

From 1980 onwards the UK has witnessed a number of trends in immigration and nationality legislation, notably the growing use of private bodies to police and enforce immigration law and the racialisation of new categories for would-be entrants to the UK (namely, visitors, asylum-seekers) as well as the continuing enforcement and in some instances tightening up of racialised laws and rules governing citizenship, the right of abode, the entry of family members, and the leave to refuse entry and deportation of those whose presence is not conducive to the public good.

Privatisation of immigration control

Privatisation has taken two forms to date. The use of private security firms to guard immigration detainees dates back to the early 1970s. From 1989, Group 4

Total Security held the contract for immigration detention work. This has involved the provision of guards at Harmondsworth, the Queen's Building and the Beehive at Gatwick. Group 4 also transports detainees between detention centres, prisons, the courts and police stations, including to and from bail and appeal hearings. Criticisms of this system include its lack of accountability, the inadequacy of staff training on race relations and the cramped and inadequate buildings. Arguably, the government not only contracted out the security work but it has also contracted out parliamentary scrutiny. In 1995 Stephen Tumin criticised the running of Campsfield, the largest privately run immigration detention centre, for its lack of experienced staff, and for creating a regime experienced as highly stressful by detainees.[2] The failure to provide information and to alleviate the sense of uncertainty was compounded by language differences (*JCWI Bulletin* 5(9) 1995: 2).

The 1987 Carriers' Liability Act made air and sea operators responsible for enabling allegedly inadmissible passengers to enter the UK. This law effectively turned airline and shipping employees into immigration officials without any training or accountability. Although twelve other EU members have similar laws, none are as strict and as tightly enforced as the UK. Moreover, none of the numerous appeals against fines imposed (£2,000 per passenger) have been successful (Cruz 1995: 13). Between 1987 and 1993 a total of £55,557,000 had been imposed, of which £25,044,000 had been paid (Bhabha and Shutter 1994: 238).

Re-inventing the racial wheel: recent changes in law and administration

Racist histories abound, many as yet unwritten, but the history of post-war immigration controls in the UK has been well documented. This has provided the legal and administrative framework within which the West Midlands Anti-Deportation Campaign has worked. In what follows we will highlight those provisions which have been of particular significance for the campaign. The 1971 Immigration Act had already made it easier for white ex-patriots to enter the country than black Commonwealth citizens with British passports with its patriality clause (i.e. having a parent or grandparent born in the UK) and the provision which allowed the Home Secretary to deport an individual whose presence was 'not conducive to the public good'. The 1981 Nationality Act tied nationality to immigration law and in the process created five different categories of nationality: British citizen; British dependent territories citizen, British overseas citizen, British subject status and British protected person status (amended by an Act in 1983 for the Falklanders/Malvinas). A sixth category was subsequently added: British national overseas status for people of Hong Kong (Hong Kong Act 1985 and Hong Kong (British nationality) Order 1986). The patriality clause was replaced by right to abode eligible for those born before 1983 who had a parent born in the UK (*JCWI Handbook*: 2).

The Immigration Act of 1988 removed the rights of settlement of wives and children settled in the UK before 1973, limited the scope for appeals for those facing deportation and increased the powers of immigration inspectors. The effect of the legislation was threefold: it provoked an immediate and dramatic increase in deportations in 1989; it led to an increased police role, both as a source of information and advice and to participate in joint raids, and finally the absence of adequate checking procedures led to the deportation of a number of British citizens, including one who ended up at Lagos airport (Cohen 1994: 65–6). The effect of this legislation can be seen in the leap in numbers of people deported – figures for the first half of 1988 showed 230 deportations, compared to 620 in the second half of 1988 and 720 in the first half of 1989. In 1986 MPs' rights to act on behalf of one of their constituents caught up in immigration procedures were reduced and visas were introduced for selected countries, notably those from the south and third world.

In the 1990s the focus shifted from immigration and nationality in relationship to black British citizens to refugees and asylum. The Asylum and Immigration Appeals Act 1993 introduced new tighter regulations for asylum-seekers such as the fingerprinting of asylum-seekers and their children on arrival, removed rights to housing, speeded up the appeal process against decisions to refuse asylum, and removed the right of appeal to visitors and many students applying to study in the UK (JCWI undated fact sheet on Asylum and Immigration Appeals Act).

In 1994 new restrictions affecting people wishing to enter the UK for different reasons were introduced. This removed the sexist character of a number of rules but did so in a wholly restrictive way. For example, young women aged 18–21 and widowed mothers under 65 have no special claims under rules. The Immigration and Asylum Act of 1996 included attempts to remove benefits for undocumented immigrants and asylum-seekers and by way of a double bind deny asylum-seekers access to employment. It introduced the training of immigration officers to spot 'illegal immigrants'. It also included a new list of countries whose citizens would require a visa to visit the UK, once again from the south and third world and in particular those countries of would-be asylum-seekers where any additional delays could be critical.

Europe-wide developments

Immigration law and policy has increasingly become the prerogative of various European bodies, including the Schengen Group, the Conference on Security and Co-operation in Europe, and the Council of Europe. Now only EU nationals and their families have freedom of movement between EU countries. British citizens and British dependent territories citizens from Gibraltar only (not Hong Kong) thus became EU nationals. Britain thus took a much tougher line than say France, which included its overseas departments like Guadeloupe as part of France for the purposes of EU status (Bhabha and Shutter 1994: 200–1). The premise of EU law is to make movement and rights of settlement as easy as possible for the millions of would-be entrants from other EU countries. This stands in marked contrast to the thrust of domestic immigration law which is to keep down the numbers of black and non-Western people (ibid.: 202).

Moreover, EU nationals do not include third-country nationals, which meant that in 1994 over eight million legal residents were denied the same freedom of movement and settlement within the EU as EU nationals. Amongst these eight million are many who are legally resident in Britain but without British passports. It is estimated that over 100,000 such people live in the Birmingham area. The upshot of the Maastricht Treaty is that immigration is one of a number of policy areas deemed to be outside the sphere of community competence.

The Schengen Treaty which came into effect in March 1995 has eliminated passport checks on the borders of its signatories and replaced these by common visa policies and more stringent checks at external borders (ibid.: 215). Meanwhile the governments and police forces exchange information with regard to restricting the rights and movements of those deemed undesirable aliens. 'Deemed' by whom is an important question because like many EU initiatives on immigration, Schengen policies are shrouded in secrecy with little accountability to the electorates of member states.

The Ad hoc group on immigration is an intergovernmental body concerned with immigration and asylum matters. It met regularly (considering it was supposed to be an *ad hoc* body!) from the late 1980s onwards and has six standing sub-groups (ibid.: 216). Like the Trevi group which deals with illegal immigration, drug trafficking and other international crime (note the ease with which those categories are linked), the *ad hoc* group's activities are characterised by secrecy and a lack of accountability. For example, whereas national traditions, agreements and conventions once dictated policies on family reunion, European policy is now based on the premise that reunification in countries of settlement is kept at a minimum (JCWI 1993: 7)

The British government's attitude to such initiatives has been to support them insofar as they appear to tighten immigration controls and resist them in those instances when the balance appears to be favouring would-be immigrants and asylum-seekers. Take, for example, European proposals in 1995 to refuse refugee status to those fleeing from persecution from non-government as opposed to government agencies. This provision, which would inevitably make refugee status even harder to attain, was conceived in the wake of the Algerian conflict and would apply particularly to Algerians fleeing from extremist fundamentalists. It also would apply to all those fleeing extremists/fascist groups so long as those groups were not in power. Whilst the British government supported this European initiative, it vetoed a proposed European-wide anti-racist initiative (*Guardian*, 25 November 1995).

West Midlands Anti-Deportation Campaign (WMADC)

WMADC brought together a range of local anti-racist activists from various backgrounds, including people with strong roots in the local Asian and African-Caribbean communities, some of whom worked in local community support organisations, trade union activists from various unions, members of the Labour Party and of smaller left parties, and a variety of non-aligned others, many of whom had an extensive background of grass-roots anti-racist work. The organisation has never been affiliated to any particular group or tendency and has consisted of both 'left and anti-racist activists' and those who come into the campaign through their own contact with immigration law, be that through family or friends. WMADC came into existence in response to further tightening of immigration control in 1988. There was already a history of successful campaigning against deportation in the West Midlands, although cases had been fought on an individual basis. WMADC sought to co-ordinate these individual campaigns and to offer practical support and advice. The original plans for an umbrella campaign highlighted some key issues around deportation cases:

1   People facing deportation needed help with the practical business of campaigning, including how to produce publicity material and how to go about getting support for their cases.
2   Individual campaigns against deportation could not mount a sustained campaign against racist and sexist immigration laws.
3   People facing deportation and other victims of racism required a range of support not offered by existing services. Early plans for WMADC outlined the need for an anti-deportation unit with paid workers – this has not happened, for reasons which will be discussed later.
4   The fight against immigration controls required support from a range of other bodies. An umbrella campaign could provide a general platform to organise support.

Early plans for WMADC proposed a nine-point platform around which campaigning could take place. The demands revealed both concerns about developments in the enforcement of immigration law and lessons learned from the experience of individual campaigns:

1   Repeal the 1971 Immigration Act and the 1981 Nationality Act.
2   Oppose all forms of internal controls, e.g. passport checks by DHSS, NHS etc.
3   Initiate a campaign within the trade union movement for a policy of no collaboration with the immigration authorities.
4   Oppose all racist and sexist immigration controls.
5   Demand that the Labour Party and trade unions adopt a position of no racist and sexist immigration controls.
6   Oppose all deportation. Protest and campaign in defence of those threatened with deportation.
7   Campaign for a general amnesty and for full recognition of employment status for all those already here and threatened by the immigration laws.
8   Oppose all racist police harassment and raids on houses and workplaces. Break links with the police.
9   Oppose racist decisions and practices of the courts and the judiciary.

However, despite these proposals, for some time campaigns against deportation in the West Midlands continued to operate on a case-by-case basis. It took another two years for the proposals for an umbrella campaign group to be re-launched – in large part as an attempt to prevent burnout among key workers.

The letter for the 1986 planning meeting (10 October) stresses these practical concerns:

> At the moment there are five campaigns in the West Midlands. . . . Important as they are there is, we believe, a desperate need to co-ordinate the work being done and to begin fighting for everyone threatened by racist immigration laws. Individual activists are spending their time attending one meeting after another in different parts of the West Midlands.
>
> Co-ordinating our efforts will utilise both our time and money. As a result we will be in a much better position to take all the issues into the Black community, the Labour and Trade Union movement. And anywhere else for that matter!

At this point, due to limited personnel and resources, an umbrella campaign became the most effective way to fight individual cases. Although campaigns were run around each case and each campaign remained autonomous and ultimately in the hands of those facing deportation, operating from an umbrella organisation proved a more efficient way of keeping energy in each campaign. WMADC continued to stress the importance of campaigning on the wider issues of state racism, but now the emphasis fell more on issues raised through individual campaigns. The new aims of WMADC reflect this refined focus:

1   To act as a contact for people under threat of deportation, encouraging campaigns and providing support and advice in setting up campaigns.
2   To publicise WMADC's activities to attract people facing or threatened with deportation.
3   To act as a focal point for activists in a position to work for anti-deportation campaigns.
4   To help co-ordinate the activities of different campaigns in the West Midlands and to support any initiative taken by individual campaigns without pre-conditions.
5   To raise the issue of deportations and racist laws within and outside bodies from which WMADC will seek support.
6   To fight against all racist and sexist immigration laws.
7   To organise support for campaigns outside the region.

These aims reflect the main points of the original platform, but now all points centre on campaigns against deportation. The wider political implications of deportation are raised through the business of individual campaigns. This is still the framework for campaigning today.

As a campaign WMADC has resisted the temptation to apply for funded posts – the political independence of the campaign is essential to its effectiveness and funding may jeopardise this. However, in conjunction with WMADC, the National Coalition of Anti-Deportation Campaigns has hired a paid worker to co-ordinate information about anti-deportation campaigns nationally – this money comes from church and charity sources. In June 1996, WMADC was awarded a grant from the National Lottery to provide an information service for asylum-seekers. This project is independent of the campaign. All political work continues to be carried out on a voluntary basis, with the agenda of work taken from the campaigns being fought at that time. It is these individual cases which show the main work of the organisation. With this in mind, we want to turn now to look in more detail at two campaigns fought in different periods.

Case 1 – Baba Bakhtaura

Baba's case was fought and won before the umbrella organisation WMADC was formed. By all accounts, the experience of this and other early campaigns (particularly the cases of Muhammed Idrish and Som Raj) were formative in proposals for a more ongoing co-ordinated campaign.

Baba came to Britain in 1979. In 1982 he was charged with 'overstaying' his visit and sentenced to two months imprisonment. The Home Office then decided to deport him. Baba appealed to the High Court against this first deportation order. At this time, a strong campaign was organised with firm support from the community. Due to this pressure, Baba won his appeal and the judge ruled that it was in the interest of the community that he stay.

The issue of community interest was central to Baba Bakhtaura's case in ways which set a precedent for campaigns which followed. Baba made his living as a folk singer, performing at weddings and temples and a wide range of religious, social and charity events. As a result of this, Baba was already a well-known figure in the Asian community, both locally and nationally, and the campaign was able to build on his existing reputation.

Baba's profession not only provided the basis for a community publicity network, it also formed the basis of another central strand in the campaign's argument. Baba is disabled – yet his singing career allowed him to remain financially independent. Baba received no state benefits – a point stressed in campaign literature. Later campaigns have also laid emphasis on these different aspects of 'the public interest' and try to argue both that people facing deportation make an invaluable contribution to their communities and that as workers they contribute to the life and wealth of the nation, instead of being 'a drain on the state'.

Unfortunately, the Home Office appealed against the High Court ruling that Baba should stay because of community interest. The Appeal Court overturned the High Court decision and once again ruled for Baba's deportation. In the light of this decision, Baba resumed his campaign on an even larger scale.

Leaflets from the campaign summarised the key facts and issues of the individual campaign and then went on to place this case in the context of wider political issues. In this mid-1980s campaign, the context described is far more comprehensive than that of more recent anti-deportation literature. Later we will discuss this shift in emphasis further. For now, we want to concentrate on the ways in which the Baba Bakhtaura campaign was informed by the wider concerns of anti-racist politics of the time, as part of our argument that the business and effectiveness of anti-deportation campaigning depends greatly on the role of this issue in larger political movements. The campaign stresses this:

Racism in Britain

Baba is one of the 60 or so black people who are deported every week under Britain's racist immigration laws. These laws also keep thousands of black families divided across continents, causing a lot of heartache. Nearly every year the British government passes more racist laws attacking the rights of black people. For Social Security, Education and Housing we are treated as illegal and have to show our passports. Now the racists are increasing their attacks on our people, burning our homes, our shops and our temples. All of this brings added fear and uncertainty to our communities.

Only we ourselves can stand up for our right to live here free from any harassment.

Our Right to Live Here

For hundreds of years Britain occupied our countries and took away great wealth, leaving only poverty and misery. After the Second World War they came and took our labour to build their 'Welfare State'. Now they say that we are a problem and make more and more laws to keep us out and send us back. But we made Britain the rich country that it is today and we have the right to live here.

(Campaign leaflet)

In 1983 Baba stood in the general election as an anti-deportation candidate – reflecting the tactic of arguing that anti-deportation campaigning was part of a wider anti-racist political platform. The campaign also stressed its connection with the labour movement. Baba gave fund-raising concerts during the 1984–5 miners' strike and his campaign gained support from Birmingham Trades Council and individual unions like NUPE, as well as from churches, temples and mosques.

The crux of Baba's case lay in the interpretation of 'the public interest'. The House of Lords ruled that Baba's cultural contribution to the Asian community meant that it was in the public interest that he stay. The Immigration Appeal Tribunal, however, resisted this suggestion, saying that, 'if this appeal were to succeed it would make a mockery of the immigration regulations'.

Baba finally won his right to stay after an appeal to the House of Lords in 1986. Many people in the Midlands remember his case (and ask about him when WMADC hold demonstrations and public events). The case developed a high profile among Asian communities, trade unionists and the wider public. Mocking the immigration regulations by introducing alternative ideas about what constitutes the public good became a standard tactic in anti-deportation campaigns in the Midlands and beyond.

Case 2 – Prakash Chavrimootoo

Prakash came to Britain in 1989 from Mauritius. She, like many other people facing deportation, came to Britain after marrying a British citizen. With her came her young son, Prem. During their twelve months leave to remain, both Prakash and Prem were subjected to domestic violence. They were forced to flee their home and came to Birmingham to rebuild their lives.

Prakash found work as a home care worker with Birmingham Social Services Department and made her home in Handsworth. Prem settled in school and in his new home. However, because Prakash had left the marriage in less than twelve months, she now faced deportation. Despite many protests and appeals, Prakash was served with a deportation order on 14 October 1995. From this time the situation became even more urgent.

Prakash is a UNISON member and her campaign was supported by her union. However, there are significant distinctions between the campaigning approaches of WMADC and UNISON.

An early leaflet produced by WMADC, although brief, retained a section headed 'Racist Immigration Laws':

> The 1988 Immigration Act is the most recent in a long line of racist immigration laws. These laws only affect Black people, and over the years they have divided many thousands of Black families. Two hundred and fifty Black people are deported every month. Now the Home Office wants to deport Prakash and Prem.

The inside of the leaflet *also* uses the slogan 'Here to Stay, Here to Fight' – an explicitly anti-racist, community-based approach to fighting immigration laws.

Leaflets produced by UNISON, on the other hand, say far less about the context of deportation as a state strategy:

> UNISON hopes not only to relieve the personal suffering of Prakash and Prem but also to raise awareness of the injustices of current legislation which results in such deportations. This legislation prevents women who come to Britain as wives of British citizens, but suffer violence or abuse at the hands of their husbands, from leaving then within twelve months of their arrival. Women are left with a horrendous choice – either stick it out with their violent husbands and risk their own lives and those of their children, or leave their marriages and risk being deported from Britain. UNISON believes that women should not be forced into such a situation, and is campaigning for the scrapping of the 12 month time limit and other racist immigration legislation.

Although there is some mention of racist laws, the focus here is the twelve-month rule and its effect on women experiencing domestic violence. The union leaflet does not mention 'black people' or the effects of racist immigration law upon their lives. Although this leaflet is also part of a campaign against deportation, there is no sense that this is part of any wider anti-racist struggle. Nor is it part of wider feminist struggles in any explicit sense – we are asked to sympathise with women as victims of violence rather than as victims of sexist and racist laws and more systematic oppression. Although the campaign is strengthened by union backing, the political energy of WMADC seems to be lost in the UNISON leaflet.

On 14 October 1995 Prakash was served with a deportation order – three immigration officials came to her house to ensure that the order was served. This meant that Prakash had exhausted the appeal process. In the eyes of the law she was an illegal immigrant and had very little comeback about her treatment. Again, the horrors of the Joy Gardiner case have brought this home – the acquittal of three of the police officers involved in this killing implies that the level of force used was necessary and that these people were only doing their job. This verdict has added to the anti-immigration frenzy overtaking Britain and has legitimated the most violent state racism. In solidarity with the family of Joy Gardiner, WMADC held a public meeting in July 1995 at which Prakash, Audrey Grant and a member of Raghbir Singh's campaign shared a platform with Myrna Simpson, Joy Gardiner's mother. Two hundred people attended.

In an interview Prakash talked about her case and how the laws and immigration rules have worked against her:

> It's a very racist and sexist law – it only affects women that come into this country. It's the 12 month rule – because I didn't stay with my husband for 12 months – that's my punishment. My marriage broke down because of domestic violence – which wasn't my fault. The Adjudicator and the Home Secretary say 'the marriage didn't last so she should go back' but both my parents are dead and I haven't got anybody to turn to. If we go back, we wouldn't have a roof over our heads. I would have no money, no job and nowhere to go. How am I going to survive? . . . And now I could be picked up and deported at any time.

The rules did allow her son Prem to appeal, which in turn might have increased Prakash's chances of staying, as she explained. But she also describes how difficult it would be for Prem to go back to Mauritius:

> So, because my son he has been in this country seven years (he came when he was six) he has a right to a full appeal now. So I hope he wins because he's grown up here in a very westernised way – and he only speaks English and he would be devastated if they sent us back. He doesn't remember anything in Mauritius – not even my family. He loves his school and he's made lots of friends – so I hope the Home Secretary will exercise his discretion in our case and let us stay.

Prakash applied for leave to take judicial review proceedings against the Home Office. Her application was to be heard by the High Court in October 1996. So, Prakash continued to fight her case with the support of the campaign which she recognises has been important in a number of ways. First in terms of publicity:

> The Campaign has been very good supporting me all the time – getting petitions, distributing leaflets – the campaign is very good with publicity – and giving me moral support as well – they arrange meetings for me and liaise with other campaigns. I would urge people in my situation to join a campaign. You cannot fight without public and campaign support. If it hadn't been for the campaign I would be back in Mauritius – a long time ago. Now, lots of people know my story because of the press, radio and TV coverage.

Many have written to the Home Secretary – so there will be hundreds of letters from people you don't know. In this way the campaign gives you confidence which you need because deportees are under a lot of pressure and stress and it affects you a lot . . .

Prakash also talked about the confidence she has gained through the campaign.

When I go and speak somewhere and the campaign members are with you – I was nervous at first giving speeches to a large group of people – and then I see people clap it gives me confidence and it makes you say to yourself I will go on fighting to the end.

I've done it so many times now. For example I spoke at the UNISON conference to well over a thousand people. So I would recommend people facing deportation to go to meetings and conferences if you get the chance. You have nothing to lose.

Overall publicity, pressure and hope are the most important benefits of a campaign:

The more the publicity, the harder it is for the Home Secretary to deport you because he has to justify the decision. I've had four appeals in six years and all of them have been turned down.

I've been to the High Court twice and Birmingham Immigration Tribunal twice so I would say to people facing deportation should never give up . . . fight for it!

Prakash's case was due to be heard on 2 October 1996, but a week before this she was arrested and detained while signing on at the police station. That afternoon, she was taken from the police station in Handsworth to Campsfield Immigration Detention Centre in Oxford. She was not allowed to see Prem before she left, although he was in the police station. Prem had been taken from school by police officers, although he had committed no offence, and plans had already been made to place him in care. Only the intervention of the campaign prevented this from happening.

When Prakash was arrested, the campaign called a demonstration outside the police station that very afternoon. In the days that followed several demonstrations were held outside Campsfield and outside the High Court at each of the hearings. Campaign members lobbied MPs, and Rodney Bickerstaff, General Secretary of UNISON, spoke about Prakash at the Labour Party Conference.

Only the strength of her campaign stopped Prakash's deportation and forced her release from Campsfield. On 17 October the Appeal Court judges granted judicial review on the grounds that the family unit of mother and son should be preserved. Prem had not been served with any removal papers and the court ruled that Prakash could not be deported without a consideration of Prem's situation.

The Home Office response to this was to serve Prem with a notice of removal in February 1997. The Major government showed its commitment to the family by trying to deport a fourteen-year-old boy to a country he cannot remember. This willingness to issue deportation orders against children has signalled a new set of dangers for families facing deportation – now children too are in the frontline.

The Labour victory in the May 1997 elections raised hopes among many anti-deportation campaigners. Plenty of promises had been made by individual MPs before the election – it remained to be seen what would happen afterwards. Unfortunately, both Jack Straw, the new Home Secretary, and Mike O'Brien, the Home Office minister with responsibility for immigration, clearly indicated their intention to maintain a hard line on immigration and asylum. Proceedings against Prakash and Prem continued and the family continued to live in fear of being picked up and deported.

In July 1997, before Prem's appeal, Prakash and Prem were granted leave to remain. Although Prakash's MP attempted to monopolise the publicity around this event, it was clear that Prakash and Prem could not have won without their long and exhausting campaign. While both Labour and Tory governments wish to downplay the effectiveness of campaigning, the experience of West Midlands Anti-Deportation Campaign proves that community campaigns can fight back against racist laws.

Conclusions: the significance of campaign politics

Three features of WMADC activity are worth mentioning: the strategic use of media, the alliances with trade unions, and individual empowerment through sustained campaign pressure.

In the first place, campaigns were built on the assumption that publicity achieved four important objectives. First, media coverage helped to put names and faces to what would otherwise have remained, as far as mainstream public perception was concerned, statistical aggregates of unwanted entrants. Second, by highlighting family circumstances, for example in Prakash's case her experience of domestic violence and the threat of separation from her son, the campaign encouraged an empathy with the situations faced by those threatened with deportation. Third, publicity made it harder for the Home Office to exercise its discretion and make its decisions behind the veil of judicial and administrative secrecy. It rendered the whole process more transparent and more accountable. Finally, by highlighting the circumstances faced in a succession of cases, it invited viewers and readers to see the connections between them and the overall inequities of the system. In other words, the succession of well-publicised cases highlighted the racist and sexist principles and practices surrounding immigration politics.

One important aim of WMADC's media strategy has been to anchor individuals to a sense of place and community. In Prakash's case the campaign emphasised her role as a local authority care worker, whilst in Prem's case the importance of his school was highlighted. Baba's role as a performer on the Asian wedding circuit was used to emphasise his 'contribution to the public good' of the Asian community, thus turning immigration laws back on their architects and administrators. Since many of the campaigns extended over several years,

WMADC has constantly looked to find ways of revitalising interest in individual cases. So, anniversaries, birthdays, mother's day (in the case of Prakash and Prem) were used as photo-opportunities. The settings were also important, again in stressing the importance of community integration. Hence cathedrals, schools and temples were often used to host such events.

Such sporadic media events not only helped to build up a picture of the person but could also be aimed at the injustices of immigration control and the targeting of those responsible for administering it. Hence WMADC held one protest outside British Airways offices in Birmingham to highlight the role of carriers in the detention of suspects. In another protest, a soup kitchen was organised outside a benefits office to highlight the consequences of the withdrawal of benefits for asylum-seekers. Of necessity some protests were less planned and more wildcat in nature in immediate response to developments. These were held at police stations, airports etc., wherever individuals were at risk from the authorities.

Needless to say WMADC has waged its media campaigns against a background of mainstream coverage of immigration which has nourished public hostility to black immigration and which in one instance even targeted the WMADC. In 1996 the organisation successfully applied for National Lottery money to fund a worker. The national tabloid and local press condemned the decision as 'PC [political correctness] gone mad'. The public furore was such that it prompted questions in the House of Commons and a prime ministerial commitment to 'look into the matter'.

WMADC has promoted links between those facing deportation and trade unions. In some cases, for example Som Raj and Mohammed Idrish, they were already active in their unions, the NUJ and NALGO. The campaign sought not only to involve deportees in their unions but also to inform fellow trade unionists of the situation facing one of their colleagues.

Strong links with trade unions enabled deportees to tap into a network of politicised people, a circuit of conferences, meetings and in some cases, e.g. UNISON, a black self-organising section of the union. These self-organising groups have provided an important alternative to mainstream union bureaucracies for black people to gain political experience. For example, UNISON's Lesbian and Gay Members' Group worked in conjunction with the union's Black Workers' Group to get minority issues onto the union's agenda.

Such links with self-organised groups within trade unions not only provided links to the wider trade union movement, but also to the Labour Party. In Prakash's case, her trade union leader, Rodney Bickerstaff, spoke about her case at the Labour Party conference, putting pressure on the Labour Party as a whole and on union-sponsored MPs in particular. This helped to ensure that cases were not just perceived in individual terms but as part of a wider political issue and that through such interventions at meetings and conferences the issues surrounding deportation would reach deep into the labour movement.

WMADC provided women like Prakash with a publicity outlet, support network, media and trade union contacts and links with other deportation cases. By her own testimony, the opportunities the campaign provided and particularly the opportunity to speak about her case to large public gatherings gave her added confidence. It lessened her sense of isolation and encouraged her to pursue her fight through to its successful outcome.

The experience of the WMADC demonstrates the importance of a pragmatic, unspectacular style of politics. By *unspectactular* we mean that such politics lacks the attention-grabbing attributes of newsworthy politics, which invariably require scandal, iconic status, violence or a combination of the above to make an impact. It also lacks the glamour of film, advertising, sports, popular music or television drama, all of which are easier media around which to weave racial narratives. This has entailed sustained, persistent campaigning and learning from the experience of one campaign and adapting to changed circumstances. Much of its effort has been aimed at taking cases out of the bureaucratic closet and forcing them into the public arena. In Baba's case the campaign successfully exploited the ambiguity of the 'public good' clause in immigration law and used it to defend Baba's right to stay in the UK.

In all cases, including both those of Baba and Prakash, the exhaustive and exhausting use of the appeals process proved to the campaign's advantage. In Prakash's eight-year campaign, it enabled Prem to stay in the country long enough to be entitled to a full appeal, although as it turned out he and Prakash were given leave to remain before this point in the campaign was reached.

Those whose cases were taken up by WMADC were empowered in several ways through their experience of the campaigns. First, they felt less isolated as the campaign was able to put them in touch with others in similar circumstances. It provided opportunities to address large public and trade union meetings and to recognise the strength and solidarity of support behind them. Finally and most importantly it led to a successful outcome, that is the right to stay in the UK.

WMADC has highlighted individual cases not only to achieve successful outcomes for the individuals concerned but also to raise public awareness of the inequities and iniquities of the system of immigration control. This kind of anti-racist politics has not relied on grand prescriptive theorising but on strategies aimed to secure concrete, *ad hoc* gains, whilst at the same time making connections across, and alliances with, other anti-racist campaigns. More than any other knowledge base it requires an understanding of the legal and political terrain on which it has waged its campaigns and the role of the media as an instrument in campaign politics. In this sense it shares postmodernism's knowledge which is relative and fragmented and a corresponding scepticism with regard to grand theory. Its politics can be best summed up as persistent and pragmatic rather than overarching and prescriptive.

Moreover, WMADC politics actually rests on an acknowledgement of the limits of politics and a corresponding recognition of the significance of global process and blocs and technological changes. It seeks to adapt to and exploit the latter in order to further the campaign's interests. The more humdrum, mundane world of this kind of anti-racist campaigning merits a place alongside newer, 'pleasure-led' forms of cultural theory and/or politics. The experience of WMADC testifies to the continuing significance of the 'black' signifier in politics, not in a way which is intended to pre-empt the use of other categories in other contexts or to suggest any kind of ranking or hierarchy of categories. Within the context of recent critiques of anti-racist politics, we are not wishing to endorse the use of such terms as 'black' in any kind of abstract or universal sense but to invoke it as part of a larger vocabulary which is sufficiently broad and inclusive to adjust to both changing circumstances *and* enduring continuities.

Our experience to date suggests that there are no set rules about how community resistance works. It seems that effective organisation can be funded or non-funded, linked to established groups or freelance – the key issue is commitment and energy over a sustained period. As the century turns, academic writing about race and politics has moved away from political prescription and become more concerned to describe the complex forces which shape our identities and interactions. Whilst we are happy to move away from the divisiveness and polarisation which characterised much previous debate between so-called reformists and those advocating a more radical political analysis and agenda for action, we remain committed to a discussion of the ways in which people organise locally and at least some discernment about what is politically effective.

Notes

1 We use 'black communities' throughout to refer to self-organising groups which have formed, in part, out of the struggle against the racially oppressive characteristics of British society. It is not meant to refer exclusively to those of African Caribbean origin but rather to any group which has been subject to such oppression. As we shall point out later, we do not use it to the exclusion of other terms but only to register its appropriateness in the context of anti-deportation politics.

2 Local support and campaign groups have organised against the establishment of immigration detention centres in their area. One of the most consistently active of these groups is the 'Close Down Campsfield Campaign', which was formed in opposition to the building of Campsfield House, a detention centre just outside Oxford. The group holds regular pickets and rallies outside Campsfield, visits and supports detainees, and continues to publicise the appalling conditions of the centre to the wider public.

10 Issues and dilemmas

'Race' in higher education teaching practices

Susie Jacobs with Nadeem Hai

In this chapter we discuss a neglected aspect of pedagogy concerning 'race', ethnicity and strategies of teaching in higher education (Neal 1995). We raise questions concerning the teaching of 'race'/ethnicity issues in social science higher education and suggest improvements in praxis. In our experience, the practice of teaching 'race' topics raises issues of greater complexity than teaching other sociology/social science courses. This is partly because the very object of study is contested and slippery. Moreover, questions of racial/ethnic/religious/cultural/national identity and affiliation are raised for both students and lecturers. Such categories often invoke deep emotion for many participants in the pedagogical process. The 'practices' we consider here concern those on social 'science'/studies courses dealing centrally with 'race'/racism. We are particularly concerned with the issues raised by non-dichotomous views of 'race' and of racism, and argue that neither pluralist multiculturalism nor essentialist forms of anti-racist education (at least, as they have been construed) can address the complex situations which arise within seminar rooms, let alone the even more fraught and complex relations in the world 'outside'. Rather, we need to explore the syntheses of features of both types of practice, and probably new ones.

This chapter is structured as follows. First, we discuss the literature on schooling, 'race' and education in Britain, drawing out themes relevant to higher education. Second, we review work published in Britain dealing with race and higher education. Third, we examine a selection of work from the United States, where there exists more discussion of race and higher education than is the case in Europe. Next we analyse some of the general issues entailed in 'multiculturalism'. In the final part of the chapter we move to a discussion of pedagogical issues in social science higher education. These include the curriculum, the role of the teacher, and conflicts in the seminar room.

The approaches of 'multiculturalism' and of 'anti-racism' – all contested – have provided a context for issues parallel to those mentioned above in primary and secondary education. To some extent, these approaches spill over into higher education. As Goldberg writes, 'How might the heterogeneously multicultural guide . . . comparisons across undifferentiated contexts and promote incorporative politics and pedagogies?' (1994: 33). At the same time, how can we maintain contact with the institutional and structural parameters of racism which bound the lives of racialised others, while (as teachers) promoting ways of thinking (and of acting) which combat racism and confront the actuality of the social construction/s of 'race' in their many manifestations? How can we emphasise the impact of racisms, and begin to make whiteness visible, while simultaneously stressing that there is no such thing as 'race' except, to paraphrase Anderson (1990), in our collective imaginations?

'Race' and schooling in Britain

Below we give a brief (and non-exhaustive) outline of the development of discourses on 'race' and schooling, then we discuss two government reports, Rampton and Swann, with reference to multicultural and anti-racist strategies.

Early analysis of 'race' in schools dwelt on issues of educational attainment and underachievement, specifically language, family and cultural background. For instance, the underachievement of the West Indian child, or the lack of language skills of Asian children, became hotly contested issues and informed much of the academic debates of the time as well as governmental responses and popular discourses. There are numerous large-scale and small-scale studies into the performance of children of West Indian origin (Tomlinson 1983: 28) and of children of Asian origin (Tomlinson 1983: 47).

Studies in the 1960s and 1970s amongst different ethnic groups tended to concentrate on underachievement and reflected concerns of white parents about the effect of the presence of children of ethnic minority families on their own children. Cultural differences, the alleged underperformance of ethnic minority children, and teacher time taken to educate ethnic minority children would, it was feared, hold back the education of white children. The Honeyford affair in 1987 illustrates this type of (racist) response.

Intelligence quotients (IQs) became an important marker in the measurement of attainment levels, discussed in Houghton (1966), Payne (1974) and Philips (1979). In influential psychology texts, such as those of Jenson (1969) and Eysenck (1971), intellectual deficiency was seen as the major cause of educational disadvantage. This is echoed in current debates surrounding the work by Charles Murray and his collaborators in the United States where it has been argued that African-American children have lower IQs than their white peers (Murray 1996).

In the 1960s the debates revolved around underachievement, due to 'culture shock', family background and language problems, among other factors (ILEA Research and Statistics Group 1968). Studies were undertaken on the subjects of language proficiency (McEwan *et al.* 1975; Edwards 1976); streaming, particularly of African-Caribbean children, into lower streams in schools (Townsend 1971; Troyna 1978); and educational 'subnormality' (Tomlinson 1981). Many of these issues were common to both African-Caribbean and South Asian children. They were described then as 'immigrant children', despite the fact that an increasing number of them had been born in Britain or had migrated at an early age. So the pathologised 'black' child was seen as having inferior forms of language, subject to assumptions that might lead him/her to being placed in lower streams, and was more likely to be classified as 'educationally sub-normal'.

African-Caribbean and South Asian parents were also concerned about poor education standards in state schools partly because they saw their children being stigmatised. Such concerns led (some) families of ethnic minorities to set up separate schooling, either in 'Saturday schools' or full-time. Separate schooling was often religiously based. Such schools, it was thought, would not only reinforce particular cultures but could also provide stringent academic standards.

From the mid to late 1970s, growing opposition emerged to individualistic explanations of racial disadvantage. The Centre for Contemporary Cultural Studies at the University of Birmingham became a 'home' for such critical perspectives. Explanations centred on the pervasive racism of contemporary society and on institutional factors rather than on pathologising 'immigrant' families and children.

On the political left and centre the emerging debate was about the best policies and strategies to combat discrimination and racism. In the early 1980s, as Minister for Education (1981–6) Keith Joseph was concerned with two main issues: to move education away from progressive pedagogies, and to bring schools in line with market forces (Jones 1989). These themes were taken up by Kenneth Baker in the Education Reform Act of 1988, which introduced a National Curriculum, including the teaching of British history with England as the central focus. The Act enshrined compulsory religious education (broadly Christian in nature).[1] Although the ideology of white Christian Britain was at its centre, the National Curriculum gave a yardstick for comparing performance (albeit viewed in a narrow manner) between pupils from various local education authorities (LEAs).

Most Conservatives saw culture as unified rather than comprised of a conflictual diversity of cultural meanings (Jones 1989: 57). Implicitly and sometimes explicitly, they saw British culture as white, Protestant, English and heterosexual. This trend was continued in the government of John Major (Skellington 1996). The 1993 Education Act supported and extended the 1988 Act; while mentioning the cultural pluralism of Britain, it did little in policy terms actually to implement such pluralism (Gilbourn 1995: 30–1). The Act attempted to deal with the disproportionate percentage of exclusions of ethnic minority children by guaranteeing the right to LEA-funded education. During this period, LEA policies and government-sponsored reports on race and schooling had some impact in shifting discourse to forms of 'multiculturalism' (see below).

The Blairite Labour government has made several changes: the abolition of assisted places (for independent schools), the establishment of a national scheme for nursery places, and the introduction of 'the market' through tuition fees in higher education. So far 'race' has not figured importantly in any 'new' Labour agenda. However, following a long campaign, the Islamia School in Brent was granted voluntary aided status, so that Islamic schools were placed on (formally) the same footing as Christian and Jewish schools receiving state funding.

'Race', multiculturalism and the Rampton and Swann reports

Having given a broad overview of some of the policy shifts around 'race' and education over the last thirty years, we now briefly turn to the Rampton and

Swann reports, important in setting the agenda for what purports to be a 'multi-cultural' education in Britain.

The Callaghan Labour government in 1979 set up the Rampton Committee (HMSO 1981) with a remit to investigate the state of education for children of all ethnic minorities, with an interim report on West Indian children who were underachieving in comparison to white and Asian children (Statham *et al.* 1991). The main finding of this report was that:

> while believing that few teachers were intentionally racist, and while not accepting that racism was the sole cause of West Indian underachievement, the committee concluded that unintentional racism (in the sense of stereo-typed, negative or patronising views of West Indian children) was widespread and did influence children's performance.
>
> (Statham *et al.* 1991: 33)

The lack of pre-school childcare, prejudice concerning the language usage of West Indian children, and inappropriate curriculum material were also cited as causing disadvantage. The Rampton Report made some progress from blaming minorities to viewing the educational system as in need of change. It stressed the need for multiculturally aware teacher training and the need for a broader, multicultural approach to education (Statham *et al.* 1991: 34).

The Swann Report (HMSO 1985) had a broader remit – how to generate an atmosphere of cultural tolerance of ethnic minority cultures in a society charac-terised by cultural diversity (Rattansi 1992: 25) – and was more detailed in its investigation and findings. Swann confirmed the findings of Rampton that West Indian and Bangladeshi pupils were doing less well than their white counterparts. The report considered whether IQ differences explained the underachievement of West Indian and Bangladeshi children but this was not found to be significant. Prejudice, based on inaccurate information, and negative stereotyping, were seen as obstacles to good 'race relations'. Socio-economic inequalities were regarded as having a part to play (Statham *et al.* 1989: 36). The main recommendations were that:

- LEAs should lead in fighting myths and stereotypes in order to bring about the acceptance of a multicultural society.
- Increased priority should be given to teaching English in schools.
- The multiplicity of languages in schools should be seen as an asset, not a liability.
- More attention should be paid to multicultural teaching methods.

After Swann there was a quasi-official accommodation to anti-racist and multi-culturalist policies despite the orientations of the national government. Indeed 'it is arguable that the Swann report put multiculturalism and at least weak versions of anti-racism on the national educational agenda' (Rattansi 1992: 13).

Within schools, 'multiculturalism' involved broader religious education in assemblies in most schools, and learning about 'othered' cultures through the celebration of festivals, arts, music and the introduction of stories with characters from different minority groups. In most cases multiculturalism did not extend to learning about systematic inequalities facing different ethnic/racialised groups. There was also a growing awareness that issues of 'race' and racism were not confined to schools in 'inner city' areas, i.e. where a number of ethnic minority children might be present, but were also relevant to all-'white' schools (Gaine 1998).

'Multiculturalism' has been critiqued for tending to fall into a patronising 'tolerance' of different cultures and for its often-cited tendency towards cultural relativism. Other points at issue are the tendency to ignore institutional contexts (Mohan 1995; Yudice 1995) as well as economic and political parameters, e.g. lack of attention to differential resources (Goldberg 1994; Turner 1993; Troyna 1992). At the same time, some versions of multiculturalism contain important dimensions of respect for diversity of cultures and beliefs.

The key features of most anti-racist approaches is the linkage with structure. Anti-racist stances in education attempted to locate oppression within socio-political and historical contexts, including those of capitalist economic structures. Institutional and popular racisms were linked to pervasive institutional racism. Anti-racist activists also sought to promote a more positive image of various racial groupings.

Anti-racism has also been critiqued since the 1980s in Britain, especially from the political right but also from the left, after the failures of racism awareness training. Among the problems raised by anti-racist strategies are tendencies to dichotomise the world in moral terms and to see race unproblematically as based on skin pigmentation. A chilling example of the failures of anti-racist policy in education was observed in 1986 in Manchester, when the schoolboy Ahmed Iqbal Ullah was killed by his schoolmate Darren Coulbourn. The Burnage Report (Macdonald *et al.* 1989), reporting on this, cited the crude model of anti-racism employed at the school as one cause of these events. Racism was located in a 'moral vacuum' and removed from other contexts such as community, class and sexual (*sic*) disadvantage. White people tended to be seen as homogeneously racist and therefore excluded from any struggle against racism. The Burnage Report argued that anti-racist policies needed to address concerns of all disadvantaged groups (including the white working class). 'Top-down' anti-racist policies tended to engender resistance rather than understanding of, and opposition to, racism.

In the 1990s, these debates dissolved as examples of false dichotomisation, an example of how postmodernist emphases upon 'difference' have had an impact upon schooling and higher education. Given continued discrimination and racism, much of it violent, against people of African and Asian origin as well as against other groupings, anti-racist strategies continue to be important. The two strategies can be seen as intertwined. It is no longer possible to equate liberal democracy with multiculturalism and to reconcile the inherent exploitation of capitalism with anti-racism (Enzensberger 1992: 15–51). For Solomos and Back (1996: 113), the ultimate aim of anti-racism is to 'develop and maintain . . . a truly multicultural society'.

Over the past thirty years there has been a partial discursive shift from path-ologising children of 'other' cultures to more pluralistic views. It is important to note that such moves coexist with continued exclusion – seen perhaps in its most overt manifestation in the high rates of exclusion of African-Caribbean and mixed-race boys from schools. But the concerns of many ethnic minority parents and children remain marginal: to have special needs recognised in diet and in use of space such as prayer rooms; Eurocentrism and Christian emphasis in curricula; and more generally, ethnic minority pupils' own experiences of schooling. Despite mixed experiences of schooling in Britain, by 1998 ethnic minority adolescents were entering higher education in large numbers.

British work on 'race' and higher education

In contrast to the large amount of work on race and schooling in Britain, relatively little has been written on 'race' and higher education. Although the teaching of 'race'-related issues in social science (and humanities) subjects has flourished since the 1980s, this interest has not translated into work on praxis. In the context of writing on teaching women's studies, it is uncommon for British academics to focus on their own practice (McNeil 1992). Most British work deals with institutional matters rather than those which require reflexivity (but see Bhattacharyya 1996; Henwood and Phoenix 1996).

One such institutional concern is that of access. Mal Leicester in *Race for a Change* (1993) deals with aspects of race teaching and provision in continuing/adult and higher education. She focuses on the potential of multicultural and anti-racist teaching and institutional practices to change the sector(s) as a whole. She deals with access courses for mature students with non-standard entry qualifications. This is a route through which a number of black students have entered higher education. It is perhaps telling that 'race' provision has often been concentrated in departments of adult and continuing education rather than being incorporated into mainstream settings.

Leicester claimed that there are disproportionately few black students (her terminology) in higher education (1993: 59). However, Modood and Shiner's detailed statistical analysis of 1992 data on the admission of ethnic minority students to universities and (ex-) polytechnics contradicts this. They analysed data from UCCA and PCAS (as was) (bodies dealing with admission to higher education) and found that ethnic minority students 'of colour' were under-represented in the old universities but had gained admission to polytechnics (now, new universities).

The authors disaggregated data for different ethnic/national groupings. After controlling for factors such as social class, age, sex, and type of school attended, some ethnic/racial differences in rates of admission to universities and polytechnics remained unexplained in statistical terms, suggesting that differential rates of admission could be due to discrimination. The main findings were that black Caribbean and Pakistani candidates remained significantly less likely to be admitted to 'old' universities, whereas several groups ('Asian-others', Bangladeshis and Chinese applicants) were significantly less likely to have been admitted to polytechnics/new universities. On the other hand, black Caribbean and Indian applicants continued to be significantly more likely to have gained admission to polytechnics.

By 1996, at a conference on race and education at the Policy Studies Institute in London, Modood was able to demonstrate that students from most ethnic minority groups (except African-Caribbean origin men) were obtaining credentials (e.g. A levels, degrees, diplomas) equivalent or (more often) in greater numbers than were their white equivalents.

By 1998, 12 per cent of higher education students were from 'non-white' ethnic minorities (Wilson 1998).[2] All groups except African-Caribbean males and Bangladeshi females were over-represented within higher education, a dramatic change within a short period of time. One interesting finding which bears comparison with the US is the high percentage of some Asian groups going to university. Issues of progression, as recently identified by HEFCE, are also of import. Many minority students remained unemployed, or employed in jobs for which they were overqualified. Thus, the push to obtain 'good' degree results is likely to be acute for many ethnic minority students, given the labour market discrimination they often face (Brown 1992). At present, the degree results of black, Asian and other ethnic minority students remains an under-researched issue, whether compared with white students, or between minority groups.

The organisational context of anti-racist and equal opportunities strategies is a second institutional matter of import addressed by Leicester (1993) and Neal (1995, 1998). The Swann Report (1985) defined institutional racism as the way in which a range of long-established systems, practices and procedures may unintentionally work against minority groups – for instance, recruitment by word of mouth. Emphasis is placed upon effects (outcomes) rather than intentions. Although this separation of 'structure' and of 'action' is unhelpful, it may be still useful to keep in mind the consequences, intentional or not, of the procedures and collective actions that make up institutions. There are still relatively few African-Caribbean, Asian and other minority staff in universities, especially at higher academic and administrative levels, which highlights the continued need to examine discrimination at institutional level.

Leicester reviewed the results of a 1991 questionnaire sent to sociology, politics, education, continuing education, history, maths and biology departments. Thirty-five universities had written anti-racist policies in place; so did seven (of 120) departments (1993: 96). The latter tended to be highly proactive in these spheres, and to have detailed policies rather than general directives. The majority gave positive responses to questions concerning equal opportunities in staff recruitment. But the closer a candidate came to the possibility of appointment, the weaker policies became. Only six responses indicated that any anti-racist staff development programmes existed, and only two departments claimed to attempt actively to recruit black/Asian staff (ibid.). One quarter of departments made special provision for ethnic minority students; however, upon closer inspection such provision was nearly always English language teaching. Some 89 per cent of departments had recruited students via access courses. Overall, Leicester describes provision as highly patchy, with some examples of 'good practice' but with wide gaps, and with some institutions making virtually no provision either for a multi-cultural or an anti-racist learning environment. She also identifies an important finding: that most anti-racist initiatives, whether in continuing or in higher education, tend to be the result of action by individuals, or sometimes small groups, rather than those of institutions. Acting without or with little institutional support, such initiatives may easily peter out.

Neal (1995) researched equal opportunities policies in two institutions. Both were 'new' universities: one was committed to equal opportunities through its location in an area of London where many black/ethnic minority peoples live; for the other 'equal opportunities' was part of a highly public profile. She found that, in both cases, the institutions concerned tended to depoliticise race issues as technical matters that could be implemented through, for instance, ethnic monitoring or anti-harassment procedures. Different constituencies often vied for 'equal opps' recognition, with gender issues sometimes assuming a higher profile than ones of race/ethnicity. Neal (1998) criticises the tendency to avoid a committed anti-racist strategy, even in institutions where 'race' issues are not completely ignored.

Leicester provides a useful tripartite division of 'models' of the university: the 'ivory tower' (the context which has existed for most 'old' universities), the 'mature' university and the 'university of market forces'. The 'mature' university model is, in her view, most compatible with anti-racist/multicultural discourses. This model is characterised as being democratic in representation and decision-making; having non-competitive entry; discussion as the basis of learning; emphasising interdisciplinarity and student-centredness and learning for empowerment. The market-force led university (model) emphasises: education for pragmatic ends; cost-effective teaching methods; highly controlled management and organisation; competition for students on courses; and 'enterprise education' (1993: 54–5). Few could dispute that the latter model is now dominant, especially in new universities, and is set to become more so. The absolute divisions made, however, do not attend to the ways that 'market-speak' can co-opt the discourse of democracy and student-centredness. Mohan, writing of the US context (see below), notes how the rubric of multiculturalism can also become another marketing strategy, as evidenced in the advertisements of some companies (1995: 377). Students in new market-led universities are seen and may see themselves as 'consumers' of 'products' (courses), which enable them to compete better in the marketplace. Further, in times of severe constraints on resources, as at present, the types of qualities and initiatives Leicester describes under the rubric of the second ('mature') model are often threatened.

The picture appears more encouraging for provision of specific courses on 'race' and related aspects. More departments in Leicester's survey reported provision of courses on race than claimed that awareness of race issues permeated their whole programme (1993: 97). She points out, 'The contradiction between anti-racist work at seminar level within an institution that does not embody fair practice in its own procedures is a common anomaly' (1993: 21).

In 1991, Thiara and Goulbourne surveyed social science courses on 'race' and ethnicity in the United Kingdom. They showed that in 1991 there existed a wide range of courses for students in education, sociology, social policy, politics and anthropology; there also existed a range of models for those planning to offer courses with this field (1991: 5). This is now somewhat dated material, but does provide a useful basis of information. Work building upon and updating this would be helpful.

In 1996, Bulmer and Solomos edited a special edition of *Ethnic and Racial Studies* on race, ethnicity and the curriculum in higher education. This welcome intervention concentrated specifically on curricular issues as well as some over-lapping questions (of ethnic minority students in institutions and on courses). Contributions covered sociology, anthropology, geography, history and psychology, but the collection omits subjects less likely to be departmentally based (cultural studies, women's studies). In the case of the latter this is particularly unfortunate, given its attention to pedagogy, subject positioning and the impact of experience. Mason, writing on sociology curricula, described the near-explosion of research and teaching on race, ethnicity, racism and anti-racism, otherness and difference, within the discipline. Bonnett, discussing teaching of 'race' within geography, stresses the contribution of cultural studies as well as sociology in widening customary geographical concerns. Jenkins, discussing social anthropology's contribution, underlines the importance of the category 'ethnicity'. In an earlier contribution discussing Eurocentrism in social sciences, Joseph, Reddy and Searle-Chatterjee (1990) also concluded that anthropology, despite its colonial origins and much of its practice, is potentially less ethnocentric than most social science discourse. This was seen as being due to its commitment to understanding cultures on their 'own' terms. Henwood and Phoenix, writing on psychology and social psychology in the *Ethnic and Racial Studies* collection, gave a valuable overview of trends, including the impact of discourse theory. Although not a survey as such, the Bulmer and Solomos collection indicates that the range of courses on 'race' has expanded during the 1990s and will probably continue to do so. How these will fit in with the gloomy outline above of most institutions' (forced) 'turn to the market' remains to be seen.

Race and higher education: some considerations from the USA

In contrast to British writing (see below), considerable attention has been paid in the United States to pedagogical issues in the teaching of race. What is there seen as a legitimate concern of teachers is more likely to be perceived in Britain as undue introspection and emphasis on personal disclosure.

We cannot attempt a comprehensive review of literature here, but we discuss some recent texts concerned particularly with curricular and more pragmatic teaching concerns. Before outlining some of the themes of this literature, we should indicate some of the differences between the US and British contexts. Comparisons are important, but they should not be made in a facile manner.

In the USA a far higher proportion of the population, up to one-half, enters university, compared with British rates of under one-third. Higher education is mainly privatised and elite institutions are able to charge very high fees.

A far higher proportion of the population, up to 28 per cent, consists of people 'of colour'. Within this, the largest grouping (13–14 per cent of the population) consists of African-Americans. The next largest group is termed 'Hispanic', with the majority population migrating from Mexico. Another 3–4 per cent consists of

East and South Asians, mainly recent migrants since the 1960s revision of previously racist immigration legislation. Only 1 per cent of the population consists of native American 'Indians'. The remaining population is mainly of diverse European origin, including 3.5 per cent Jews and larger numbers of other descendants of Southern and Eastern European immigrants.

The history of African-Americans, the descendants of slaves, stands out within this context of a society composed of people with highly disparate origins. While many African-Americans are in fact mixed-race, due to the sexual power of slavemasters over slave women, in the USA any African ancestry is taken to be a sign of 'blackness'. Racism against African-Americans is not the only form found in the country; it is certainly the most longstanding and intense, despite some diminution since the civil rights movement (Pettigrew 1994). This is reflected in the highly disadvantaged position of most African-Americans, although about one-fifth to one-quarter of African-Americans now belong to middle/upper income groupings.

Many overlapping concerns unite social science/cultural studies work on race in the two national contexts; however, the tenor of works remains distinct. The relative insularity of US discourses is unsurprising given the country's history, size and global dominance. Moreover, the category 'black' was formulated around the enslavement of African peoples; as Miles puts it, 'the specificity of the category "black" is over determined by the fact that it was forged as a racially specific discourse linking the notions "slave", "African", "Negro" and "race"' (Miles 1994: 194). While this history and its legacies are important in the British context, they have more immediate resonance in the USA since large-scale slavery existed within national boundaries. The other 'side' of the dichotomy, whiteness, was predicated on the possibility of all European groupings, even low-status ones, being able to assimilate on a relatively privileged basis (at a minimum, their labour was not forced) as 'white'.

Due to this history, continuing discrimination and the fact that, unlike in Britain, rates of racial intermarriage are low in the US, the terms 'black' and 'white' are little questioned, in academic writing let alone in popular discourse. Popular and academic discourses emphasise race/ethnicity over class as social classification.

It is curious that the longstanding presence of one minority, 'Hispanics' (see *Latin American Perspectives* 75, 1992, for debates over definition), whose 'race' is contested, has not been more disruptive of the centrality of the black/white dichotomy. Although cultural globalisation is occurring, to some extent it has not had any thoroughgoing impact on these discourses, which still display firmly national characteristics.

In recent years, equal opportunities policies, which allowed a degree of discretion to university authorities concerning selection of candidates in order to maintain racial/ethnic/gender balance in student populations, has increased the proportion of African-American and other ethnic minorities 'of colour' in student bodies. At the University of California at Berkeley, for instance, half of the student body consists of people 'of colour'. With the recent Supreme Court decision overturning such policies, proportions of students of colour have fallen drastically.

At the prestigious University of Texas Faculty of Law, the proportion of black and Hispanic students has declined dramatically since administrators and academics can no longer take into account very small differentials in achievement test scores. There are high percentages of 'Asian', especially Chinese-origin, students in universities, leading to claims of the 'over-representation of Asians', parallel to earlier 'quota' policies attempting to curtail Jewish admission to universities (Woo 1990). It may be interesting to see if similar processes occur in Britain.

In teaching terms, there has existed, at least in some subjects such as English, cultural studies, anthropology and sociology, greater emphasis on 'multiculturalism' than has existed in Britain. The backlash against this and the emphasis on essentialism has led to 'multicultural wars' within some US faculties. Today, right-wing rhetoric concerning 'political correctness' has become extraordinarily popular (Berlant and Warner 1994: 111). Mohan is able to write that after the 'culture wars' of the 1980s, both public and academic cultures are making room for some form of multiculturalism. Despite offensives from the right, colleges and universities are discreetly implementing pluralist criteria (Mohan 1995: 374). There is now a body of US writing concerning multiculturalism in institutions of higher education.

This literature overlaps with the British debate on 'race' and higher education cited, but deals differently with issues. One concern is the definition of 'multi-cultural' itself: the term 'anti-racist' is little-used. Peter McLaren's (1994) categorisation of multiculturalism is influential. He divides multicultural discourses into conservative, liberal, left liberal and critical. Conservative or corporatist multiculturalism does not view whiteness as a form of ethnicity; the white middle class operate an ideology of assimilation, see the USA as a monolingual country, and there is no interrogation of 'high status' knowledge. Most variants of this 'school' are articulated by white people; however Black Nationalist 'melanin theory' is another form of conservative multiculturalism. Liberal multiculturalism, according to McLaren, is a form of ethnocentric humanism, while also highlighting obstacles to 'progression', especially within education. 'Left liberal' multiculturalism emphasises cultural difference and tends to exoticise Otherness. This variant emphasises the role of 'authentic experience' and the politics of social location; it also, according to McLaren, tends to be a-theoretical (1994: 52). Lastly, critical or 'resistance' multiculturalism, influenced by postmodernism, asserts that signs and significations, including racial ones, are unstable and shifting. Representations of race as well as class and gender are understood to be the result of larger social struggles over signs, meanings and institutional structures.

A second concern in this literature relates to struggles against the conservative/corporatist interpretations which predominate in the USA (Goldberg 1994; Kincheloe and Steinberg 1997), and which have appropriated the (originally ironic) term 'politically correct'. Attacks from the right on 'politically correct' strategies, including teaching strategies, form part of contemporary 'multicultural wars'. This includes the renewed debate on 'race and IQ', which rarely receives serious social science platform in Britain (with perhaps the exception of some, isolated, psychology departments) except as an example of a racist debate. Virtually all US theoretical and political currents, except the extreme, white supremacist right, feel impelled to accept some form of 'multiculturalism'. A third and important theme concerns more practical, pedagogic issues: we draw upon this literature in the discussion below.

Much of the critical work on multiculturalism in the US by writers such as Bhaba, Giroux, Goldberg, hooks and McLaren comes from the field of cultural studies as well as from education faculties (e.g. Kincheloe and Steinberg 1997). Some of this has crossed national boundaries, referring to British work, especially that of Stuart Hall and Paul Gilroy, as well as that of Carby, Parekh and Jeater. Without wishing to reify disciplinary boundaries, much US sociology (of race/ethnicity) remains firmly focused on American concerns, including the particular US 'race relations' problematic (see Pincus and Erlich 1994; Arthur and Shapiro 1996), especially the situation of a racialised 'underclass'.

Multiculturalism, anti-racism, essentialism

Debates concerning multiculturalism, the meaning(s) of 'race' and ethnicity, otherness, and essentialised versions of the above, underpin those over pedagogy. Such 'abstract' matters form a backdrop to not-so-abstract conflicts within and without seminar rooms.

A focus on what is termed identity politics, essentialist multiculturalism, left essentialism, or anti-racism should not obscure the fact that there are other, essentialised culturalist politics, including explicitly racist ones This is particularly the case in the USA, due to the organisational strength of the (mainly Christian) right, but is also so, albeit more diffusely, in Britain – despite the image of a new 'rainbow nation'. 'Monoculturalism' remains the dominant form. However small essentialist cultural/ethnic/political groupings are in general, they are of great importance in any discussions of race, race politics, cultural forms, resistances, policies and related issues.

As Mohan points out, the central questions of relativism (linked to multiculturalism) are by no means trivial:

> How do we understand and engage with difference and alterity without reducing them to images of ourselves or incorporating them into our frames of intelligibility, thereby replicating the insularity and violence of Eurocentric encounters with others? How do we get off the well-worn paths . . . of dealing with otherness and learn to listen to others articulating desires on its own terms? Motivated by a respect for others' selves, spaces, contexts and histories, relativism has put on the intellectual agenda, the investigation of crucial social and political interests served by the repressions and absences in dominant frameworks of understanding the world.
>
> (Mohan 1995: 383)

'Identity politics' can provide spaces for the exploration of individual and group backgrounds, affirm ethnic and racialised cultures which are often denigrated, and rediscover submerged histories (or, at times, 'herstories'). Identity politics too, can provide important possibilities for self-direction (Goldberg 1994). All of these factors are important in classrooms.

However, even in its less 'essentialist' forms, relativism usually fails in establishing responsible dialogue between different cultures (Mohan 1995). 'Left essentialist' (Kincheloe and Steinberg's term) multiculturalists often connect (the category) difference to a historical past of cultural authenticity where the essence of a particular identity developed – or an essence that transcends the forces of historical and social context and power (1997: 20).

If identity politics can be affirming, it can also be excluding. Kincheloe and Steinberg remind us that: 'Some versions of anti-racism often assume that only authentically oppressed people can possess moral agency, e.g. a white person cannot criticise a Latino. In such essentialised identity politics, one would have to submit proper credentials before offering an opinion on race or gender' (1997: 21). This politics of location holds that the basis of epistemological authority is a set of 'authentic' experiences. Goldberg is even more critical of the (dominant) simplistic versions of cultural relativism:

> This failure [of cultural studies] has enabled a more or less uncontested (re)emergence of dangerous claims to truth: racialised representations of the underclass in terms of poverty of culture; Holocaust denials; conspiratorial Jewish corporate and political powers; Jews qua Jews as slave traders and owners; Muslim terrorists in Bosnia . . .
>
> (1994: 15)

Such representations show how misleading is Kincheloe and Steinberg's use of the term 'left' to describe a form of essentialism. Gilroy more properly terms such orientations as 'cultural nationalist' (1993b). As such, critiques of them must be similar to those made of ideas of 'community' and 'nation': the arbitrary drawing of boundaries; exclusivity; lack of attention to – or suppression of – internal differences, particularly the disruptions of gender, sexuality and class; the problem of who represents the nation/community/people, etc.; and (for some) an inherent tendency to racism or at least xenophobia.

Most people who support identity politics are not, of course, virulent cultural nationalists; however, it is of importance to note the congruence between nationalism and at least some forms of cultural relativism.

Some responses to essentialism from US writers have been highly critical. The main responses have been to formulate models of multiculturalism which are somewhat more flexible and which aim for socio-economic as well as cultural change, as in the outline of 'critical multiculturalism' (McLaren 1994). Giroux, for instance, sees schools and other public institutions as 'border institutions': teachers and students can become 'border crossers' (1994: 329). Despite the attraction of this conception, cultures are seen as intact entities, albeit ones with permeable boundaries.

US-based critiques do not query the conceptual basis of the term 'race' beyond a cursory recognition that is in part a social construction. The category 'white' is now more often discussed (Roediger 1991; Frankenburg 1993) but the categories tend to emerge as very bounded rather than deconstructed (but see Marable 1995 on blackness). Kincheloe and Steinberg write that groups like the Irish, Italians and Jews (in the USA) do not always know that they are white, and refer to their ethnicities as a first source of identity (1997: 21). The option of using the term ethnicity to denote more fluid categories (Anthias 1990; Anthias and Yuval-Davis 1992; Barth 1969; Hall 1992) appears not to be an option in this debate, due perhaps to the unfortunate history of the concept in the USA. It is still used mainly to refer to differences among white groups, although this appears to be changing with the migration of groups little-represented before the 1960s, notably Asians from various countries.

Yudice's work (1995) is an exception to the tendency to see whiteness in essentialist 'racial' terms and does begin to interrogate the idea of whiteness. He critiques the idea that whiteness automatically grants privilege. He argues that whites, especially working-class whites, must be able to assert a white identity which does not necessarily emulate blacks/Hispanics, if multiculturalism is to have any resonance for them. However, he reacts with extreme anger to the suggestion that Jews are not necessarily white or automatically privileged (Lerner 1993 cited in Yudice) despite his acknowledgement that he grew up in an area in which multiple racisms, including anti-Semitism, existed. He asserts that Lerner – and perhaps Jews more generally? – wish to gain from racism by divesting themselves of whiteness, and that Lerner himself is opportunistic and racist (1995: 261). However, the (also white) readers of *Race Traitor* – who wish to 'abolish the white race' – are accused only of *naïveté* (1995: 271). A charitable analysis of this reaction is that race and racism are seen as essentially based on skin colour: i.e. it is assumed that this is how 'race' has been constructed in the USA historically and still is at present, therefore most US Jews are 'white', although in a European past and an East European present such a category would have been nonsensical.

Goldberg argues for a more robust form of relativism. Against the abandoning of evaluative judgement by some multiculturalists and postmodernists, such relativism would allow distinctions to be drawn between more or less accurate truth claims and more or less justifiable values (vs. the right or the good) (1994: 15). He maintains that the category 'heterogeneity' should become a central, organising one for multiculturalists: irrepressible traces of heterogeneity dot any mapping of human history (see Dyson 1994 for discussion of African-Americans in this context).

In Britain, explicit debates around these issues have been more firmly based in the discipline of sociology than in cultural studies. They have also more radically deconstructed the idea of 'race' as a shared construction, and as having any biological content. The work of Miles, Gilroy, Hall, Anthias and Yuval-Davis and others have been crucial in this respect. While approaching the subject from different directions, Hall and Gilroy, for instance, stress that the racial formation signified by 'black' has been used as a site of resistance and mobilisation. Others such as Brah disrupt the idea of culture as an entity with fixed boundaries and determinate 'matter' within these boundaries. The latter uses the words of the 'Chicago Cultural Studies Group'[3] to describe 'the flattened homogenized model of culture in anthropology' (1994: 134). Gilroy, arguing against 'ethnic absolutism', writes: 'cultures . . . even in situations of brutality, are never sealed off from one another' (1993a: 2). Moreover, 'the refusal to accept syncretic inter-dependency [of cultures] . . . has been associated recently with . . . an over integrated notion of pure culture' (1993: 31–2). Work based on political economy, notably that of Miles (also Anthias 1990; Carter 1996), has distanced itself more radically from the idea of race, substituting the concepts of racialisation and ethnicity (see also Hall 1992). Thus in Britain, the earlier 'race relations' discourse is being supplanted, using concepts such as difference (itself criticised in turn for its lack of critical purchase; see Brah 1996; Chicago Cultural Studies Group 1994), diaspora, hybridity and syncretism. The latter stress fluidity rather than fixity.

This amounts to a highly sophisticated discourse – another example of (hybridised) British ingenuity that deserves export. How does such a discourse translate into teaching concerns and teaching praxis within higher education? In the following sections we survey some general issues concerning curricula, the subject positions of lecturers and students, and conflicts within lecture/seminar settings. We ask if and how such issues are informed by the changes in 'race' discourse outlined above.

The curriculum

The development of any subject curriculum is always a matter of construction of knowledge. Lecturers develop curricula according to their own interests, existing knowledge-bases, political positions and whatever debates and discourses are current. Student interest may help to form the curriculum on some courses.

Given the paucity of recent research it is difficult to discuss in detail what is taught on contemporary British higher education 'race' courses. Thiara and Goulbourne's survey (1991) indicated that the majority of courses taught in the early 1990s were, perhaps not surprisingly, British-based, and concentrated on institutional aspects, for instance 'race' and immigration law, the media, education and policing, as well as the black experience in Britain, historically and at present. Some courses were social policy oriented. In 1991, few contained comparative material; those which did, usually drew on US or South African experience. However, a very small number compared differing European experiences. Where sociological theories were mentioned, these were most often Marxist, social psychological and feminist, with some emphasis on discourse as a matter of inquiry. At that time, most although not all of the courses surveyed tended to fit into the 'race relations' problematic.

Discourses have shifted, including the emphasis on 'discourse' itself, and so have people. It seems fair to assume, despite lack of contemporary detail, that current debates and concerns over concepts such as identity, difference, hybridity and diaspora play some part in current 'race' courses, despite the undoubted difficulties in presenting such complex material. Some concern with definitions of 'race' and other terms such as ethnicity, nation, racialisation and blackness/whiteness was apparent in the 1991 survey. It is probable, too, that what Miles terms the current concern with naming has become more central, and may have displaced analysis of why racism occurs (1994).

The literature referred to earlier does not focus on curriculum matters, being posed at more general levels. One topic is the importance of teaching history. Kincheloe and Steinberg, for instance, write: 'Any critical multicultural curriculum must be grounded on rigorous historical scholarship that explores not only excluded . . . histories but also the construction of public memory in both subjugated and dominant groups' (1997: 231). They cite W. E. B. DuBois's insights. Giroux writes, 'Multiculturalism itself signifies a terrain of struggle around the reformulation of memory and national identity' (1994: 336). And Miles puts forward a generally accepted structural (in his case, Marxist) view that any serious teaching of 'race' must contain a historical dimension.

Even if there is agreement on this point (and many 'cultural studies' oriented courses omit a historical dimension), problems do not end there. Whose/which history/ies are taught? A strong – and understandable – tendency in teaching race is to construct the 'object' of study in terms of racialised communities, with any attention to gender or class divisions added on. Further, which racialised communities should be studied? To cite two issues: although one might expect students to know of the history of black slavery, in the USA or the Caribbean, this is often not the case even for black/African-origin students. A similar comment might be made about the Holocaust. Unlike the subjects of slavery and colonialism, the Holocaust appeared on a very small minority of courses (2–3), perhaps because that subject does not fit easily within the British post-war race problematic. Even less often taught, until recently, are the histories of Asian groupings, of the Irish, or of other minority groupings within Europe. Movement away from a certain degree of British parochialism has the merit of unearthing different histories, it lends (additional) complexity to (the) story/ies of 'race', and it also tends to unsettle any notion that 'race' as a categorical attribute carried exclusively by non-white groups.

The subject position/s of teachers

The issue of subject positioning – of both teachers and students – is brought to the fore by feminist work, as well as by postmodern currents. Another – separate – issue is the need for more African-Caribbean and Asian teachers in higher education. We should first ask how 'subject positioning' should be construed. Should it be seen (as it usually is in the contexts discussed) in terms of 'race', of ethnicity/nationality/religion? What about other aspects of subject positioning and sources of identity, particularly gender, age, class, disability or more idiosyncratic factors? How, if at all, do teachers' subject positionings affect questions such as choice of curriculum, or teaching strategies?

The need for more ethnic/racialised minority teachers in higher education is often conflated with the need for 'role models'. This is baggage from debates over race and schooling, in which the black teachers' presence is seen as needing particular justification, and the role these teachers are assumed to play especially *vis-à-vis* ethnic minority schoolchildren. The relatively few African-Caribbean/ Asian-origin higher education teachers in British institutions may be cast as role models. Thus, the complex question (of subject positioning) is sometimes reduced to a seemingly much simpler one.

As Anita Allen (1994) points out, lecturers/professors are usually (seen as) role models in the sense of 'ethical templates': 'Role models are individuals who inspire others to believe that they too may be capable of high accomplishment' (citing Thompson and Sher in M. Cohen 1977). There are valid arguments for role models (see Hooks 1994; Leicester 1993). Allen, writing of US black women law professors (i.e. lecturers), comments that black women academics can assume nurturing roles, particularly for other black women, who may badly require such support to avoid marginalisation in 'the academy'. The role model can take on an important emblematic status for students. Bhattacharyya writes that an assumption concerning black teachers (and presumably others in 'oppressed' statuses?) is that the bad experiences the teacher has suffered will aid communication with students who have suffered similarly (1996: 165). She, and we (and, presumably, the students cited), feel that there are only some elements of truth in this argument.

Bhattacharyya comments that shared experience does not immediately mean that all the individuals affected can successfully negotiate teaching situations (ibid.). Allen notes that the idea of 'role models' perpetuates the idea that black women (or other groupings) are inferior intellectuals. She argues further that it presumes that white teachers have no role to play in addressing the special needs of black students (1994).

Another issue is that black/minority teachers may play a symbolic role for institutions as well as students and other staff: 'the black teacher is wheeled on as some institutional response to a whole set of racial difficulties' (Bhattacharyya 1996: 166). While we need more black/Asian/minority lecturers, this should not translate into a new racialised oppression in which these lecturers must carry institutional needs and expectations.

These observations return us to questions of essentialism and authenticity. It is often assumed that teachers of 'race' should themselves be minority group members (ideally African or Asian origin, or Jewish at a pinch). A lecturer's possibly painful/demeaning experience of racism is not seen as an experience that might be shared, from which others might learn, but as one lending 'authenticity'. Only those endowed with such authenticity can speak with authority (as lecturers, but also as students); those lacking in authenticity cannot discuss the issue of 'race'. As Fuss writes, 'Personal consciousness of individual oppressions, lived experience – in short, identity politics – can act both to authorize and to de-authorize speech' (1989: 116).

This question is logically separate from those of numbers of black teachers, representation and role models. Ethnic minority social science/humanities teachers may not – and often do not – wish to teach race as this may make them feel ghettoised. Their academic interests may simply lie elsewhere. The presence of a 'minority' teacher on a race course may signal both to the institution and to other staff that the space of race teaching is 'filled'. In this scenario, African/Asian-origin/etc. people carry 'race' issues and non- marked others sense that they do not have to do so: 'race' is being 'dealt with'. We should not load the question of 'representation' onto courses on race. Neither should it be assumed that the presence of Asian/black teachers automatically translates into non-Eurocentric curricula – although members of particular groups may be sensitive to particular forms of racism and teaching materials. Henwood and Phoenix warn us that (in psychology) the presence of large numbers of female students and growing numbers of female lecturers have not had significant impact on gender-biased assumptions of mainstream teaching in the discipline (1996).

Although some Asian/Muslim/African/Irish-origin teachers do wish to assume the position of 'role model', others may not wish to assume pastoral roles in addition to other duties. Our intuition is that, as fiscal and academic pressures increase for all staff, fewer will be able to take on extra nurturing, regardless of their personal inclinations.[4] We note that female staff are often expected to take on pastoral roles and are likely to meet much 'everyday' rather than official disapproval should they fail to do so. Institutions may need to seek wider solutions to meeting the needs of students facing racism/s.

Experience is an important basis of knowledge. Regardless of a person's own experiences of racism (or sexism, able-bodyism) one has no direct experience beyond her/his own life, and even this experience is processed through abstract knowledge. Even if we assume that individuals of one grouping share a collective consciousness (of Partition, the Holocaust, US slavery, police brutality), we cannot expect members of one group to understand the racisms of other minority groups. Individuals are positioned according to other social divisions as well as individual/family experience. Every individual processes information differently. We do not wish to deconstruct totally experiences of racism, or of collective consciousness; these exist, but are nevertheless variable as are racial/ethnic categorisations.

To acknowledge a role for 'experience' does not amount to the essentialist view that only African/Asian/Jewish-origin teachers can teach race because of their 'authentic experience' and that a white English male (seen in England as 'non-ethnic'), cannot, or is at best an inferior teacher. The practice (from women's studies) of acknowledging one's own subject position remains important but does not solve all problems. All lecturers occupy power positions *vis-à-vis* their students. 'Positioning' oneself risks that one facet of identity (ethnicity/'race'/religion) becomes frozen and essentialised within the classroom. However, such positioning at least acknowledges that the teacher, like the student, is an individual located socially and culturally. This observation should not, of course, hold true only on 'race' courses. The difference, in our experience, between such courses and others is that the lecturer may not be able to act otherwise. The challenge remains concerning how the lecturer can acknowledge his/her own position without lapsing either (for African-Caribbean/Asian/other minority staff) into essentialism of experience or (for 'unmarked'/white staff) into unproductive defensiveness and apology for commitment to 'race' issues.

Conflicts

'Race' seminars and classrooms are often sites of conflict. Dissension and miscommunication may occur between lecturers and students and, even more commonly, among students. Although a number of teachers stated that conflicts occurred in this teaching more frequently than in other social science subjects (e.g. sociological theory, sociology of health), the British literature is nearly silent on this aspect (see Henwood and Phoenix 1996). As with other practical pedagogical issues, US literature is more forthcoming, although it is possible that overt clashes may occur more frequently in US seminar rooms.[5] Goldberg, citing Graff (1988), exhorts teachers to 'teach the conflicts' rather than to seek avoidance strategies. Hooks counsels teachers not to despair when they encounter conflict in multicultural classrooms (1994: 33); she challenges the idea that the classroom should necessarily be a safe and harmonious place.

Students undertake 'race' courses for a variety of reasons. Aside from 'normal' reasons for doing courses (academic interest; compulsory nature of course; to obtain specific academic/vocational qualifications; to further conceptual understanding; more mundanely, to make up a required option/number of credits) students may have additional motivations for studying 'race' material. These include: desires to work out personal identity matters; to work through experiences of racism; to understand (and sometimes to affect) global racialised conflicts; and to combat racism. Thus 'race' courses frequently carry an extra loading of expectation, over and above those of other courses. In some cases, a race course may be the main – or only – space in which such issues can be openly discussed. This may apply particularly to those students who feel racially/ethnically marginalised within departments and institutions.

Conflicts among students can take a variety of forms; for the sake of discussion here, we categorise these into:

- Overt/intentional racist expressions (in general uncommon on race courses apart from some forms such as anti-Gypsy expressions).
- Expression of unconsciously held stereotypes.
- Conflicts occurring through the medium of ' identity politics'. While this has been critiqued, we should note its positive side. Within seminar rooms, expressions of experience may provide some students with their first opportunities to speak about these issues (Kincheloe and Steinberg 1997). Expressions of 'unmarked' white/English experience does not have to take a self-conscious form because it is already universalised and normative.

Another twist to this situation may arise when, in predominantly white/English/ Christian classes, minority students may feel pressured to assume the role of 'indigenous authority' (Hooks 1994). Some students are comfortable sharing experience; others meet this situation with silence and withdrawal. A common reaction, expressed by students in individual discussions (see note 6), is anxiety at 'being looked at'. Concern over the 'gaze' of others in the classroom may be an inhibiting factor in open discussion, especially for female students.

Friction, disagreement and tension within seminar rooms normally takes place, by definition, in the teacher's presence. S/he is meant to manage situations; to ensure that a minority student is not positioned as a resource by other students; to mediate conflicts; to allow space for all to speak while encouraging analytical thought. Conflicts between lecturers and students may take the forms mentioned above, although in this case mediated by unequal power relations, which make any conflicts more acute for students. The student who feels subject to semi-covert stereotyping by other students may at times be able to express anger/dismay about this; but similar feelings about lecturers may not be expressed because they are more dangerous. Lecturers may also be subject to racism (see below), but students are not in powerful positions so these may be less immediately threatening (although still painful) and lecturers are inhibited in self-expression, lest they lose their neutral/mediating roles in the classroom.

One of the authors has interviewed twenty-seven lecturers in Britain teaching 'race'-based courses. The material in the following sections is based on these interviews, from a workshop on teaching 'race' and from group and individual discussions with students carried out at intervals over the past four years.[6]

Of lecturers interviewed, several expressed concern about the ratio of 'experiential' vs. 'analytical' content within race seminar settings. Aware of students' needs to pass examinations/write formal essays, (some) lecturers were anxious that seminars should contribute concretely to analytical learning (i.e. that which is assessed in most academic settings) as well as to be sites for exploration of identity/experience. This, we note, was not from a naive separation between theory and experience/practice, but limitations of time. Given the discrimination many African/Asian-origin students will face in the labour market, this consideration may be of special import. Lecturers also felt that academic space ought to be partly directed by students in ways they saw fit and useful.

Another teaching concern was that the deconstructionist paradigm could be experienced by undermining the position of some students of African and African-Caribbean-origin. This is prefigured in US writings: 'Anti-essentialist displacement must not be seen as a convenient way of silencing students' (Fuss 1989: 117). Hooks echoes this: 'The critique of identity politics should not be a new, chic way of silencing those from marginalized groups' (1994: 83). Hooks notes that teachers may have to distance themselves from students' needs for immediate affirmation and to learn patience. 'It may take time for students to experience paradigmatic shifts as positive' (1994: 42). Indeed, we would argue, such shifts are often experienced as threatening. For some, the notion that 'race' is a social construction is liberating; for others, the idea that that which has constrained and oppressed one throughout life is imagined, or that differences between blood groups have more biological import (Harris 1995), is close to devastating. It may be necessary to devote much time and 'space' within seminars to allow for discussion of students' own theoretical and personal reactions.

The situations faced by teachers of 'race' are very complex. Nearly all university teachers, of course, face complex seminar situations. But those involving 'race' may carry particular emotional charge. The following is a small sample of situations cited by social science lecturers in interviews concerning 'race' teaching.

> White English working-class student to white English female middle-class lecturer:
>   'Jewish people have culture and they have money, too. Black people, they have culture. We don't have anything.'

> African-Caribbean English male to white male lecturer of European origin and to class:
>   'This is our experience, after all: this is what the course is about. What business do you have telling us about our experience?'

Situation faced by Asian-origin female lecturer:

The seminar group is predominantly white, two-thirds female. The lecturer does not wish to offer personal experiences to highlight social issues or to represent black/Asian womanhood. The students, especially women, become frustrated and angry, wishing her to be more 'open'.

White European-origin female lecturer:

'Ethnicity may at times be a "mode of struggle", a reaction to racism.'

Muslim female student:

'Do you mean that Muslim identity is only a reaction? That it has no value in itself!?'

African-Caribbean male lecturer:

'Will there ever be a day when I have a mainly black group? I am the "other" in my own classroom.'

Jewish male to white English male lecturer:

'What right do you have to talk about domestic violence in the Jewish community? These matters are dealt with internally and it is not a big problem anyway. Our main problem, what we have to deal with now, is growing anti-Semitism.'

Situation faced by African-Caribbean origin female lecturer:

'In many seminars I face an insidious struggle for control. The group is mainly white. Some students try to undermine me in small ways. Others just look on . . . I don't think that white teachers face this – or maybe it is partly due to gender . . .'

White Welsh female student in a group comprised of a wide 'racial'/ethnic/religious mix, who largely agree:

'But Romanies do make a nuisance for neighbours, don't they? I know they have their own rules and such, but they create a big mess.'

Space does not allow us to unpack each of these intricate situations here. We simply wish to point out that 'race' lecturers faced with such interactions are enjoined to respond rapidly and incisively, but in a manner which does not undermine students or 'put them down', as this can only be unproductive in the long run. Lecturers may need to 'live with' frustration and ambiguity because deeply held beliefs and senses of identity may be at stake.

Moreover, discussion of 'race' issues may involve painful memory and emotion, whether collective or individual, historical or contemporary. Teachers need to 'contain' much emotion, including sometimes their own, within the classroom. There is some reference to this factor within US writing, but silence in Britain. To acknowledge overtly that discussions in 'race' classrooms may involve emotional aspects for some, would not halt dissension or conflict, but might ease many situations. Another consideration is that few academics have the training to deal with feelings which might arise, either for themselves of for students; nor do there exist general models – at least outside psychoanalysis – upon which they might draw. Whether or not British higher education seminar rooms are seen by lecturers (and students) as legitimate spaces for the voicing of emotion, strong feeling concerning 'race', racism and racialised experience can be banned. Racialised/ethnic/national and religious categories of identity are often linked to collective trauma, historical and contemporary, and feelings about these may 'surface' even if this is part of normative models of seminar-room interaction.

Conclusion

Shifting discourses concerning 'race' and racism, ethnicity and multiculturalism, have marked work on schooling and 'race' in Britain. In higher education, British social science/cultural studies theorists have developed a sophisticated discourse on 'race', but research on how this translates into university teaching is at an early stage. This contrasts with the situation in the USA, where a more essentialist discourse coexists with concern over teaching practicalities, such as conflict.

With the entry to ethnic minority students into British higher education in larger numbers, more work is being undertaken. At the time of writing, research on recruitment of ethnic minority staff to institutions of higher education is being undertaken at the University of Bristol. A sub-committee of the HEFCE-funded SSP2000 initiative is concerned with 'race'/ethnicity, issues of ethnic minority student recruitment and progression (Bird and Middleton 2000). This will add to the work which we have discussed on student recruitment, equal opportunities policies, the spread of courses including 'race' issues and other curriculum matters. There is scope for more work on subjects including the experiences of minority students from different groupings, course curricula and the interaction between 'multicultural' and 'anti-racist' strategies.

Drawing on Leicester (1993), Neal (1995 and 1998) and Bhattacharrya (1996), we would like to emphasise the connections between individual lecturers/departments and institutional strategies. The less an institution as a whole deals with 'race' issues, the more individual lecturers on race courses will be expected to 'solve' wider problems. Minority lecturers, and race courses, will continue to be seen as emblematic, and the (many) individual initiatives which do occur will be less effective.

In this chapter we have pursued a more specific focus, that of strategies on social science courses which discuss 'race' as a central concern. According to the experience of lecturers and students interviewed (note 6), teaching such subjects often involves conflict and contestation as part of learning processes. The content of such contestation depends upon a variety of factors, including (*inter alia*) the lecturer's positioning (not only ethnic/racial), the theoretical frame used, overall course content, student background and expectations, and the personalities of lecturer/s and students.

'Race' classrooms (at least, at times) provide space for the exploration of feelings/experience and their connection with wider concepts, but they are unlikely to be able to 'solve' definitely any of the problems arising. Bhattacharyya puts it well (and bravely):

> one of the uncertain points which interests me . . . [is] the point at which an honest attempt at political education must talk about what is not possible . . . Living with the discomfort of . . . inadequate compromises is what we are left with . . .
>
> (1996: 162)

Giroux writes that one of the aims of 'insurgent multicultural' teaching is to 'get students beyond a world they already know in order to challenge and to provoke their inquiry' . . . (1994: 340). Facilitating such learning requires many areas of teaching skill, both intellectual and interpersonal. If conflicts occur, so do exchanges, enrichment and the gaining of greater depth and breadth of understanding for both students and lecturers.

As we have emphasised, we need a broader discussion of the immediate pedagogical (and theoretical) practicalities of 'race' teaching as well as the experiences of students and of teachers on these courses. Limited and contingent answers may be possible; some compromises may be more satisfactory than others.

Notes

1 Parents could withdraw children from such assemblies, and some concessions were made in geographical areas where the majority population was non-Christian (in practice usually Muslim).
2 See Wilson 1998. This stated that 12 per cent of higher education staff belong to 'non-white' ethnic minorities, but this was a production error; the text should read that 12 per cent of higher education students are from 'non-white' minorities (Wilson, pers. comm., 4 January 1999).
3 The Chicago Cultural Studies Group was formed temporarily to write the article.
4 Fee-paying students, whatever their 'race'/ethnicity, may have high expectations of staff in pastoral capacities.
5 US students may speak out more readily; there is (to generalise) less fear of 'saying the wrong thing', and expression of feelings and experience is far more acceptable. Although these observations are the stuff of national stereotypes, they also describe behavioural norms.
6 Susie Jacobs has collected data on the subjects discussed, by means of:
  - interviews, in person and by telephone, with fifteen teachers of social science courses specifically dealing with 'race' in higher education (1996–7);
  - organisation of a workshop on 'teaching race', at the British Sociological Association Conference, University of Reading, April 1996;
  - less structured discussions with students of 'race' over some years;
  - semi-structured discussions with approximately twelve teachers of 'race' issues in social science and allied subjects;
  - S. Jacobs, J. Batsleer and E. Burman chaired a day conference on teaching race in higher education at Manchester Metropolitan University, February 1997;
  - N. Hai and S. Jacobs held a small group interview with undergraduate students of race, March 1998.

Bibliography

Afshar, H. 1994 'Women and the politics of fundamentalism in Iran', *Women Against Fundamentalism Journal* 5: 15–20.

Ahmed, S. 1997 ' "It's a sun-tan isn't it?" Autobiography as an identificatory practice', in H. Mirza (ed.) *Black British Feminism: A Reader*, London: Routledge.

Agulhon, M. 1989 *Marianne au pouvoir. L'imagerie et la symbolique républicaine de 1880 à 1914*, Paris: Flamarrion.

Alleg, H. 1958 *La question*, Paris: Editions de Minuit.

Allen, A. 1994 'On being a role model', in D. Goldberg (ed.) *Multiculturalism: A Critical Reader*, Oxford: Blackwell.

Alund, A. 1995 'Alterity in modernity', *Acta Sociologica* 38: 311–22.

Amselle, J.-L. 1996 *Vers un multiculturalisme français? L'empire de la coutume*, Paris: Aubier.

Anderson, B. 1990 *Imagined Communities: Reflections on the Origin and Spread of Nationalism*, London/New York: Verso.

—— 1995 'Ice empire and ice hockey: two fin de siècle dreams', *New Left Review* 214: 146–50.

Anderson, J. (ed.) (2001) *Transnational Democracy*, London: Routledge.

Andrews, G. R. 1991 *Blacks and Whites in São Paulo, Brazil, 1888–1988*, Madison: University of Wisconsin Press.

Anthias, F. 1990 'Race and class revisited: conceptualising race and racisms', *Sociological Review* 38(3): 19–42.

—— 1992a 'Connecting "race" and ethnic phenomena', *Sociology* 26(3): 421–38.

—— 1992b *Ethnicity, Class, Gender and Migration, Greek Cypriots in Britain*, Aldershot: Avebury.

—— 1994 'Race conscious policies in Britain', *Innovation* 7: 239–58.

—— 1998a 'Evaluating "Diaspora": beyond ethnicity', *Sociology* 32(3): 557–80.

—— 1998b 'The limits of ethnic diversity', *Patterns of Prejudice* 32(4): 5–20.

—— 1998c 'Rethinking social divisions: some notes towards a theoretical framework', *Sociological Review* 47(2): 505–35.

—— 2000 *The Location of difference and the politics of location*, unpublished paper to conference on Feminist Utopias, Toronto, November 8–12, 2000.

—— 2001 'New hybridities, old concepts', *Ethnic and Racial Studies*, 24(4): 619–41.

—— forthcoming 'New British Cypriot Identities'.

Anthias, F. and Kelly, P. M. (eds) 1996 *Thinking about 'The Social'*, London: Greenwich University Press.

Anthias, F. and Yuval-Davis, N. 1983 'Contextualising feminism – gender, ethnic and class divisions', *Feminist Review* (Winter): 62–75.

—— 1992 *Racialized Boundaries: Race, Nation, Gender, Colour and Class and the Anti-racist Struggle*, London: Routledge.

Anzaldua, G. 1987 *Borderlines/La Frontera*, San Francisco: Spinster/Aunt Lute Books.

Appadurai, A. 1990 'Disjuncture and difference in the global cultural economy', in M. Featherstone (ed.) *Global Modernities*, London: Sage.

Arthur, J. and Shapiro, A. 1996 *Color, Class, Identity: The New Politics of Race*, Boulder: Westview.

Assiter, A. 1996 *Enlightened Women: Modernist Feminism in a Postmodern Age*, London: Routledge.

—— 1999 'Citizenship revisited', in N. Yuval-Davis and P. Werbner (eds) *Women, Citizenship and Difference*, London: Zed Books.

Back, L. 1996 *New Ethnicities and Urban Culture*, London: UCL Press.

Bakhtin, M. M. 1981 *The Dialogic Imagination: Four Essays by MM Bakhtin*, London: Emerson & Holquist, University of Texas Press.

—— 1986 *Speech Genres and Other Late Essays*, Austin: University of Texas Press.

Balibar, E. 1984 'La société metisée', *Le Monde*, Paris.

—— 1990 'Paradoxes of Universality', in D. Goldberg (ed.) *Anatomy of Racism*, Minneapolis, MN: University of Minnesota Press.

—— 1991a 'Es gibt keinen staat in Europa: racism and politics in Europe today', *New Left Review* (March/April): 5–19.

—— 1991b 'The Nation Form. History and Ideology', in E. Balibar and I. Wallerstein (eds) *Race, Nation, Class: Ambiguous Identities*, London: Verso.

—— 1992 *Les frontieres de la démocratie*, Paris: La Decouverte.

—— 1994 *Lieux et noms de la verité*, Paris: L'Aube.

—— 1997 *La crainte des masses. Politique et philosophie avant et après Marx*, Paris: Galilee.

—— 1998 *Droit de cité. Culture et politique en démocratie*, Paris: L'Aube.

Balibar, E. and Wallerstein, I. 1988 *Race nation classe, les identités ambiques*, Paris: La Découveste.

Banuri, T. 1990. 'Modernisation and its discontents: a cultural perspective on theories of development', in F. Apfell Marglin and S. A. Marglin (eds) *Dominating Knowledge*, Oxford: Clarendon Press, pp. 73–101.

Barth, F. 1969 *Ethnic Groups and Boundaries*, Boston: Little Brown & Co.

Barthelemy, M. 2000 *Associations: Un Nouvel Age de la Participation?*, Paris: Presses de Sciences Po.

Bauman, Z. 1991 *Modernity and Ambivalence*, Cambridge: Polity.

—— 1992 *Intimations of Postmodernity*, London: Routledge.

—— 1998 *Globalization: The Human Consequences*, New York: Columbia University Press.

Berlant, L. and Warner, M. 1994 'Introduction to critical multiculturalism', in D. Goldberg (ed.) *Multiculturalism: A Critical Reader*, Oxford: Blackwell.

Berlin, I. 1956 'The two Freedoms', in I. Berlin, and R. Wolheim. *Symposium on Equality*, Aristotelian proceedings, London.

Berthelier, R. 1994 *L'homme maghrebin dans la litterature psychiatrique*, Paris: L'Harmattan.

Beveridge, W. 1942 *Report on Social Insurance and Allied Services*, London: HMSO.

Bhabha, H. 1990 *Nation and Narration*, London: Routledge.

—— 1994 *The Location of Culture*, London/New York: Routledge.

Bhabha, J. and Shutter, S. 1994 *Women's Movement: Women under Immigration, Nationality and Refugee Law*, Stoke on Trent: Trentham Books.

Bhattacharyya, G. 1996 'Black skin, white boards: learning to be the "Race" lady in British higher education', *Parallax* 2: 161–71.

Bird, J. and Middleton, C. 2000 *Institutional Racism in Sociology and Social Policy*, London: HEFCE.

Birnbaum, P. 1989 'Sur l'étatisation révolutionnaire: l'abbé Gregoire et le destin de l'identité juive', *Le Debat* 52 (janvier/février): 157–73.

—— 1991 *Les Fous de la Republique: Histoire politique des juifs d'Etat, de Gambetta à Vichy*, Paris: Fayard.

—— 1993 *'La France aux Français'. Histoire politique des haines nationalistes*, Paris: Seuil.

Blum, L. 1938 *Contre le racisme. Discours prononcé le 26 novembre 1938 au banquet du Congrès de l'Anti-racisme*, Paris: Editions de droit de vivre.

Blumel, A. 1949 'Grandeur de ce combat', *Droit et Liberté* 29(1): 1.

Bonacich, R. 1973 'A theory of middleman minorities', *American Sociological Review* 38: 583–94.

Bonnett, A. 2000 *Anti-Racism*, London: Routledge.

Borne, D. 1977 *Petits bourgeois en revolte? Le mouvement Poujade*, Paris: Flammarion.

Bouamama, S. 1994 *Dix ans de marche des Beurs. Chronique d'un mouvement avorté*, Paris: Desclee de Brouwer.

Bourdieu, P. 1990 *The Logic of Practice*, Stanford: Stanford University Press.

Brah, A. 1996 *Cartographies of Diaspora: Contesting Identities*, London/New York: Routledge.

Brown, C. 1984 *Black and White Britain: The Third PSI Survey*, London: Heinemann.

Brown, R. 1992 'Same difference: the persistence of disadvantage in the racial employment market', in P. Braham, A. Rattansi and P. Skellington (eds) *Racism and Anti-racism*, London: Sage/Open University.

Brubaker, R. 1992 *Citizenship and Nationhood in France and Germany*, Cambridge, MA: Harvard University Press.

Bulmer, M. and Solomos, J. 1996 'Race, ethnicity and the curriculum', *Ethnic and Racial Studies* 19(4): 777–88.

—— 1998 'Introduction: re-thinking ethnic and racial studies', *Ethnic and Racial Studies* 21(5): 819–37.

Burke, J. 1999 'Reconciling cultural diversity with a democratic community: Mestizaje as opposed to the usual suspects', *Citizenship Studies* 3(1): 119–40.

Burney, E. 1988 *Steps to Social Equality: Positive Action in a Negative Climate*, London: Runnymede Trust.

Butler, J. 1990 *Gender Trouble*, London: Routledge.

Cabinet Office, Women's Unit 1999 *Living without Fear*, London: Cabinet Office, Women's Unit.

Cain, H. and Yuval-Davis, N. 1990 'The "equal opportunities community" and the anti-racist struggle', *Critical Social Policy* (Autumn): 5–26.

Cambridge, A. and Feuchtwang, S. 1990 *Anti-racist Strategies*, Aldershot: Avebury.

Carby, H. 1982 'White woman listen! Black feminism and the boundaries of sisterhood', in CCCS (ed.) *The Empire Strikes Back: Race and Racism in 70s Britain*, London: Hutchinson.

CARF (Campaign Against Racism and Facism) 1981 *Southall: The Birth of a Black Community*, London: CARF/ Institute of Race Relations.

—— 1991 *Newham – The Forging of a Black Community*, London: CARF/Newham Monitoring Project.

Carmichael, S. and Hamilton, C. 1968 *Black Power: The Political Liberation in America*, Boston: Cape.

Carter, B. 1996 'Race, racisms and realism', Paper to BSA Conference, Worlds of the Future, University of Reading.

Castells, M. 1975 'Immigrant workers and class struggles in advanced capitalism: the western European experience', *Politics and Society* 5(1), p. 33–66.

Castles, S. 1999 'International migration and the global agenda', *International Migration* 37(1): 5–19.

Castles, S. and Kosack, G. 1973 *Immigrant Workers and Class Structure in Western Europe*, Oxford: Oxford University Press/IRR.

Castles, S. and Miller, M. J. 1993 *The Age of Migration: International Population Movements in the Modern World*, London: Macmillan.

Césaire, A. 1956 [1939] *Cahiers d'un retour au pays natal*, Paris: Presence Africaine.

Chicago Cultural Studies Group 1994 'Critical Multiculturalism', in D. Goldberg (ed.) *Multiculturalism: A Critical Reader*, Oxford: Blackwell.

Choudry, S. 1996 *Pakistani Women's Experiences of Domestic Violence in Great Britain*, London: Home Office Research and Statistics Directorate.

Cisse, M. 1999 *Parole de sans-papiers*, Paris: La Dispute.

Clifford, J. 1992 'Travelling cultures', in L. Grossberg, C. Nelson and P. Treichler (eds) *Cultural Studies*, London: Routledge.

—— 1994 'Diasporas', *Cultural Anthropology* 9(3): 302–38.

—— 1997 *Routes: Travel and Translation in the Late Twentieth Century*, Cambridge, MA: Harvard University Press.

Cloonan, M. and Street, J. 1998 'Rock the vote: popular culture and politics', *Politics* 18(1): 33–8.

Cohen, A. 1974 *Urban Ethnicity*, New York: Tavistock.

Cohen, J. and Arato, A. 1995 *Civil Society and Political Theory*, Boston: MIT Press.

Cohen, M. 1977 *Equality and Preferential Treatment*, Princeton: Princeton University Press.

Cohen, P. 1988 'The perversions of inheritance', in P. Cohen and H. Bains (eds) *Multiracist Britain*, London: Macmillan.

—— 1992 ' "Its racism what dunnit". Hidden narratives in theories of racism', in J. Donald and A. Rattansi (eds) *Race, Culture and Difference*, London: Sage.

Cohen, R. 1993 'Notions of diaspora: classical, modern and global', UNESCO-CRER International Seminar, Emerging Trends and Major Issues in Migration and Ethnic Relations in Western and Eastern Europe, University of Warwick.

—— 1994 *Frontiers of Identity: the British and Others*, London: Longman.

—— 1997 *Global Diasporas: An Introduction*, London: University College London Press.

Collins, P. 1992 *Black Feminist Thought: Knowledge, Consciousness and the Politics of Empowerment*, Boston: Unwin Hyman.

Conan, E. and Rousso, H. 1994 *Vichy, un passe qui ne passe pas*, Paris: Fayard.

Conklin, A. 1997 *A Mission to Civilize: The Republican Idea of Empire in France and West Africa 1895–1930*, Stanford: Stanford University Press.

Connolly, C. 1990 'Splintered sisterhood: anti-racism in a young women's project', *Feminist Review* 36, (Autumn): 52–64.

—— 1991 'Washing our linen', *Feminist Review* 37 (Spring): 68–77.

Costa-Lascoux, J. 1990 *Anti-discrimination in Belgium, France and the Netherlands*, Strasbourg Committee of Experts on Community Relations, Council of Europe.

Council of Europe 2000 'Tous différents tous egaux: du principe à la pratique. Contribution Européenne à la conference mondiale contre le racisme, la discrimination raciale, la xenophobie et l'intolerance qui y est associée', Strasbourg: Council of Europe.

Coutant, P. 1997 'L'anti-racisme en crise', *M* (janvier–fevrier): 50–4.

Cruz, A. 1995 *Shifting, the Responsibility: Carriers' Liability in the Member States of the EU and North America*, Stoke on Trent: Trentham Books.

Datafolha 1995 *300 Anos de Zumbi: Os Brasileiros e o Preconceito de Côr*, São Paulo: Datafolha.

Daly, M. 1993 *Communitarianism: Belonging and Commitment in a Pluralist Democracy*, Belmont, CA: Wadsworth Publishing Company.

Damas, L. 1939 'Misère noire', *Esprit* 81(june): 333–54.

Danese, G. 1998 'Transnational collective action in Europe: the case of migrants in Italy and Spain', *Journal of Ethnic and Migration Studies* 24(4): 715–34.

Daniel, W. 1968 *Racial Discrimination in England*, London: PEP/Penguin.

de Lepervanche, M. 1980 'From race to ethnicity', *Australian and New Zealand Journal of Sociology* 16(1): 24–37.

Dewitte, P. 1985 *Les Mouvements nègres en France 1919–1939*, Paris: L'Harmattan.

Diawara, M. 1992 'Interview with VY Mudimbre', in V. Mudimbe (ed.) *The Surreptitious Speech: Presénce Africaine and the Politics of Otherness 1947–1987*, Chicago/London: University of Chicago Press.

Dickanson, O. P. 1992 *Canada's First Nations*. Toronto: McClelland and Stanley.

Diop, A. 1997 *Dans la peau d'un sans-papiers*, Paris: Seuil.

D'Souza, D. 1995 *The End of Racism*, New York: Free Press.

Dubet, F. 1987 *La Galère*, Paris: Fayard.

Dumont, L. 1972 *Homo Hierarchicus*, New York: Paladin.

Dyson, E. 1994 'Essentialism and the complexities of racial identity', in D. Goldberg (ed.) *Multiculturalism: A Critical Reader*, Oxford: Blackwell.

Edwards, J. 1988 'Justice and the bounds of welfare', *Journal of Social Policy* 18.

Edwards, V. 1976 'Effects of dialect on the comprehension of West Indian children', *Educational Research* 18(2): 83–95.

Einaudi, J.-L. 1991 *La bataille de Paris: 17 octobre 1961*, Paris: Seuil.

Enzensberger, H. 1992 'The great migration', *Granta* 42: 15–51.

Evans, D. 1993 *Sexual Citizenship: The Material Construction of Sexualities*, London: Routledge.

Evans, M. 1997 *The Memory of Resistance: French Opposition to the Algerian War 1954–1962*, Oxford/New York: Berg.

Evregenis, D. 1985 'Committee of Inquiry into the Rise of Fascism and Racism in Europe, Report on findings of the inquiry', Strasbourg: European Parliament.

Eysenck, H. 1971 *Race, Intelligence, Education*, London: Morris Temple Smith.

Fabre, M. 1991 *From Harlem to Paris: Black American Writers in France 1840–1980*, Chicago: Chicago University Press.

Falk, R. 1995 'The world order between inter-state law and the law of humanity: the role of civil society institutions', in D. Archibugi and D. Held (eds) *Cosmopolitan Democracy*, Cambridge: Polity.

Fanon, F. 1952 *Peau noire masques blancs*, Paris: Seuil.

—— 1956 'Racisme et culture', *Présence Africaine* 8–9–10(juin–novembre): 122–31.

—— 1961 *Les damnés de la terre*, Paris: Gallimard.

Fassin, D., Morice, A. and Quiminal, C. 1997 *Les lois de l'inhospitalité. Les politiques de l'immigration à l'épreuve des sanspapiers*, Paris: La Decouverte.

Featherstone, M. 1990 *Global Culture: Nationalism, Globalisation and Identity*, London: Sage.

Fentress, J. and Wickham, C. 1992 *Social Memory*, Oxford: Blackwell.

Feuchtwang, S. 1990 'Racism: territoriality and ethnocentricity', in A. Cambridge and S. Feuchtwang (eds) *Anti-racist Strategies*, Aldershot: Avebury.

Fillieule, O. 1993 *Sociologie de la protestation. Les formes de l'action collective dans la France contemporaine*, Paris: L'Harmattan.

Fine, R. 1994 'The "New nationalism" and democracy: a critique of pro patria', *Democratization* 1(3): 423–43.

Finer, S. 1958 *Anonymous Empire*, London: Pall Mall Press.

Ford, G. 1992 *Europe: The Rise of Racism and Xenophobia*, London: Pluto.

Foucault, M. 1971 *L'ordre du dicours*, Paris: Gallimard.

—— 1977 *Language, Counter-memory, Practice. Selected Essays and Interviews*, Oxford: Blackwell.

—— 1980 *Power/Knowledge. Selected Interviews and Other Writings 1972–1977*, Harvester Wheatsheaf.

Frankenburg, R. 1993 *White Women: Race Matters*, London: Routledge.

Friedman, J. 1997 'Global crises, the struggle for cultural identity and intellectual porkbarelling: cosmopolitans versis locals, ethnics and nationals in an era of de-hegemonisation', in P. Werbner and T. Modood (eds) *Debating Cultural Hybridity*, London: Zed Books.

Fuss, D. 1989 *Essentially Speaking: Feminism, Nature and Difference*, New York: Routledge.

Gabriel, J. 1998 *Whitewash: Racialised Politics and Media*, London: Routledge.

Gaine, C. 1998 *No Problem Here: A Practical Approach to Education and 'Race' in White Schools*, London: Hutchinson Education.

Gallissot, R. 1985 *Misère de l'anti-racisme*, Paris: Arcantere.

Geddes, A. 1995 'Immigrant and ethnic minorities and the EU's democratic deficit', *Journal of Common Market Studies* 33(2): 197–217.

Geisser, V. 1997 *Ethnicité républicaine. Les élites d'origine maghrebine dans le système politique français*, Paris: Presses de Sciences Po.

Gibb, R. 1995 'The politics of (collective) identity: theoretical issues in the study of a French anti-racist movement', paper for conference on Anthropological Understandings of the Politics of Identity, Queens University Belfast, 15–17 December.

Giddens, A. 1991 *Modernity and Self-identity: Self and Society in the Late Modern Age*, Cambridge: Polity Press.

—— 1994 *Beyond Left and Right: The Future of Radical Politics*, Cambridge: Polity Press.

Gilbourn, D. 1995 *Racism and Anti-racism in Real Schools*, London: Open University Press.

Gill, S., Mayor, B. and Blair, M. (eds) 1992 *Racism and Education*, London: Sage/Open University.

Gilroy, P. 1987a Problems in Anti-Racist Strategy, London: Runymede Trust.

—— 1987b *There Ain't no Black in the Union Jack*, London: Hutchinson.

—— 1992 'The end of anti-racism', in J. Donald and A. Rattansi (eds) *Race, Culture and Difference*, London: Sage.

—— 1993a *The Black Atlantic*, London: Verso.

—— 1993b *Small Acts: Thoughts on the Politics of Black Cultures*, London: Serpent's Tail.

—— 1997 'Diaspora and the detours of identity', in K. Woodward (ed.) *Identity and Difference*, London: Sage.

—— 1998 'Race ends here', *Ethnic and Racial Studies* 21(5: 838–47).

—— 2000 *Against Race: Imagining Political Culture Beyond the Color Line*, Cambridge MA: Harvard University Press.

Girardet, R. 1968 'L'apotheose de la "plus grande France": L'idée coloniale devant l'opinion francaise 1930–1935', *Revue francaise de science politique* 18(6): 1085–114.

—— 1972 *L'idée coloniale en France 1870–1962*, Paris: Hachette.

—— 1987 'Autour de la notion de tradition politique. Essai de problematique', *Pouvoirs* 42(septembre): 5–14.

Giroux, H. 1994 'Insurgent multiculturalism and the promise of pedagogy', in D. Goldberg (ed.) *Multiculturalism: A Critical Reader*, Oxford: Blackwell.

Gleick, J. 1990 *Chaos – die Ordnung des Universums*, Munich: Droemersche Verlagsanstalt.

Goffman, E. 1974 *Frame Analysis*, New York: Harper and Row.

Goldberg, D. 1990 *Anatomy of Racism*, Minneapolis: University of Minnesota Press.

—— 1993 *Racist Culture*, Oxford: Blackwell.

—— 1994 *Multiculturalism: A Critical Reader*, London: Blackwell.

Gordon, P. 1989 *Citizenship for Some? Race and Government Policy 1979–1989*, London: Runnymede Trust.

Gorz, A. 1970 'Immigrant labour', *New Left Review* (May): 28–31.

Graff, G. 1988 'Teach the conflicts: an alternative to educational fundamentalism', in B. Craige (ed.) *Literature, Language, Politics*, Athens GA/London: University of Georgia.

Guidice, F. 1992 *Arabicides*, Paris: La Decouverte.

Guillaumin, C. 1972 *L'idéologie raciste. Genese et language actuel*, Paris: Mouton.

—— 1992 'Usages théoriques et usages banals du terme "race"', *Mots* 59–65.

Habermas, J. 1992 'Citizenship and national identity: some reflections on the future of Europe', *Praxis International* 12(1).

Hall, S. 1976 *Resistance through Rituals*, London: Hutchinson.

—— 1981 'Notes on deconstructing "the popular"', in R. Samuel (ed.) *People's History and Social Theory*, London: Routledge and Kegan Paul.

—— 1990 'Cultural identity and diaspora', in J. Rutherford (ed.) *Identity: Community, Culture, Difference*, London: Lawrence & Wishart.

—— 1992 *Modernity and its Futures*, Cambridge: Open University Press.

—— 1992 'New ethnicities' in J. Donald and A. Rattansi (eds) *Race, Culture and Difference*, London: Sage.

—— 1998 'Aspiration and attitude: reflections on Black Britain in the nineties' in Frontiers/Backyards, special issue of *New Formations* (Spring) 33: 38–46.

Hall, S. and du Gay, P. 1996 *Questions of Cultural Identity*, London: Sage.

Hall, S. and Held, D. 1989 'Citizens and citizenship', in S. Hall and S. Jacques (eds) *New Times*, London: Lawrence & Wishart.

Hall, S., Held, D. and Mcgrew, T. (eds) 1992 *Modernity and its Futures*, Cambridge: Polity Press.

Hamon, H. and Rotman, P. 1979 *Les porteurs de valises. La résistance française a la guerre d'Algérie*, Paris: Seuil.

Hanchard, M. G. 1994 *Orpheus and Power: The Movimento Negro of Rio de Janero and São Paolo, Brazil*, Princeton: Princeton University Press.

Hannigan, J. 1985 'Alain Touraine, Manuel Castels and social movement theory: a critical appraisal', *Sociological Quarterly* 26(4): 435–54.

Harding, S. 1991 *Whose Science? Whose Knowledge? Thinking from Women's Lives*, Milton Keynes: Open University Press.

Harris, D. 1987 *Justifying State Welfare: The New Right v the Old Left*, Oxford: Blackwell.

Harris, M. 1995 *Cultural Anthropology*, 4th edn, New York: HarperCollins.

Hasenbalg, C. A. and Silva, N. do Valle 1992 'Raça e oportunididades educacionais no Brasil', in Nelson do Valle Silva and Carlos A. Hasenbalg, *Relações Raciais no Brasil Contemporâneo*, Rio de Janeiro: Rio Fundol/IUPERJ.

Hazareesingh, S. 1994 *Political Traditions in Modern France*, Oxford: Oxford University Press.

Hebdige, D. 1979 *Subculture: The Meaning of Style*, London: Routledge.

Hechter, M. 1987 'Nationalism as group solidarity', *Ethnic and Racial Studies* 10(4): 415–26.

Heineman, B. 1972 *The Politics of the Powerless: A Study of the Campaign Against Racial Discrimination*, Oxford: Oxford University Press.

Heitmeyer, W. 1988 *Rechtsextremistische Orientierungen bei Judenlichen. Empirishche Ergebnisse und Erklarungsmuster einer Untersuchung zur politischen Sozialisation*, Munich: Weinheim.

Held, D. 1991 'Between state and civil society', in Andrews, G. (ed.) *Citizenship*, London: Lawrence & Wishart.

—— 1995 *Democracy and the Global Order*, Cambridge: Polity Press.

Helie-Lucas, M. 1993 'Women's struggles and strategies in the growth of fundamentalism in the Muslim world: from entryism to internationalism', in H. Afshar (ed.) *Women in the Middle East: Perceptions, Realities and Struggles for Liberation*, London: Macmillan.

Helmreich, S. 1992. 'Kinship, nation and Paul Gilroy's concept of diaspora', *Diaspora* 2(2): 243–9.

Henwood, K. and Phoenix, A. 1996 "Race" in psychology: teaching the subject', *Ethnic and Racial Studies* 19(4): 841–63.

Hewitt, R. 1986 *White Talk, Black Talk: Inter-racial Friendship and Communication amongst Adolescents*, Cambridge: Cambridge University Press.

—— 1996 *Routes of Racism: The Social Basis of Racist Action*, Stoke on Trent: Trentham.

Hickman, M. and Walter, B. 1995 'Deconstructing Whiteness: Irish women in Britain', *Feminist Review* 50 (Summer): 5–19.

—— 1997 *Discrimination and the Irish Community in Britain: A Report of Research Undertaken for the CRE*, London: Commission for Racial Equality.

Hill-Collins, P. 1990 *Black Feminist Thought*, London, HarperCollins.

Hirst, D. 1997 'Terror zealot is tamed by market force', *The Guardian* (26 September): 17.

Hirst, P. and Thompson, G. 1996 *Globalisation in Question*, Cambridge: Polity.

HMSO 1981 *West Indian Children in Our Schools: Report of the Committee of Inquiry into the Education of Children from Ethnic Minority Groups*, London: HMSO.

—— 1985 *Education for All: Report of the Committee of Inquiry into the Education of Children from Ethnic Minority Groups*, London: HMSO.

Hobsbawm, E. and Ranger, T. 1983 *The Invention of Tradition*, London: Cambridge University Press.

Hooks, B. 1993 *Black Looks: Race and Representation*, Boston: South End.

—— 1994 *Teaching to Transgress*, London: Routledge.

Houghton, V. 1966 'A Rreport on the scores of West Indian immigrant children and English children on an individually administered test', *Race* 8(1).

House, J. 1996 'Muslim communities in France', in G. Nonneman, T. Niblock and B. Szajkowski (eds) *Muslim Communities in the New Europe*, Aldershot: Garnet/Ithica.

—— 1997 'Anti-racism and anti-racist discourse in France from 1900 to the present day', unpublished paper, Department of French, University of Leeds.

Howe, S. 1993 *Anticolonialism in British Politics: The Left and the End of the Empire 1918–1964*, Oxford: Oxford University Press.

Huq, R. 1995 'Fragile alliance', *Red Pepper* (February): 10–11.

Hyman, P. 1979 *From Dreyfus to Vichy: The Remaking of French Jewry 1906–1939*, New York: Columbia University Press.

Ignatieff, M. 1993 *Blood and Belonging: Journeys into the New Nationalisms*, London: BBC Books/Chatto & Windus.

ILEA Research and Statistics Group 1968 'Language proficiency', London: ILEA.

Imache, A. 1934 'La repression s'aggrave! Le vrai visage de l'imperialisme', *El Ouma* IVe année (28 décembre: 1).

IM'média/REFLEX 1997 *Sans-Papiers: Chroniques d'un mouvement*, Paris: Editions Réflex/IM'média.

International Council on Human Rights Policy 2000 'The Persistence and Mutation of Racism', Versiox: ICHRP.

International Human Rights Law Group 2000 'Bellagio Consultation on the UN World Conference Against Racism', vol. 2001.

Jack, B. 1996 *Negritude and Literary Criticism: The History and Theory of Negro-African Literature in French*, Westport, CT: Greenwood Press.

Jayasuriya, L. 1991 'Citizenship, democratic pluralism and ethnic minorities in Australia', in R. Nile (ed.) *Immigration and the Politics of Ethnicity and Race in Australia and Britain*, London: Bureau of Immigration Research Australia: Sir Robert Menzies Centre for Australian Studies, University of London.

Jazouli, A. 1986 *L'action collective des jeunes maghebins de France*, Paris: CIEMI/ L'Harmattan.

—— 1992 *Les Années Banlieues*, Paris: Seuil.

JCWI (Joint Council for the Welfare of Immigrants) 1993 *Right to Family Life For Immigrants in Europe*, London, JCWI.

—— 1995 *Immigration and Nationality Handbook*, London: JCWI.

Jenkins, B. 1990 *Nationalism in France. Class and Nation since 1789*, London/New York: Routledge.

Jenson, A. 1969 'How far can we boost IQ and scholastic abilitiy?', *Harvard Educational Review* 39(1).

Johnson, R. and Pattie, C. 1997 'Fluctuating party identification in Great Britain: patterns longitudinal study', *Politics* 17(2): 67–77.

Jones, K. 1989 *Right Turn: The Conservative Revolution in Education*, London: Hutchinson.

Joppke, C. 1996 'Multiculturalism and immigration: a comparison of the United States, Germany and Great Britain', *Theory and Society* 25(4): 449–500.

Joseph, G., Reddy, V. and Searle-Chatterjee, M. 1990 'Eurocentrism in the social sciences', *Race and Class* 31(4): 1–26.

Jules-Rosette, B. 1998 *Black Paris: The African Writers' Landscape*, Chicago: University of Illinois Press.

Juri'c-Pahor, M. 1993 'Zur Konstruktion des Geschlechterverhaltnisses in nichtdominanten ethnischen Gruppen', in N. Fremde (ed.) *Wissenschaftlerinnen in der europaischen Ethnologie*, Vienna: Wiener Frauenverlag.

Kahn, J. 1995 *Final Report of the Consultative Commission on Racism and Xenophobia*, Brussels: Permanent Representatives Committee/General Affairs Council 6906/1/95.

Kastoryano, R. 1994 'The transnational migration network of non-Europeans within Europe', *Esprit* 3–4: 171–7.

Keck, M. and Sikkink, K. 1999 'Transnational advocacy networks in international and regional politics', *International Social Science Journal* 51(1): 89–101.

Kincheloe, J. and Steinberg, S. 1997 *Changing Multiculturalism*, Buckingham: Open University Press.

King, J. 1995 'Ethnic minorities and multilateral European institutions', in A. Hargreaves and J. Leaman (eds) *Racism, Ethnicity and Politics in Contemporary Europe*, Aldershot: Edward Elgar.

Kingdon, J. 1984 *Agendas, Alternatives and Public Policy*, Boston: Little Brown.

Klug, F. 1999 'Human rights as a set of secular ethics, or where does the responsibilities bit fit in?' *Patterns of Prejudice* 33 (2): 65–72.

Knowles, C. 1992 *Race, Discourse and Labourism*, London: Routledge.

Knowles, C. and Mercer, S. 1990 'Feminism and anti-racism: an exploration of the political possibilities', in A. Cambridge and S. Feuchtwang (eds) *Anti-racist Strategies*, London: Gower.

Kosselleck, R. 1982 'Begriffsgeschichte and social history', *Economy and Society* 11(4): 409–27.

Kristeva, J. 1993 *Nations without Nationalism*, New York: Columbia University Press.

Kuper, L. 1975 *Science and Society*, London: UNESCO, Allen & Unwin.

Kymlicka, W. 1995 *Multi-cultural Citizenship: A Liberal Theory of Minority Rights*, Oxford: Clarendon Press.

Laclau, E. and Mouffe, C. 1985 *Hegemony and Socialist Strategy*, London: Verso.

Langley, J. 1973 *Pan-Africanism and Nationalism in West Africa 1900–1945: A Study in Ideology and Social Classes*, Oxford: Clarendon Press.

Latin American Perspectives 1992 'Special Issue on Hispanic Identities in the USA', *Latin American Perspectives* 75.

Lebovics, H. 1992 *True France: The Wars over Cultural Identity, 1900–1945*, Ithaca/London: Cornell University Press.

Lecache, B. 1944 *Lettre ouverte aux anti-racistes*, Paris: Service de Presse Anti-raciste.

Leicester, M. 1993 *Race for a Change in Continuing and Higher Education*, Buckingham: Society for Research into Higher Education/Open University.

Lerner, M. 1993 'Jews are not white', *Village Voice*, 18 May.

Levinas, E. 1987 *Collected Philosophical Papers*, Dordrecht: Martinus Nijhoff Publishers.

Liauzu, C. 1982 *Aux origines des tiers-mondismes. Colonises et anticolonialistes en France 1919–1939*, Paris: L'Harmattan.

Lister, R. 1990 *The Exclusive Society: Citizenship and the Poor*, London: Child Poverty Action Group.

—— 1998 *Citizenship: Feminist Perspectives*, Basingstoke: Macmillan.

Lloyd, C. 1994 'Universalism and difference: the crisis of anti-racism in Britain and France', in A. Rattansi and S. Westwood (eds) *On the Western Front: Racism, Ethnicity, Identities*, London: Polity.

—— 1995 *The Irish Community in Britain: Discrimination, Disadvantage and Racism: An Annotated Bibliography*, London: University of North London Press.

—— 1996 'Anti-racist ideas in France: myths of orgin', *The European Legacy: Towards New Paradigms* 1 (1): 126–31.

—— 1997 'Struggling for rights: African women and the 'Sanspapiers' movement in France', *Refuge* 14, (2): 31–4.

—— 1998a 'Anti-racist mobilisations in France and Britain in the 1970s and 1980s', in D. Joly (ed.) *Scapegoats and Social Actors: The Exclusion and Integration of Minorities in Western and Eastern Europe*, London: Macmillan.

—— 1998b *Discourses of Anti-racism in France*, Aldershot: Ashgate.

—— 1998c 'Rendez-vous manques: feminisms and anti-racisms in France: a critique', *Modern and Contemporary France* 6 (1): 61–74.

—— 1999a 'Organising across borders: Algerian women's associations in a period of conflict', *Review of African Political Economy* 26(82): 479–90.

—— 1999b 'Une enquete policière mise en accusation', *Différences* 207 (mai): 8.

—— 2000 'Cent ans de vie associative: table ronde avec Jean-Michel Belorgey, Martine Bartelemy et Catherine Wihtol de Wenden', *Différences* (décembre): 8–10.

Long, M. 1988 *Etre Français aujourd'hui et demain*, Paris: 10/180.

Lorcin, P. 1995 *Imperial Identities: Stereotyping, Prejudices and Race in Colonial Algeria*, London: Taurus.

MacDonald, I., Bhavnani, R., Kahn, L. and John, G. 1989 *Murder in the Playground: The Report of the MacDonald Inquiry into Racism and Racial Violence in Manchester Schools*, Manchester: Longsight Press.

McEwan, E., Gipps, C. and Summer, R. 1975 *Language Proficiency in the Multi-Racial Junior School*, Slough: NFER.

McEwan, M. 1995 *Tackling Racism in Europe*, Oxford: Berg.Macey, D. 1998 'The Algerian with the knife', *Parallax* 4(2): 159–67.

Macey, D. 1998 'The Algerian with the knife', *Parallax* 4(2): 159–67.

Mackay, C. 1937 [1935] *A Long Way from Home: An Autobiography*, London: Pluto.

McLaren, P. 1994 'White terror and oppositional agency: towards a critical multiculturalism', in D. Goldberg (ed.) *Multiculturalism: A Cultural Reader*, Oxford: Blackwell.

MacLaren, P. and Torres, R. 1999 'Racism and multicultural education: rethinking 'race' and 'whiteness' in late capitalism', in S. May (ed.) *Critical Multiculturalism*, London: Falmer Press.

McLuhan, M. 1964 *Understanding Media*, London: Routledge.

MacMaster, N. 1997 *Colonial Migrants and Racism: Algerians in France 1900–62*, Basingstoke/London: Macmillan.

McNeil, M. 1992 'Pedagogical praxis and problems: reflections on teaching about gender relations', in A. Hinds, A. Phoenix and J. Stacey (eds) *Working Out: New Directions in Women's Studies*, Brighton: Falmer.

Macpherson, W. 1999 'Inquiry into the matters arising from the death of Stephen Lawrence on 22 April 1993', London: Stationery Office, http://www.official-docments.co.uk/document/cm42/4262/4262.htm.

Mannheim, K. 1929 *Ideology and Utopia*, London: Routledge and Kegan Paul.

Marable, M. 1995 *Beyond Black and White: Transforming African-American Politics*, London: Verso.

Margalit, A. and Harbertal, M. 1998 'Liberalism and the right to culture' in M. Mautner, A. Sugi and R. Shami (eds), *Multiculturalism in a Jewish Democratic State*, Tel-Aviv: Tel-Aviv University, Ramat Press, pp. 93–106.

Marrus, M. 1971 *The Politics of Assimilation: A Study of the French Jewish Community at the Time of the Dreyfus Affair*, Oxford: Clarendon Press.

Marshall, T. 1950 *Citizenship and Social Class*, Cambridge: Cambridge University Press.

—— 1975 *Social Policy in the Twentieth Century*, London: Hutchinson.

—— 1981 *The Right to Welfare and Other Essays*, London: Heinemann Educational.

Marx, K. 1975 'On the Jewish question', *Early Writings*, Harmondsworth: Penguin.

May, S. 1999 *Critical Multiculturalism*, London: Falmer Press.

Mead, G. H. 1934 *Mind, Self and Society*, Chicago: Chicago University Press.

Memmi, A. 1957 *Portrait du colonise*, Paris: Payot.

Miles, R. 1989 *Racism*, London: Routlege.

—— 1993 *Racism after 'Race Relations'*, London: Routledge.

—— 1994 'Explaining racism in contemporary Europe', in A. Rattansi and S. Westwood (eds) *On the Western Front: Racism, Modernity, Identity, Polity*, Cambridge: Polity.

Modood, T. 1992 *Not Easy Being British*, Stoke on Trent: Lunnymede Trust/Trentham.

—— 1994a *Ethnic Minorities and Higher Education: Why Are There Differential Rates of Entry?*, London: PSI.

—— 1994b 'Political blackness and British Asians', *Sociology* 28(4): 859–76.

—— 1996a 'Access of ethnic minority students to higher education in Britain', paper for PSI Day Conference on Race and Higher Education, May, London.

—— 1996b '"Race" in Britain and the politics of difference', in D. Archard (ed.) *Philosophy and Pluralism*, Cambridge: Cambridge University Press.

—— 1997 *Church, State and Religious Minorities*, London: PSI.

Modood T., Berthoud, R., Lakey, J., Smith, P. and Virdee, S. 1997 *Ethnic Minorities in Britain: Diversity and Disadvantage*, London: PSI.

Mohan, R. 1995 'Multiculturalism in the nineties: pitfalls and possiblities', in C. Newfield and R. Strickland (eds) *After Political Correctness: The Humanities and Society in the 1990s*, Boulder: Westwood.

Mouffe, C. 1992 'Democratic citizenship and the political community', in C. Mouffe (ed.) *Dimensions of Radical Democracy: Pluralism, Citizenship, Community*, London: Verso.

Murray, C. 1996 *Charles Murray and the Underclass: The Developing Debate*, London: IEA Health and Welfare Unit/*The Sunday Times*.

Neal, S. 1995 'A question of silence? Anti-racist discourses and initiatives in higher education: two case studies', in M. Griffiths and B. Troyna (eds) *Anti-racism, Culture and Justice in Education*, Stoke on Trent: Trentham Books.

—— 1998 *The Making of Equal Opportunities Policies in Universities*, Milton Keynes: Open University Press.

Neveu, C. 1994 'Is "black" an exportable category to mainland Europe? Race and citizenship in a European context', in J. Rex and B. Drury (eds) *Ethnic Mobilisation in a Multi-Cultural Europe*, Aldershot: Avebury.

Nicolet, C. 1994 *L'idée republicaine en France (1789–1924). Essai d'histoire critique*, Paris: Gallimard.

Noiriel, G. 1991 *La tyrannie du national. Le droit d'asile en Europe 1793–1993*, Paris: Calmann-Levy.

—— 1992 *Le creuset Français. Histoire de l'immigration XIXe–XX siècle*, Paris: Seuil.

Nord, P. 1995 *The Republican Moment: Struggles for Democracy in Nineteenth-Century France*, Cambridge, MA: Harvard University Press.

Novick, P. 1968 *The Resistance versus Vichy: The Purge of Collaborators in Liberated France*, London: Chatto and Windus.

Office of Multicultural Affairs 1989 *National Agenda for Multicultural Australia*, Canberra: Australian Government Printing Service.

Okin, S. 1999 *Is Multiculturalism Bad for Women?* Princeton: Princeton University Press.

Oldfield, A. 1990 *Citizenship and Community: Civic Republication and the Modern World*. London: Routledge.

Paraf, P. 1931 'Défense d'Israel . . . Défense de l'Humanité', *Bulletin de la LICA* 12(mars): 2.

—— 1993 'Liberal responses to cultural diversity', paper for COST Conference, Multiculturalism and Diversity, Vienna.

—— 2000 *Rethinking Multiculturalism*, Basingstoke: Macmillan.

Patel, P. 1995 'The impact of Hindu fundamentalism in Britain', *Women Against Fundamentalism* 7: 31–4.

—— 1999 'Difficult alliances: treading the minefield of identity and solidarity politics', *Soundings* 12 (Summer): 115–26.

Pateman, C. 1988a 'The fraternal social contract', in J. Keane (ed.) *Civil Society and the State: New European Perspectives*, London/New York: Routledge.

—— 1988b *The Sexual Contract*, Oxford: Polity.

—— 1996 *Democratization and Citizenship in the 1990s*, Oslo: Institute for Social Research.

Payne, J. 1974 *Educational Priority EPA Surveys and Statistics*, London: HMSO.

Peled, Y. 1992 'Ethnic democracy and the legal construction of citizenship: Arab citizens of the Jewish state', *American Political Science Review* 86(2): 432–42.

Pettigrew, T. 1994 'New patterns of prejudice: the different worlds of 1964 and 1984', in F. Pincus and H. Erlich (eds) *Race and Ethnic Conflict*, Boulder: Westview.

Pettman, J. 1992 *Living in the Margins: Racism, Sexism and Feminism in Australia*, Sydney: Allen & Unwin.

Philips, C. 1979 'Educational underachievement in different ethnic groups', *Educational Research* 21(2): 116–30.

Phizacklea, A. and Miles, R. 1980 *Labour and Racism*, London: Routledge and Kegan Paul.

Pierre-Bloch, J.-P. 1936 'Tous mobilisés contre le racisme', *Le Droit de Vivre* 47(3): 1.

Pieterse, J. 1995 'Globalisation as hybridisation', in M. Featherstone (ed.) *Global Culture*, London: Sage.

Pincus, F. and Erlich, H. 1994 *Race and Ethnic Conflict*, Boulder: Westview.

Polac, C. 1994 'Quand les "immigres" prennent la parole', in P. Perrineau (ed.) *L'engagement politique. Declin ou mutation*, Paris: Presses de la Fondation nationale des sciences politiques.

Prochaska, A. 1990 *Making Algeria French: Colonialism in Bone 1870–1920*, Cambridge: Cambridge University Press.

Ramsbotham, O. and Woodhouse, T. 1996 *Humanitarian Intervention in Contemporary Conflict*, Cambridge: Polity.

Ranciere, J. 1998 'The cause of the other', *Parallax* 7 (4): 36–49.

Rassool, N. 1997 'Fractured or flexible identities? Life histories of "black" diasporic women in Britain', in H. Mirza (ed.) *Black British Feminism: A Reader*, London: Routledge.

Räthzel, N. 1994 'Harmonious Heimat and disturbing *Ausländer*', *Feminism and Psychology* 4(1): 81–98.

—— 1995 'Aussiedler and Ausländer: transforming German national identity', *Social Identities* 1(2): 263–82.

—— 1996 'Frauensolidaritat gegen nationale Grobmachtpolitik und Alltagsrassismen?', in B. Fuchs and G. Habinger (eds) *Rassismen und Feminismen*, Vienna: Promedia.

—— 1997 *Gegenbilder. Nationale Identitaten durch Konstruktionen des Anderen*, Osnabruk: Leske und Budrich.

—— 1999: Workers of migrant origin in Germany: forms of discrimination in the labour market and at the workplace. In John Wrench, Andrea Rea and Nouria Ouali (eds) *Migrants, Ethnic Minorities and the Labour Market*, Basingstoke: Macmillan In association with Centre for Research in Ethnic Relations, University of Warwick, pp. 33–53.

Rattansi, A. 1992 'Changing the subject? Racism, culture and education', in J. Donald and A. Rattansi (eds) *Race, Culture and Difference*, London: Sage/Open University Press.

—— 1994 'Western racisms, ethncities and identities in a postmodern frame', in A. Rattansi and S. Westwood (eds) *Racism, Modernity and Identity: On the Western Front*, Oxford: Blackwell.

—— 1999 'Racism, "postmodernism" and reflexive multiculturalism', in S. May (ed.) *Critical Multiculturalism*, London: Falmer Press.

Rayski, A. 1950 'La presse anti-raciste sous l'occupation hitlerienne. Receuil de journaux, tracts, appels, proclamations et brochures édités par les organisations juives de la Résistance et divers autres mouvements pendant l'occupation de la France de 1940 à 1944', Centre de documentation de l'UJRE.

Rea, A. (ed.) 1997 *Racisme et Antiracisme en Europe*, Brussels: Editions Complexes.

Rex, J. 1986 *Race and Ethnicity*, Milton Keynes: Open University Press.

—— 1996 *Ethnic Minorities in the Modern Nation State*, Aldershot: Avebury.

Rex, J. and Drury, B. 1994 *Ethnic Mobilisation in a Multi-Cultural Europe*, Aldershot: Avebury.

Reynolds, H. 1996 *Aboriginal Sovereignty: Three Nations, One Australia?*, Sydney: Allen & Unwin.

Robertson, R. 1995 'Globalisation: time-space and homogeneity-heterogeneity', in M. Featherstone (ed.) *Global Modernities*, London: Sage.

Robbins, D. 1994 *Observatory on National Policies to Combat Social Exclusion: Third Annual Report*, Lille: EEIG.

Robins, D. 1991 'Tradition and translation: national culture in its global context', in J. Corner and S. Harvey (eds) *Enterprise and Heritage: Crosscurrents in National Culture*, London: Routledge.

Roche, M. 1987 'Citizenship, social theory and social change', *Theory and Society* 16: 363–99.

Roediger, D. 1991 *The Wages of Whiteness: Race and the Making of the American Working Class*, London: Verso.

Root, M. 1996 *Multiracial Experience: Racial Borders as the New Frontier*, Thousand Oaks: Sage.

Rosanvallon, P. 1992 *Le sacre du citoyen. Histoire du suffrage universel en France*, Paris: Gallimard.

Rosenthal, G. 1948 *Rapport sur la question noire*, Paris: Congres national de l'alliance anti-raciste.

Ross, K. 1995 *Fast Cars, Clean Bodies: Decolonization and the Reordering of French Culture*, Cambridge, MA: MIT Press.

Rousso, H. 1990 *Le Syndrome de Vichy de 1944 à nos jours*, Paris: Seuil.

Rowe, W. and Scheling, V. 1991 *Memory and Modernity: Popular Culture in Latin America*, London: Verso.

Rudelle, O. 1987 'La tradition républicaine', *Pouvoirs* 42(septembre): 31–42.

Sabatier, P. 1988 'An advocacy coalition framework of policy change and the role of policy-oriented learning therein', *Policy Sciences* 21: 129–68.

Sacks, O. 1990 *Awakenings*, London: Picador.

Sahgal, G. and Yuval-Davis, N. 1992 *Refusing Holy Orders: Women and Fundamentalism in Britain*, London: Virago.

Salomon, M. 1948 'D'un juif à des Negrès', *Présence Africaine* 5: 774–9.

Sandel, M. 1982 *Liberalism and the Limits of Justice*, Cambridge: Cambridge University Press.

Sartre, J.-P. 1948 *Anti-Semite and Jew*, New York: Schoken.

—— 1964 'Portrait du colonise,', in J.-P. Sartre (ed.) *Situations V*, Paris: Gallimard.

SBS (Southall Black Sisters) 1990 *Against the Grain*, London: Southall Black Sisters.

Schierup, C.-U. 1995 'Multiculturalism and universalism in the USA and EU Europe', paper for workshop, Nationalism and Ethnicity, Berne, March.

Schor, R. 1992 *L'antesemitisme en France pendant les auuéss 30. Prelude a Vichy*, Brussels: Complexe.

Schutz, A. 1970 [1932] *On Phenomenology and Social Relations*, Chicago [1932]: University of Chicago Press.

—— 1996 [1950] 'The stranger', in F. Anthias and M. Kelly (eds) *Thinking about the Social*, London: Greenwich University Press.

Scott, J. W. 1996 *Only Paradoxes to Offer: French Feminists and the Rights of Man*, Cambridge, MA: Harvard University Press.

Seidman, G. 2000 *Adjusting the Lens: What do Globalizations, Transnationalism, and the Anti-Apartheid Movement Mean for Social Movement Theory?*, Michigan: University of Michigan Press.

Shafir, G. 1998 *The Citizenship Debates: A Reader*, Minneapolis: Minnesota University Press.

Sharma, S., Hutnyk, J. and Sharma, A. 1996 *Disorienting Rhythms*, London: Zed Books.

Shukla, S. 1997 'Building diaspora and nation: the 1991 "Cultural Festival of India"', *Cultural Studies* 2(2): 296–315.

Silverman, M. 1988 'Questions of nationality and citizenship in the 1980s', *Modern and Contemporary France* 34 (July): 10–16.

—— 1992 *Deconstructing the Nation: Immigration, Racism and Citizenship in Modern France*, London: Routledge.

Simeant, J. 1998 *La cause des sanspapiers*, Paris: Presses de Science Po.

Simmel, G. 1950 [1908] 'The stranger', in A. Wolff (ed.) *The Sociology of Georg Simmel*, New York: Free Press.

Sivanandan, A. 1974 *Race, Class and the State*, London: Institute of Race Relations.

—— 1982 *A Different Hunger: Writings on Black Resistance*, London: Pluto.

—— 1985 'RAT and the degradation of the black struggle', *Race and Class* XXVI: 1–33.

—— 1995 'La trahison des clercs', *New Statesman*, 14 July, pp. 20–1.

Skellington, R. 1996 *'Race' in Britain Today*, London: Sage.

Skidmore, T. E. 1993 [1974] *Black into White: Race and Nationality in Brazilian Thought*, Durham: Duke University Press.

Sklair 1991 *Sociology of the Global System*, London: Harvester Wheatsheaf.

Solomos, J. and Back, L. 1996 *Racism and Society*, London: Macmillan.

Sooben, P. 1990 'The origins of the Race Relations Act', Research Paper in Ethnic relations, CRER, University of Warwick.

Soucy, R. 1986 *French Fascism: The First Wave 1924–1933*, New Haven: Yale University Press.

—— 1995 *French Fascism: The Second Wave 1933–37*, New Haven: Yale University Press.

Soundings 1999 'Special issue on transversal politics', *Soundings* 12.

Soysal, Y. 1994 *Limits of Citizenship: Migrants and Postnational Membership in Europe*, Chicago: University of Chicago Press.

Spivak, G. 1993 'Can the subaltern speak?', in P. Williams and I. Chrisman (eds) *Colonial Discourse and Post-Colonial Theory: A Reader*, Hemel Hempstead: Harvester Wheatsheaf.

Stasiulis, D. and Yuval-Davis, N. 1995 *Unsettling Settler Societies: Articiulations of Gender, Ethnicity, Race and Class*, London: Sage.

Statham, J., Mackinnon, D., Cathcart, H. and Hales, M. 1991 *The Education Fact File*, London: Hodder & Stoughton.

Stedward, G. 1997 'Agendas, arenas and anti-racism', unpublished PhD thesis, Department of Politics, University of Warwick.

Sternhell, Z. 1985 *Maurice Barres et le Nationalisme français*, Brussels: Complexes.

—— 1987 *Ni droite ni gauche. L'idéologie fasciste en France*, Brussels: Complexes.

Stolcke, V. 1995 'Talking culture: new boundaries, new rhetorics of exclusion in Europe', *Current Anthropology* 16(1): 1–23.

Stoler, A. 1995 *Race and the Education of Desire: Foucault's History of Sexuality and the Colonial Order of Things*, Durham, NC: Duke University Press.

Stone, J. 1985 *Racial Conflict in Contemporary Society*, London: Fontana Press.

Stonequist, E. 1937 *The Marginal Man*, New York: Scribner.

Stora, B. 1986 *Messali Haadj: Pionnier du nationalisme algérien 1898–1974*, Paris: L'Harmattan.

—— 1987 *Nationalistes algériens et Révolutionnaries français au temps du Front Populaire*, Paris: L'Harmattan.

—— 1992 *Ils venaient d'Algérie. L'immigration algérienne en France 1912–1992*, Paris: Fayard.

Taguieff, P.-A. 1979 'La nouvelle droit a l'oeil nu', *Droit et Liberte* 386 (décembre): 21–3.

—— 1980 'Présence de l'heritage nazi: des "nouvelles droites" intellectuelles au "revisionnisme"', *Droit et Liberté* 387 (janvier): 11–17.

—— 1990 *La force du prejuge. Essai sur le racisme et ses doubles*, Paris: Gallimard.

—— 1991 *Face au racisme*, Paris: La Decouverte.

—— 1995 *Les fins de l'anti-racisme*, Paris: Michalon.

—— 1996 *La république menacée (entretiens avec Philippe Petit)*, Paris: Textuel.

—— 1999 [1990] 'The new cultural racism in France', *Telos* 83 (Spring 1990); also excerpted in Martin Bulmer and John Solomos (eds) *Racism*, London: Oxford University Press.

Tamir, Y. 1998 'Two concepts of multiculturalism', in M. Mautner, A. Sagi and R. Shamir (eds) *Multiculturalism in a Jewish and Democratic State*, Tel Aviv: Tel Aviv University, Ramat Press.

Tarrow, S. 1995 'The Europeanisation of conflict: reflections from a social movements perspective', *West European Politics* 18(2): 223–51.

Tartakowsky, D. 1998 *Le pouvoir est dans la rue. Crises politiques et manifestations en France*, Paris: Aubier.

Taylor, C. 1994a 'Examining the politics of recognition', in A. Gutman (ed.) *Multiculturalism*, Princeton, NJ: Princeton University Press.

—— 1994b 'The politics of recognition', in A. Gutmann (ed.) *The Politics of Recognition*, Princeton, NJ: Princeton University Press.

Telles, E. 1992 'Segregation by skin color in Brazil', *American Sociological Review* 57.

—— 1994 'Industrialization and racial inequality in employment: the Brazilian example', *American Sociological Review* 59.

Thiara, R. and Goulbourne, H. 1991 *Courses in Race and Ethnic Relations in Higher Education in Britain*, Coventry: Centre for Research in Ethnic Relations, University of Warwick.

Tizard, B. and Phoenix, A. 1993 *Black, White or Mixed Race? Race and Racism in the Lives of Young People of Mixed Parentage*, London: Routledge.

Tomlinson, S. 1981 *Educational Subnormality – A Study in Decision-Making*, London: Routledge and Kegan Paul.

—— 1983 *Ethnic Minorities in British Schools*, Aldershot: Gower.

Touraine, A. 1969 *La société post-industrielle*, Paris: La Decouverte.

—— 1993 'Le racisme aujourd'hui', in M. Wieviorka (ed.) *Racisme et modernité*, Paris: La Decouverte.

Townsend, H. 1971 *Immigrant Pupils in England – the LEA response*, Slough: NFER.

Troyna, B. 1978 'Race and streaming: a case study', *Educational Review* 30(1): 59–65.

—— 1992 'Can you see the join? An historical analysis of multicultural and anti-racist policies', in D. Gill, B. Major and M. Blair (eds) *Racism and Education*, London: Open University/Sage.

Turner, B. 1990 'The two faces of sociology: global or national?', in M. Featherstone (ed.) *Global Culture*, London: Sage.

—— 1993 *Max Weber: From History to Modernity*, London/New York: Routledge.

—— 1998 'National citizenship and cosmopolitan virtue: some issues with globalization', paper to departmental seminar, University of Greenwich, November.

Twine, F. W. 1997 *Racism in a Racial Democracy: The Maintenance of White Supremacy in Brazil*, New Brunswick, NJ: Rutger University Press.

Unesco 1951 *Race and Science*, New York: Columbia University Press.

—— 1972 *Apartheid*, Paris: Unesco.

—— 1980 *Sociological Theories: Race and Colonialism*, Paris: Unesco.

—— 1982a *Living in Two Cultures: The Socio-cultural Situation of Migrant Workers and their Families*, London: Gower/Unesco.

—— 1982b *Racisme, science et pseudo-science*, Paris: Unesco.

United Nations 1997 'Third decade to combat racism and racial discrimination and the convening of a world conference on racism, racial discrimination, xenophobia and related intolerance, Resolution 52/111', New York: United Nations.

Vidal-Naquet, P. 1962 *La raison d'état*, Paris: Minuit.

Wallerstein, I. 1990 'Culture as the ideological battleground of the modern world-system', in M. Featherstone (ed.) *Global Culture*, London: Sage.

Wallman, S. 1979 *Ethnicity at Work*, London: Macmillan.

Walzer, M. 1994 'Comment', in A. Gutmann (ed.) *Multiculturalism and the Politics of Recognition*, Princeton, NJ: Princeton University Press.

Waters, M. 1995 *Globalization*, London: Routledge.

Webster, E. and Adler, G. 1999 'Toward a class compromise in South Africa's "double transition": bargained liberalization and the consolidation of democracy', *Politics and Society* 27 (3).

Weinburg, D. 1977 *A Community on Trial: The Jews of Paris in the 1930s*, Chicago: University of Chicago Press.

Werbner, P. 1997 'Essentialising essentalism, essentialising silence: ambivalence and multiplicity in the constructions of racism and ethnicity', in P. Werbner and T. Modood (eds) *Debating Cultural Hybridity: Multi-cultural Identities and the Politics of Anti-racism*, London: Zed Books.

—— 1999 'Global pathways: working-class cosmopolitans and the creation of transnational ethnic worlds', *Social Anthropology* 7(1): 17–37.

Werber, P. and Modood, T. 1997 *Debating Cultural Hybridity. Multi-cultural identities and the Politics of Anti-racism*, London, Zed Books.

West, C. 1992 'The new cultural politics of difference', in R. Ferguson, M. Gever, T. Minh-ha and C. West (eds) *Out There: Marginalisation and Contemporary Cultures*, Cambridge MA: MIT Press.

Wieviorka, M. 1993a 'Conclusion: anti-racisme, democratie et identités', in M. Wieviorka (ed.) *Racisme et modernité*, Paris: La Decouverte.

—— (ed.) 1993b *Racisme et modernite*, Paris: La Decouverte.

—— 1995 *The Arena of Racism*, translated by C. Turner, Thousand Oaks, CA: Sage.

—— 1997 'Is it so difficult to be an anti-racist?', in P. Werbner and T. Modood (eds) *Debating Cultural Hybridity*, London: Zed Books.

Wihtol de Wenden, C. 1988 *Les Immigrés et la Politique*, Paris: Presses de la Fondation Nationale des Sciences Politiques.

—— 1997 'Que sont devenues les associations civiques issues de l'immigration', *Hommes et Migrations* 1206(mars–avrill): 53–66.

Wilkinson, H. and Muglan, G. 1995 *Freedom's Children*, London: Demos.

Williams, R. 1958 *Culture and Society*, London: Chatto and Windus.

Willis, P. 1979 *Learning to Labour: How Working-Class Kids get Working-Class Jobs*, London: Hutchinson.

Wilson, A. 1987 *Mixed Race Children: A Study of Identity*, London: Allen and Unwin.

Wilson, T. 1998 'New universities are now the norm', *The Lecturer* (December): 23.

Winant, H. 1994 'Racial formation and hegemony: global and local developments', in A. Rattansi and S. Westwood (eds) *Racism, Modernity, Identity*, London: Polity.

—— 2001 *The World is a Ghetto: Race and Democracy Since World War II*, New York: Basic Books.

Winock, M. 1992 'Le mythe fondateur: l'affaire Dreyfus', in S. Berstein and O. Rudelle (eds) *Le modele républicain*, Paris: Presses Universitaires de France.

Woo, D. 1990 'The overrepresentation of Asian Americans – a red herring', *Sage Race Relations Abstracts* 15(2).

Woodal, C. 1993 'Arabicide in France: an interview with Fausto Guidice', *Race and Class* 35(2): 21–33.

Wrench, J. 1995 'Racism and occupational health and safety: migrant and minority women and "poor work"', Coventry: Centre for Comparative Labour Studies, University of Warwick.

Wrench, J. and Solomos, J. 1993 *Racism and Migration in Western Europe*, Oxford: Berg.

Young, I. 1988 *The Sexual Contract*, Cambridge: Polity.

—— 1989 'Polity and group difference: a critique of the ideal of universal citizenship', *Ethics* 99: 250–74.

—— 1995 *The Sexual Contract*, Cambridge: Polity.

Young, J. 1988 *Writing and Rewriting the Holocaust: Narrative and the Consequences of Interpretation*, Bloomington: Indiana University Press.

Young, R. 1995 *Colonial Desire: Hybridity in Theory, Culture and Race*, London/New York: Routledge.

Yudice, G. 1995 'Neither impunging nor disavowing whiteness does a viable politics make: the limits of identity politics', in C. Newfield and R. Strickland (eds) *After Political Correctness: The Humanities and Society in the 1990s*, Boulder: Westview.

Yuval-Davis, N. 1987 *The Jewish Collectivity and National Reproduction in Israel*, London: Zed Books.

—— 1991 'The citizenship debate: women, ethnic processes and the state', *Feminist Review* 39 (Winter): 58–68.

—— 1993 'Gender and nation', *Ethnic and Racial Studies* 16 (4): 621–631.

—— 1994 'Women, ethnicity and empowerment', in K. Bhavnani and A. Phoenix (eds), *Shifting Identities, Shifting Racisms: A Feminism and Psychology Reader*, London: Sage.

—— 1997a 'Ethnicity, gender relations and multiculturalism', in P. Werbner and T. Modood (eds) *Debating Cultural Hybridity*, London: Zed Books.

—— 1997b *Gender and Nation*, London: Sage.

—— 1997c 'Women, citizenship and difference', *Feminist Review* 57: 4–27.

—— 1999 'The multi-layered citizen: citizenship in the age of globalisation', *International Feminist Journal of Politics* 1(2): 299–322.

Yuval-Davis, N. and Vargas, G. 1999 'Latin American feminism in the 1990s – conversation with Gina Vargas in October 1998', *International Feminist Journal of Politics* 1(2): 299–322.

Yuval-Davis, N. and Werbner, P. 1999 *Women, Citizenship and Difference*, London: Zed Books.

Index